NATIONAL SCHOOL LIBRARY

Standards

for Learners, School Librarians, and School Libraries

Purchases of AASL publications fund advocacy, leadership, professional development, and standards initiatives for school librarians nationally.

ALA Editions purchases fund advocacy, awareness, and accreditation programs for library professionals worldwide.

NATIONAL SCHOOL LIBRARY
Standards

for Learners, School Librarians, and School Libraries

American Association
of School Librarians
TRANSFORMING LEARNING

An imprint of the American Library Association

CHICAGO | 2018

The American Association of School Librarians (AASL), www.aasl.org, a division of the American Library Association (ALA), empowers leaders to transform teaching and learning. AASL is the only national professional membership organization focused on school librarians and the school library community. AASL has more than 7,000 members and serves school librarians in the United States, Canada, and around the world. Having supported the profession for 65 years, AASL understands the current realities and evolving dynamics of your professional environment and is positioned to help members transform teaching and learning through school library programs.

© 2018 by the American Library Association

Extensive effort has gone into ensuring the reliability of the information in this book; however, the publisher makes no warranty, express or implied, with respect to the material contained herein.

For clarity and consistency, this reprint includes an updated index and the following text changes: "teacher" to "educator," "student" to "learner," and the addition of "school" preceding some instances of "library" and "librarian."

ISBNs
978-0-8389-1579-0 (paper)
978-0-8389-1658-2 (PDF)
978-0-8389-1659-9 (ePub)
978-0-8389-1660-5 (Kindle)

Publication downloads available from the American Association of School Librarians are designed for single users only. The Single User License allows the use of e-book titles and materials under a model of one-copy, one user. Contact AASL at <aasl@ala.org> to discuss other types of licensing requests.

Library of Congress Cataloging-in-Publication Data

Names: American Association of School Librarians, author.
Title: National school library standards for learners, school librarians, and school libraries / American Association of School Librarians.
Description: Chicago : ALA Editions, an imprint of the American Library Association, 2018. | Includes bibliographical references and index.
Identifiers: LCCN 2017028752| ISBN 9780838915790 (pbk. : alk. paper) | ISBN 9780838916582 (pdf) | ISBN 9780838916599 (epub) | ISBN 9780838916605 (kindle)
Subjects: LCSH: School libraries—Standards—United States. | Education—Standards—United States | School librarians—Rating of—United States. | Students—Rating of—United States.
Classification: LCC Z675.S3 A438 2018 | DDC 027.802/18—dc23 LC record available at https://lccn.loc.gov/2017028752

⊚ This paper meets the requirements of ANSI/NISO Z39.48-1992 (R2009) (Permanence of Paper).

Printed in the United States of America
22 21 20 19 18   5 4 3

CONTENTS

PART II: STANDARDS INTEGRATED FRAMEWORKS

PART III: ASSESSMENT AND EVALUATION

PART IV: SCENARIOS FOR PROFESSIONAL LEARNING

APPENDICES

PREFACE

FOR THE PAST TWO YEARS, I HAVE HAD THE HONOR OF CHAIRING THE
AASL Standards and Guidelines Editorial Board. The editorial board's work, AASL's
National School Library Standards, represents collaboration propelled by vision,
conviction, and heart. While I know not one among us would step forward to take
credit for this accomplishment, I do want to bring attention to some special contributors.

First and foremost, this game-changing work would not have happened without AASL Executive Director Sylvia Knight Norton and her leadership. Sylvia had
the foresight to envision how new, bold national standards would advance school
librarians and their important contributions to learning.

Working tirelessly alongside Sylvia has been Stephanie Book, a peerless professional who generously shared her brain with everyone who contributed to the
standards. Stephanie, I hold you in high regard and deep affection—thank you for
keeping us organized, guided, and reminded; thank you especially for always weav-
ing our sometimes-disjointed ideas together into actionable items. You will forever
have a place in my pantheon of project whisperers.

KRC Research was instrumental in setting the scene for the new standards by giving the editorial board tools and strategies to gather community input in an open,
engaging atmosphere. I would like to thank Mark Richards for spearheading KRC's
efforts and for guiding all of us to facilitate and gain deep understanding of current
school librarians' needs.

The AASL Standards and Guidelines Implementation Task Force, led by Mary Keeling, allowed the editorial board to bring together KRC's research results and the *National School Library Standards* in an innovative, actionable plan that elevated our work even further. The implementation task force was the other half to our whole; we began as colleagues, but we finished as sisters.

Our work was made all the more impactful by the powerful editing of Cheryl A. Cherry. So much more than a proofreader, Cheryl read our drafts closely, objectively, and from the point of view of our intended audience. She raised issues and made connections that have allowed us to produce the highest quality, most intentional standards and supports.

Our intellectual work was complemented by the work of the graphic designers at Distillery and the team of professionals in ALA Publishing. Both groups helped us develop the eye-catching color and iconography scheme and book layout to meet school library professionals' ongoing needs. This look and feel united the work of the editorial board and implementation task force in a visually appealing way that underscored the interconnection between the two groups' products.

As a seasoned editor and a professor, I am no stranger to group writing projects; all too often, the number of writers has an inverse relationship with the pace and quality of the results. Not in this case. The editorial board, expertly curated by the 2014–2015 AASL Executive Committee and guided by Stephanie Book, quickly found rhythm, synergy, and simpatico that helped us forge ahead through competing priorities, personal challenges, and intellectual exhaustion. Being the designated leader of colleagues I deeply respect and with whom I enjoy rich conversation, shared values, and "R&G," has been a life-changing experience. Thank you all.

—*Marcia A. Mardis*
July 10, 2017

ACKNOWLEDGMENTS

AASL gratefully acknowledges the following:

AASL Standards and Guidelines Editorial Board, 2015–2017

   Marcia A. Mardis, chairperson

   Susan D. Ballard

   Elizabeth Burns

   Kathryn Roots Lewis

   Kathy Mansfield

   Deborah Rinio

   Kathleen Riopelle Roberts

AASL Board Liaisons

   Ken Stewart, 2015–2016

   Rob Hilliker, 2016–2017

AASL Executive Director: Sylvia Knight Norton

AASL Staff Liaison: Stephanie Book, Manager, Communications

Community Research Consultation Process

For the first time in decades AASL used a multilayered survey, data, and research approach to inform the revision and remodeling of its learning standards and program guidelines for the profession. AASL would like to acknowledge the important impact the participants in this process have had on this work. The feedback and experiences gathered brought valuable insight to this critically important standards revision project. Your contributions have influenced learning for the next decade or more! AASL knows that you have many demands on your time and cannot thank you enough for your commitment to AASL and to your profession.

Participants in the Community Research Consultation Process
- AASL Standards and Guidelines Online Survey, September 2015
- AASL National Conference Focus Groups, November 2015
- AASL Affiliate State Conference Focus Groups, February 2016–May 2016
  - » Alaska Association of School Librarians
  - » California School Library Association
  - » New Hampshire School Library Media Association
  - » Pennsylvania School Librarians Association
  - » South Carolina Association of School Librarians
  - » Texas Association of School Librarians
  - » Wisconsin Educational Media and Technology Association
- AASL Standards Peer Reviewers, December 2016

KRC Research, Washington, DC
- Mark Richards, Senior VP, Management Supervisor
- Karin Cantrell, Research Director
- Beth Eagleton, Research Analyst

PART I

Introduction and Overview

1

Meet Your New Standards

WELCOME TO THE *NATIONAL SCHOOL LIBRARY STANDARDS,* FEATURING the *AASL Standards Integrated Framework,* your revitalized American Association of School Librarians standards for learners, school librarians, and school libraries. While not intended to be a curriculum, these standards are designed to guide your interactions with learners, educators, and stakeholders, as well as help you to engage in deep, effective professional practice.

Standards are everywhere—for the products we buy, the food we eat, the topics we teach, on and on. But why are standards important for school librarians? School librarianship is a profession and, as a profession, is governed by hallmarks that include a set of professional standards that define its members' practice (Shulman 1998). Because our profession tracks and embraces change, we have revitalized our 2007 standards to ensure that school librarians are working within a framework for dynamic, exciting learning leadership.

In this introduction, we want to take you through our process, beginning with a historical synopsis of national school library standards and then turning to the process we used to create the new *National School Library Standards for Learners, School Librarians, and School Libraries* and finally an overview of the standards' content and uses.

How Did We Get Here?
A Brief History of School Library Standards

The *National School Library Standards* reflects a long tradition of standards for learners, school librarians, and school libraries.

FOUNDATIONAL WORK, 1920–1959: In the 1920s C. C. Certain, under the aegis of the American Library Association (ALA), the National Education Association (NEA), and the North Central Association of Colleges and Secondary Schools, released *Standard Library Organization and Equipment for Secondary Schools of Different Sizes* (NEA et al. 1920) and *Elementary School Library Standards* (NEA and ALA 1925), standards to describe what secondary and elementary school libraries should look like and the types of services the school librarian should provide. In addition to program administration tasks, these early standards also established an instructional role for school librarians (Elkins 2014).

The Certain standards' focus on high-quality instruction and student engagement placed school librarians at the center of teaching and learning. By 1945 national efforts toward school accreditation and quality assurance led to the next set of professional standards, *School Libraries for Today and Tomorrow: Functions and Standards* (ALA et al. 1945), standards for elementary and secondary schools in a single document. In these standards, school librarians were expected to have deep knowledge of their collections and to be knowledgeable about their learners' reading abilities and preferences. The 1945 standards also specified that school librarians should participate in curriculum development and support the school's curriculum with relevant materials. School librarians were also expected to assist with remedial programs to enhance learners' reading and study skills.

By 1960 multimedia materials were becoming increasingly common in schools and *Standards for School Library Programs* (AASL 1960) reflected this development. These professional standards recommended that the school librarian curate and maintain multimedia resources in addition to print materials. These standards focused on the qualities of the services school librarians provided rather than the school library in which they may have provided those services.

The growth of school library multimedia resources and services led to a new set of professional standards: *Standards for School Media Programs* (AASL and NEA 1969); these standards now called the school library a "media center." The instructional role of the school librarian encompassed assisting learners and educators in media design and production; helping learners to develop listening, viewing, and reading skills; working with learners to evaluate and select materials; and providing educators with professional-development opportunities.

STANDARDS AND SOCIETAL CHANGE, 1961–1987: In response to rapid social and demographic change, public education funding in the late 1960s and early 1970s expanded to include programs for bilingual education, learners with disabilities, and efforts to equalize education access (Rudy 2003). In response, a new set of professional standards for school librarians, *Media Programs: District and School* (AASL and AECT 1975), reflected a greater emphasis on the school librarian's role in teaching learners to communicate ideas through media creation as well as through information use.

In the 1975 standards school librarians were expected to integrate their program into the school's instructional program, and to evaluate the efficacy of their programming and instruction (Elkins 2014). School librarians were still expected to assist educators with curriculum but now at a much deeper level; they were called on to facilitate course development, instructional design, and the "creation of alternative modes of learning" (AASL and AECT 1975, 13). School librarians were also expected to engage with the community to "transmit information about media program objectives and functions to develop public awareness and support" (AASL and AECT 1975, 55).

INFORMATION POWER ERA, 1988–2006: During the 1980s, computer technology became more widely available in schools. As a result, school library professional standards broadened their focus on multimedia to include digital media in *Information Power: Guidelines for School Library Media Programs* (AASL and AECT 1988). Commonly referred to as "Information Power 1," these professional standards gave

FIGURE 1.1

A historical timeline of the evolution of AASL standards and guidelines.

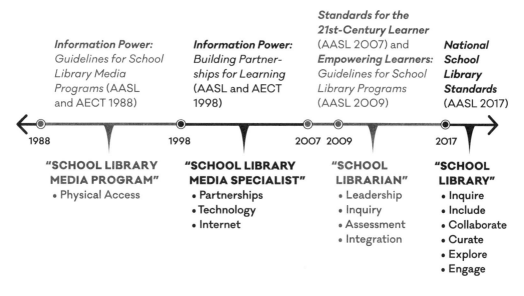

school librarians three primary roles: information specialist, teacher, and instructional consultant.

The information specialist role included traditional librarianship activities: providing access to materials in adequate numbers and of acceptable quality; guiding users in the selection of appropriate resources; and managing the collection. The teacher role focused on the content and skills that school librarians should be teaching to and fostering in learners: information skills, copyright and privacy, constitutional rights, critical thinking, and lifelong learning. The teacher role also expanded to include providing professional development to other educators and offering instruction to parents about supporting learners. The instructional consultant role added the expectation that school librarians would not only lead instructional activities but also assess them. *Information Power* explicitly stated that school librarians were to act as leaders who made the school library an "integral part of teaching and learning in the school" (AASL and AECT 1988, 43).

By the late 1990s, computers connected to the Internet were widely available in schools, allowing users global information access. This unprecedented level of access to information led to *Information Power: Building Partnerships for Learning* (AASL and AECT 1998). This unprecedented set of standards, known as "Information Power 2," included specific instructional standards with indicators, and subject-area connections were included. *Information Power: Building Partnerships for Learning* described four roles of the school librarian: teacher, instructional partner, information specialist, and program administrator. Though these roles were not remarkably different from the roles identified in the previous set of professional standards, the roles were reframed to accommodate the notion of global connection and information access (Elkins 2014). For the first time, the standards did not address the facilities aspects of school librarianship, such as numbers of books per student.

EMPOWERING LEARNERS, 2007–2017: In response to AASL's 2006 Strategic Plan, in 2007 and 2009, AASL published its next set of learning standards and program guidelines in three parts. In 2007 AASL released *Standards for the 21st-Century Learner,* a stand-alone document that included common beliefs and student learning standards. The nine common beliefs articulated foundational concepts, ranging from the centrality of reading to educational equity to diversity. These common beliefs provided a philosophical backdrop for standards that focused on learners' key abilities (skills); common ethical, legal, interpersonal, and communication behaviors proactively exercised by independent learners (responsibilities); ongoing beliefs and attitudes that guide thinking and intellectual behavior (dispositions);

reflections on one's own learning and learning processes (self-assessment strategies). Instead of being a curriculum guide or a scope and sequence of skills needed at each grade level, these standards were a framework for multiple literacies and designed for use in collaborative instruction delivered with the classroom educator benchmarked to points in a learner's development (Johns 2008).

In 2009 AASL embedded the *Standards for the 21st-Century Learner* into *Empowering Learners: Guidelines for School Library Programs*, which largely served as a reaffirmation and extension of the school librarians' roles as instructional partners, information specialists, leaders, teachers, and program administrators. These standards and guidelines reflected an awareness that the focus of school librarianship moved from the school library as a confined place to one with fluid boundaries that is layered to meet diverse needs and influenced by an interactive global community. Guiding principles for school library programs focused on building flexible learning environments with the goal of producing successful learners skilled in multiple literacies. *Empowering Learners* advanced school libraries and their programs to meet the needs of the changing school library environment and was guided not only by AASL's 2007 *Standards for the 21st-Century Learner* but also by AASL's 2009 *Standards for the 21st-Century Learner in Action*. *Empowering Learners* built on a strong history of guidelines to ensure that school librarians went beyond the basics to provide goals, priorities, criteria, and general principles for establishing effective school libraries and their programs.

Standards for the 21st-Century Learner in Action (AASL 2009c) was an in-depth look at the strands in the *Standards for the 21st-Century Learner* and the indicators within those strands. The purpose of the "in action" book was to demonstrate how the skills, dispositions, responsibilities, and self-assessment strategies identified in the standards related to one another; the book contained benchmarks and examples to show how school librarians could put the learning standards into action.

Together, these three documents allowed school librarians to "travel beyond information literacy to address multiple literacies, reflecting our students' twenty-first-century participatory culture" (Johns 2008, 6).

As the timeline in Appendix B shows, school librarianship is a profession that regularly synchronizes its work with societal, social, and educational change. Ongoing evaluation, revision, and remodeling of AASL's learner, school librarian, and school library standards is critical to both the association and the profession. Built on a strong history of standards and guidelines published by AASL, this new version of national school library standards are timely, transformative, and reflect the reimagined roles of school librarians and school libraries in the educational environment.

FIGURE 1.2

Timeline of AASL standards development process.

Planning

In this phase the AASL Standards and Guidelines Editorial Board began work by reviewing the existing AASL standards and guidelines documents. We noted what we liked and disliked as well as which topics seemed outdated or were missing. We also discussed preferred delivery modes. Our discussions then turned to the standards and guidelines produced by other education and information organizations and our alignment with these groups' missions and standards. We concluded this phase with future-casting the profession based on prevailing societal, technological, and educational trends.

Survey

In this phase, the AASL Standards and Guidelines Editorial Board worked with KRC Research to develop and deploy an online survey. This survey was designed to capture school librarians' use of the standards and guidelines, as well as their preferences, challenges to use, and priorities for future standards documents. This phase concluded with an infographic report on our survey findings, which was shared with the AASL community.

Focus groups

The AASL Standards and Guidelines Editorial Board and KRC Research developed and deployed a focus group protocol that KRC researchers used with groups of local, district, and state school library stakeholders at the AASL National Conference in November 2015. Editorial board members later used the same protocol with school librarians at state conferences. The phase culminated with collaborative analysis and review. The editorial board then shared an executive summary report with the AASL membership and the professional community.

Standards Drafting

In the final phase the AASL Standards and Guidelines Editorial Board integrated all collected data and drafted the learner, school librarian, and school library standards. To support your implementation efforts, we included additional pieces, such as assessment guides, hypothetical case studies, and lists of further readings.

Your Voice, Your Standards

In September 2015 AASL began a multilayered survey, data, and research process to revise and remodel its learning standards and school library program guidelines. This research and community-input process allowed us to make measured, informed decisions about how and where you wanted us to update our current recognized, respected, and widely used standards. Figure 1.2 provides an overview of the research phases and timeline.

In the initial community research survey phase, AASL commissioned KRC Research to broadly involve and engage members and stakeholders in assessing school librarians' current needs and envisioning ideal standards for the years ahead. AASL and the editorial board worked closely with KRC to develop a national survey and to conduct national and affiliate focus groups. In the course of these activities, over 1,300 of you shared your views and provided us with the evidence we needed to create a document for your future. Figure 1.3 summarizes the major survey results.

The editorial board used findings from the online survey to determine key areas for subsequent focus group discussion. In November 2015, at the AASL National Conference, forty attendees participated in six focus groups dedicated to standards

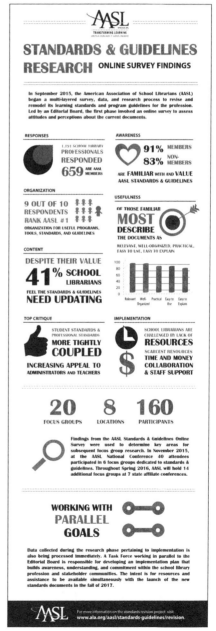

FIGURE 1.3
Summary of AASL community survey findings.

Led by the AASL Standards and Guidelines Editorial Board, the first phase of research involved an online survey to assess attitudes and perceptions about the current standards documents (Source: <http://www.ala.org/aasl/standards/research/infographic>.)

and guidelines. Throughout spring 2016, AASL held fourteen additional focus group discussions at seven state affiliate conferences, including Alaska, California, New Hampshire, Pennsylvania, South Carolina, Texas, and Wisconsin. States were selected based on the occurrence of their state conferences within the AASL research window and on achieving input from school librarians across the country and from both urban and rural districts.

From survey and focus group responses we learned you value your standards and guidelines, but feel they are underutilized. You told us that with refinement, many of the current concepts continue to be relevant. You asked us to improve and simplify the current presentation to enable your use. Finally, you identified opportunities to use the standards to make positive differences with learners and educators and in communities.

The initial response to your feedback is reflected in the title of this work. In your school communities, you observed the word "guidelines" diminished the importance of school library directives to educators, administrators, and parents. To ensure that this document is considered as important and rigorous as curriculum standards or teacher education standards, we have titled this document *National School Library Standards for Learners, School Librarians, and School Libraries.* The title also signals that the content presented here is the official standards of the national association for school librarians—the American Association of School Librarians. In a field crowded with professional organizations and initiatives, the *National School Library Standards* stand apart as the official position of the national association.

We also made additional changes in language to enhance the clarity and usefulness of this document. We use four terms consistently: learner, school librarian, school library, and educator. These terms are used instead of student, any variations of the school librarian job title, and school library program. Learners are self-directed and life-spanning; school librarian is the officially adopted title of AASL; and the streamlined term school library encompasses more than just programming and reinforces the school library's centrality and ubiquity within a learning environment. Finally, we use educator because we honor your perspective that student support takes many forms within and beyond the classroom and school day. Our aim is to enable everyone reading these standards to clearly identify how they may be applied and see themselves as both a user and a beneficiary of them.

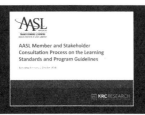

To read the full executive summary, including research from both the online survey and focus group phases, visit <http://www.ala.org/aasl/standards/research/exec-summary>.

Common Beliefs

1. The school library is a unique and essential part of a learning community.
2. Qualified school librarians lead effective school libraries.
3. Learners should be prepared for college, career, and life.
4. Reading is the core of personal and academic competency.
5. Intellectual freedom is every learner's right.
6. Information technologies must be appropriately integrated and equitably available.

COMMON BELIEFS

As we (members of the AASL Standards and Guidelines Editorial Board) reviewed the *Standards for the 21st-Century Learner* Common Beliefs and *Empowering Learners: Guidelines for School Library Programs,* and listened to the school library community, most school librarians reported that our existing guiding documents reflected current learning environments and professional best practices. The standards in this new document reflect an evolution of the earlier standards, updated with guiding assumptions informed by AASL's official position statement on the definition of an effective school library (AASL 2016c), reflecting the definition contained in the Every Student Succeeds Act (ESSA). As a result of these reviews, we identified the following common beliefs as central to the profession.

1. The school library is a unique and essential part of a learning community.

The school library is a third space for learning, a space between the classroom and home, important for on-site, personalized, and self-directed learning. The school library learning environment is a great place to be around people, yet still focus in on work (Williams 2015). Effective school libraries dynamically provide access and opportunity for all K–12 learners. Under the leadership of the school librarian, the school library provides learners with access to resources and technology, connecting classroom learning to real-world events. By providing access to an array of well-managed resources, school libraries enable academic knowledge to be linked to deeper, personalized learning. School libraries staffed with qualified professionals provide an approachable, equitable, personalized learning environment necessary for every learner's well-rounded education.

2. Qualified school librarians lead effective school libraries.

An effective school library is led by a qualified school librarian. As leaders, school librarians display high levels of persistence, overcome significant obstacles, support a range of stakeholders to achieve their goals, and play key roles in guiding their organizations through change (Collins and Porras 1997). As effective school librarians lead, they foster participatory and personalized inquiry in school libraries that are adequately staffed and resourced. Qualified school librarians perform interlinked, interdisciplinary, and cross-cutting roles as instructional leaders, program administrators, educators, collaborative partners, and information specialists (AASL 2009b; AASL 2016b–f). As an instructional leader, the school librarian contributes to curricular decisions and facilitates professional learning. As an instructional collaborator and educator, the school librarian develops information-literacy and digital-literacy instruction for all learners. And, as the school library administrator, the school librarian oversees and manages the school library and works with school and community partners. These partnerships result in expanded and improved resources and services for all learners.

3. Learners should be prepared for college, career, and life.

Our work proceeded from the assumption that the purpose of learners' education is to empower learners to pursue academic and personal success, whether in inquiry, advanced study, emotionally and intellectually rewarding professional work, or community readiness. Education is a process of continuous improvement, and exists within and beyond the school building and school day. The school library is an expansive learning environment in which fostering learners' personal interests and curricular mastery prepares them for success. The school library is centered on using a variety of engaging and relevant resources to locate and evaluate information, provide digital learning opportunities, and develop a culture of reading. To ensure equitable learning opportunities, effective school libraries include high-quality, openly licensed digital and print resources, technology tools, and robust broadband access (AASL 2016b).

Improvement science, developed by the Carnegie Foundation for the Advancement of Teaching (Bryk 2015; Bryk et al. 2015), offers school librarians a powerful lens through which to view educational decisions with colleagues. This approach calls for educators to make learners' and educators' engagement problem specific and user centered. Learning begins with the question "What specifically is the problem we are trying to solve?" and is co-developed to engage participants early and often. Improvement science also takes into account the reality that variation in performance is the core problem to address. The critical issue is not determining what works, but rather what works, for whom, and under what set of conditions.

In response to this idea, the AASL Standards and Guidelines Editorial Board used inclusion and equity as its conceptual starting points, with the acknowledgment that local data and systemic structures shape educational opportunity but can—with evidence-based decisions, community engagement, and innovative leadership—be maximized for all learners. Every Shared Foundation in this document is based in improvement science; the Competencies track improvement within the Domains.

4. Reading is the core of personal and academic competency.

Through the school library, the school librarian

- supports, supplements, and elevates learners' literacy experience by guiding them and involving them in motivational reading initiatives;
- uses story and personal narrative to engage learners; and
- has up-to-date technology and digital and print materials that include curated open educational resources.

School librarians' skills in the selection and evaluation of resources are critical in providing learners, staff, and families with open, unrestricted access to a high-quality collection of reading materials in multiple formats that reflect readers' personal interests and academic needs. School librarians take a leadership role in organizing and promoting literacy projects and events that encourage learners to become lifelong learners and readers (AASL 2016e).

5. Intellectual freedom is every learner's right.

School librarians are responsible for fostering one of America's most cherished freedoms: the freedom of speech and freedom to hear what others have to say. Learners have the right to choose what they will read, view, or hear. Learners are expected to develop the ability to think clearly, critically, and creatively about their choices, rather than allowing others to control their access to ideas and information (AASL 2016e). The school librarian's responsibility is to develop these dispositions in learners, educators, and all other members of the learning community. Read more about school library users' rights in the resources in the Suggested Further Reading list and about school librarians' responsibility to ensure learners' rights in Appendices D and E.

6. Information technologies must be appropriately integrated and equitably available.

Information technology pervades every aspect of learning and life. However, not every learner and educator has equal access to technology and the technological supports needed to apply information technology appropriately to learning tasks.

Educators and learners must be proficient in their use of available information technology. Education leaders and policymakers should strive to provide sufficient access to up-to-date, robust technology and connectivity. An effective school library plays a crucial role in bridging digital and socioeconomic divides.

YOUR ROLES WITHIN DOMAINS

The *National School Library Standards* build on familiar and appropriate aspects of previous standards. You told us that you valued the five interconnected school librarian roles articulated in *Empowering Learners:*

Leader: The school librarian is "a teacher and a learner who listens to and acts upon good ideas from peers, educators, and learners. Leadership also requires increased professional commitment and thorough knowledge of the challenges and opportunities facing the profession. By becoming an active member of the local and global learning community, the school librarian can build relationships with organizations and stakeholders to develop an effective school library program and advocate for student learning" (AASL 2009b, 17).

Instructional Partner: "The school librarian collaborates with classroom teachers to develop assignments that are matched to academic standards and include key critical-thinking skills, technology and information literacy skills, and core social skills and cultural competencies. The school librarian guides instructional design by working with the classroom teacher to establish learning objectives and goals, and by implementing assessment strategies before, during, and after assigned units of study...[C]ommunication with classroom teachers and learners now takes place virtually, as well as face-to-face" (AASL 2009b, 17).

Information Specialist: "As an information specialist, the school librarian uses technology tools to supplement school resources, assist in the creation of engaging learning tasks, connect the school with the global learning community, communicate with students and classroom teachers at any time, and provide [continuous] access to school library services. The school librarian introduces and models emerging technologies, as well as strategies for finding, assessing, and using information. He or she is a leader in software and hardware evaluation, establishing the processes for such evaluation to take place...[The] school librarian must be versed in the theoretical grounding and practical application of [copyright and fair use] laws in order to teach the ethical use of information to the learning community" (AASL 2009b, 17).

Teacher: "As teacher the school librarian empowers learners to become critical thinkers, enthusiastic readers, skillful researchers, and ethical users of information. The school librarian supports students' success by guiding them to read for understanding, breadth, and pleasure; use information for defined and self-defined purposes; build on prior knowledge and construct new knowledge; embrace the world of information and all its formats; work with each other in successful collaborations for learning; constructively assess their own work and the work of their peers; [and] become their own best critics (AASL 2009b, 18).

Program Administrator: "As program administrator, the school librarian ensures that all members of the learning community have access to resources that meet a variety of needs and interests. The implementation of a successful school library program requires the collaborative development of the program mission, strategic plan, and policies, as well as the effective management of staff, the program budget, and the physical and virtual spaces. To augment information resources available to the learning community, the school librarian works actively to form partnerships with stakeholders and sister organizations at local and global levels. The school librarian also addresses broader educational issues with other teachers in the building, at the district level, and at the professional association level" (AASL 2009b, 18).

In our focus groups, many members of the community reported that these five roles of school librarians (leader, instructional partner, information specialist, teacher, and program administrator) were valid, but not exercised one at a time. Many of you felt that you simultaneously performed two or more of these roles and that defining the roles in isolation led to a lack of professional discourse around how the learning process required school librarians to perform several roles simultaneously.

To honor this viewpoint, in this version of the AASL Standards, we have retained the roles but embedded the roles' respective responsibilities within the functional Domains (Think, Create, Share, and Grow) established in AASL's *Standards for the 21st-Century Learner* (2007). As school librarians engage in activities within the Domains, they may be exercising multiple roles in personalized ways. The AASL Standards Domains reflect Domains of Learning: cognitive, psychomotor, and affective (Anderson and Krathwohl 2001; Bloom et al. 1956), with the addition of a developmental domain. These four AASL Standards Domains describe a continuum on which school librarians and school libraries empower learners to master competencies, access resources, and use tools to do the following:

> **Think:** Inquire, think critically, and gain knowledge. This is a cognitive domain.
> **Create:** Draw conclusions, make informed decisions, apply knowledge to new situations, and create new knowledge. This is a psychomotor domain.
> **Share:** Share knowledge and participate ethically and productively as members of our democratic society. This is an affective domain.
> **Grow:** Pursue personal and aesthetic growth. This is a developmental domain.

FIGURE 1.4
Learners experience school librarians' roles through domains.

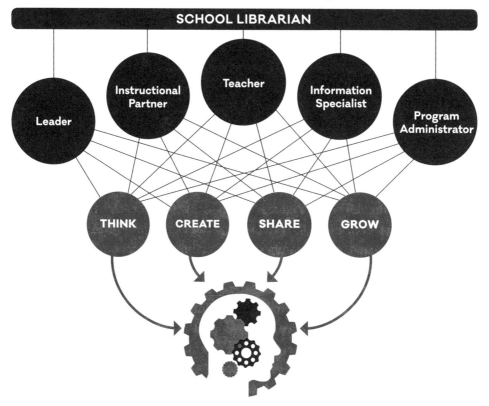

Roles and Domains dynamically combine to allow school librarians and learners to personalize their growth; this "webbing" of roles and Domains is illustrated in Figure 1.4.

As Figure 1.4 shows, learners are at the center of school librarians' practice. As learning leaders, school librarians enact, model, and communicate the Competencies in these Domains through their teaching; collaborating with other educators; demonstrating expertise in finding, evaluating, curating, and ethically using information; and administering the school library. For example, a school librarian leading a multidisciplinary unit will move fluidly through the roles of instructional partner, information specialist, and teacher as the school librarian guides learners through thinking, creating, sharing, and growing in pursuit of new knowledge. When school librarians enact a role, it is not the role that directly affects the learner; rather, it is the school librarian's expression of the role within a learning domain that affects the learner. This domain-based approach to organizing the standards ensures that school librarians are able to personalize their professional practice and growth, continuously tailoring their school library to local needs, their own strengths, and learners' benefit.

Structure and Purpose of Your New Standards

Like other sets of learning, professional, and program standards, the AASL Standards are not a curriculum; rather, they provide you with guidance and structure as you develop a curriculum tailored to your local priorities and needs.

The contents of the standards are designed to be used two ways:

1. As personalized guides: Learners and school librarians can enter the standards at the point most appropriate to the learning task or professional activity and use the standards to guide decisions about actions to develop specific competencies.
2. As progressions: Learners and school librarians first engage with the standards at the level of Think, and once mastery of the Competencies related to Think are achieved, progress through Create, Share, and Grow.

The AASL Standards frameworks are composed of Shared Foundations, explanatory Key Commitments, competency Domains, Competencies, and Alignments. These core components are presented first as individual frameworks for learners (page 34), school librarians (page 47), and school libraries (page 59); these individual frameworks provide an overview of the standards' content. The core components are then presented in integrated frameworks (see Part II) for each of the Shared Foundations, as illustrated in figure 1.5; this view integrates the Competencies for learners and school librarians, and the Alignments for school libraries under each of the six Shared Foundations. These integrated frameworks underscore the interdependence of the three standards sets. No standards set or Shared Foundation can be effectively executed independent of the other two sets.

As figure 1.5 shows, each standards framework contains five levels:

SHARED FOUNDATION: This level describes the core values that learners, school librarians, and school libraries should reflect and promote. The six Shared Foundations of Inquire, Include, Collaborate, Curate, Explore, and Engage were derived from our research and community input. Each Shared Foundation is also inherent in your Common Beliefs.

KEY COMMITMENT: The Key Commitments spell out the essential components of the Shared Foundations. Consider Key Commitments as expanded definitions of the Shared Foundations.

DOMAINS: As mentioned earlier in this chapter, the interlinked nature of school librarians' roles is translated into the learning categories of Think, Create, Share, and Grow.

FIGURE 1.5

Overview of the *AASL Standards Integrated Framework.*

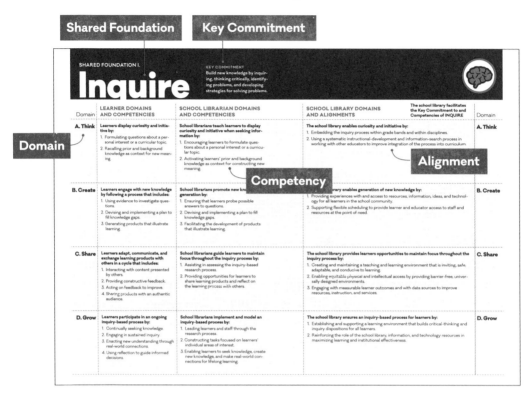

COMPETENCIES: For learners and school librarians the Key Commitments are put into practice by doing the actions that demonstrate mastery of the core Competencies included in each functional Domain. Think, Create, Share, and Grow may be seen as a continuum mirroring the inquiry process, from discovery and questioning through to sharing the results of one's work and reflecting on the process. The Competencies are not intended to be only linear, but may be used as a progression of knowledge, skills, and dispositions.

ALIGNMENTS: In school libraries the Key Commitments are expressed by the Alignments included in each functional Domain.

As figure 1.5 shows, within each Shared Foundation, standards for learners, school librarians, and school libraries contain the same functional Domains. Each section of the standards was designed to reflect the others, ensuring that standards-related activities would be mutually reinforcing, simultaneously building capacity among learners, school librarians, and the school library.

In Part II of this book we devote a chapter to each of the integrated standards frameworks. Each of these chapters presents the standard and then is anchored with details that explain the Competencies and best practices, which include practices school librarians can use to get started with effective implementation of the standards. For more about AASL's Implementation Plan, please see Appendix A.

Your Language of Growth and Competency

A notable shift in this set of standards is from the language of outcomes to the language of competency. We decided to frame learners' activities in terms of competencies to ensure that AASL's standards

- put the learner at the center, focus on growth, and acknowledge that learners are smart in different ways;
- employ a pedagogical philosophy, assessment techniques, and reporting systems that build upon and leverage learners' prior learning;
- focus on learners' growth, with appropriate supports every step of the way; and
- enable learner voice, choice, and agency (i.e., the ability to act) (Bloom 1968; Calkins and Vogt 2013).

Competencies and learning outcomes are two related educational terms that can create confusion. Competencies and outcomes can be written to describe the learning gained by a learner in individual courses (course outcomes) or for the program as a whole (program outcomes), but competencies and outcomes are not the same thing. Throughout this document we use the following working definitions:

> ***competency:*** A *general* statement that describes the desired knowledge, skills, and dispositions of a learner completing a learning experience. Competencies commonly define the applied skills and knowledge that enable people to successfully perform in professional, educational, and other life contexts.
>
> ***outcome:*** A very *specific* statement that describes exactly what a learner will be able to do in some measurable way. More than one measurable outcome may be defined for a given competency (Huba and Freed 2000), and outcomes may be assessed through quantitative and qualitative means. Outcomes demonstrate growth over time (Abbott 2013a).

The goal of competency-based education is to support learners' growth through personalized learning experiences. Part III of this book contains information about assessment.

Connecting with Stakeholders:
Personas Bring the Standards to Life

As the editorial board and the implementation task force have developed the standards and the implementation plan, we have spent extensive time talking about our audience. Who will use the standards? What are their needs? To fully envision the broad base of stakeholders, the implementation task force turned to the concept of *personas* to guide their work, and they shared their work with the editorial board.

The notion of personas derives from the field of marketing in which a key activity is to define customer segments (or, in our case, user segments) (Osterwalder and Pigneur 2010; Mulder and Yaar 2007). User segments are groups of individuals that are similar in specific ways relevant to our standards design and outreach; examples of these similarities are age, gender, professional experience, roles, and interests (Osterwalder et al. 2014). In the context of school libraries, customer or user segments include learners, school librarians, other educators, administrators, parents, and other stakeholders in the learning community.

We used personas to help us better understand our users on a more-personal level. After considering the results of the 2015 national AASL survey of members' and other stakeholders' views on the standards, a series of AASL-commissioned focus groups conducted throughout the country, and a 2013 AASL Branding Task Force survey (AASL 2015), the standards implementation task force constructed character profiles to represent different groups who share similar traits, beliefs, attitudes, and values with regard to school libraries. Personas allowed both the editorial board and the task force to get a deeper understanding of our users: their wants, needs, and motivations (Mulder and Yaar 2007). Our personas are designed to cut across categories of stakeholders and unify them into fewer, but clearly defined, user groups that we want to reach with the standards.

FOR MORE INFORMATION on the AASL Standards and Guidelines Implementation Task Force's process or for more-detailed profiles of the personas, the implementation plan can be found on the AASL Standards website at **<www.standards.aasl.org/implementation>**.

Importantly, personas offer us a user-centered shared vocabulary, facilitating both our professional conversations and our personal reflective practice. They allow us to better understand ourselves and those we serve. When we consider a next step, we might ask ourselves, "What does Patty need?" or "What would Margot do or think?" or "How might Inez contribute?" While our seven personas cannot hope to represent the diverse needs and perspectives of every individual stakeholder nationwide, they have certainly helped us extend our vision beyond our own experiences.

Below are short descriptions of the personas that guided our work. We invite you to look for yourself and your stakeholders in the descriptions, and to consider how these personas, or other personas you create based on local data, might play a role in your own local implementation efforts. Connecting with our stakeholders throughout the country has been an integral part of our work, and we hope these personas help you bring the standards to life in your own communities.

AS YOU'RE READING the standards, consider:

- Who are my stakeholders?
- Which personas resonate with me because of parallels with my community and experiences?
- How could I use or adapt these personas to guide my own work with the standards?
- How are my stakeholders' needs different from my own?
- Who could be early allies in my work with the new AASL Standards?

NOAH WHO NEEDS SUPPORT
(School Librarian)

Noah is an established librarian who will be moving from elementary to middle school level starting this fall. With his move to a new school and different grade levels, Noah feels like a first-year school librarian all over again. He is comfortable with technology, and at his old school he sought out leadership roles in the school, but right now Noah is concerned about establishing collaborative learning opportunities with other educators in his new school. The management of school library space and resources sometimes feels overwhelming to Noah, and he is eager to learn from other school librarians. He knows about the American Association of School Librarians and occasionally visits the ALA and AASL websites for resources like the ALA Youth Media Award winners and AASL annual lists of Best Apps for Teaching and Learning and Best Websites for Teaching and Learning. He is unsure, however, of how to become more involved with this professional network of experienced school librarians. His time is at a premium, and he spends it helping students after school and planning lessons that align to content-area standards. To date, his only connection with AASL has been his use of the Best Apps and Best Websites lists. In a recent district professional development day, his district school library supervisor mentioned the new AASL Standards. He wonders how he will introduce the standards to his new principal and educator colleagues. How can he use the standards to help educators meet the literacy demands of the national content standards in English/language arts, mathematics, and science?

INEZ THE INNOVATOR
(School Librarian)

Inez has been a high school librarian for twelve years during which she has served as a leadership team member in her school. She is a prolific user of social media and early adopter of technology. Although she has been a member of her state library organization, she has been more actively involved in state and national educational technology organizations. Now, Inez is curious about the new AASL Standards, and she plans to use them to help her identify areas in which she can grow. Though she's been a member of AASL for a few years, she's just starting to think about how she can contribute to and learn from the profession through national connections and leadership.

MARGOT THE MENTOR
(District School Library Supervisor, State Organization Leader, or State Department Leader)

Margot has been a district school library supervisor for nine years. In her leadership role, she directs district core teams for literacy and digital transformation. She's an active user of Twitter, Facebook, and Pinterest and connects regularly with other members of AASL, ALSC, and YALSA. She wonders what the new AASL Standards will look like in practice and how they will affect learning outcomes. Margot is also concerned about what she'll need to do to build capacity among her school librarians to make long-term changes to their practice.

ATHENA THE ACADEMIC
(Library and Information Science Pre-Service Educator and Researcher)

Athena has been teaching in a pre-service LIS program for several years, and her courses are designed around AASL's 2007 *Standards for the 21st-Century Learner.* A member of ALISE (Association for Library and Information Science Education) and AASL's ESLS (Educators of School Librarians Section), she wants to ensure her learners are prepared to lead learning in K–12 schools. She is eager to adjust her pre-service curriculum to reflect the new standards. Athena is a member of AASL's Community of Scholars and has attended the AASL CLASS Research Symposium. She is frequently asked to present at conferences and is eager to engage in research that examines the impact and implementation of the new standards.

LEON THE LEAD LEARNER
(Principal)

Leon has been a principal for three years, and he relies on his school librarian for help with tech support for the school's tablets recently purchased with grant funds. He knows his school librarian is busy and well-respected by educators, but he's not entirely sure what she does beyond helping him with his technology needs, making colorful displays, and recommending books to students and educators. Leon is committed to building a culture of innovative teaching and learning in his school, and he has a sense that his school librarian can help—he's just not quite sure how. He appreciates the focus on open, equitable access to resources and opportunities that his school librarian has created in the school library, and he's looking for ways to learn more about how the school library and school librarian can help him achieve his goals for the school.

TONY THE TEACHER
(Classroom Educator)

Tony has been teaching sixth grade for 10 years. He has little experience partnering with the school librarian in his middle school. His time is at a premium; he spends it helping students after school and planning lessons that align to content-area standards. To date, his only connection with AASL has been his use of the Best Apps and Best Web-

sites. His school librarian mentioned the new AASL Standards in a recent faculty meeting, and he wonders now about collaborating with her to integrate technology and inquiry into his instruction and to help him meet the literacy demands of the national content standards in English/language arts, mathematics, and science.

PATTY THE PARENT
(Parent, Guardian, and Community Member)

Patty, who arrived in the country five years ago, works full time. Her early shift allows her to be home shortly after her child arrives home from school. (In the morning she drops off her younger children, still toddlers, with her sister who lives in an apartment downstairs.) Patty's home country did not have school libraries; therefore, she is not aware of the resources they provide or the relationships they foster that will be valuable to her children as they move through school. When her child tells her about a class visit to the school library, Patty wonders whether the school library is learner- and parent-friendly, and how it will support her children's learning experiences. She also wonders if the school library has resources she can use and activities in which she can get involved. Patty is eager to learn more about the school library but unsure how to approach the school librarian.

Of course, no set of personas represents the range of stakeholders that are instrumental for the support of effective school libraries. For more about the implementation task force's work, please see Appendix A.

Getting Started with Your Standards: Scenarios for Professional Learning

Part IV of this book contains a series of case studies to illustrate authentic scenarios through which district-level supervisors and building-level school librarians can envision putting the AASL Standards into action. In many instances, these case studies will include the personas developed for implementation as well as additional members of related user segments. Each case study concludes with discussion questions that can be used for self-reflection, group professional development, and pre-service education.

Growing with Your Standards: Evaluation and Assessment

To enable you to thrive in a competency-based learning environment, Part III details how to measure success in an AASL Standards–driven learning environment. Assessment approaches for learners and school librarians are presented in detail. Also included are strategies for assessing school libraries.

Assessment is the process of objectively understanding the state or condition of a learner or an educator; this understanding is achieved through observation and measurement. Assessment of learning requires measuring progress toward mastering a competency; assessment of teaching means taking a measure of its effectiveness. Formative assessment is measurement for the purpose of improving teaching or learning while it is happening. In contrast, summative assessment is what we typically call "evaluation." Evaluation is the process of observing and measuring an outcome or learning product, ideally comparing it to a standard. Evaluation of school librarians is a means of measuring professional performance over the course of a specified period of time. The focus of the standards is on in-service building- and district-level personnel. They are not intended to address or articulate performance expectations for beginning school librarians. Rather, the evaluation of novice professionals should be modified to reflect expectations expressed in the ALA/AASL Standards for the Initial Preparation of School Librarians (AASL n.d.1.).

The sample instrument components and detailed approaches in Part III of this book will help you devise and use assessment and evaluation strategies that support effective implementation of the AASL Standards.

Questions for Reflective Practitioners

Many great philosophers and educational theorists (Aristotle, John Dewey, Donald Schon) have challenged us to examine established ideas and techniques, and then further develop responses and practices based on our reflections. The new standards allow us to pose questions and develop ideas on how these standards may impact our daily activities and practice. Practitioners at each career stage have a collection of beliefs, examples, and practices to draw upon. These form the basis for initial reflective thoughts. Using these unique previous experiences as points of reference, we can situate ourselves and our practices within the new standards and develop the habits of reflective practitioners.

The reflective practitioner thinks about what the new standards present. This step challenges readers to examine the standards, to explore what may be different or new in the document, or to think about situating the standards in a specific educational context. What do you see in the standards that is different or changed from previous iterations of school library standards or other sets of standards in education? Next, reflective practitioners synthesize this understanding and make personal meaning. So, what do you think about the use of the standards as they apply to your practice and your school library? Finally, reflective practitioners think of future actions. What will you do to best implement the standards? How will you use the standards to guide future work? Various points in the text present opportunities to reflect on how these standards may best be implemented. Some questions for reflective practitioners follow.

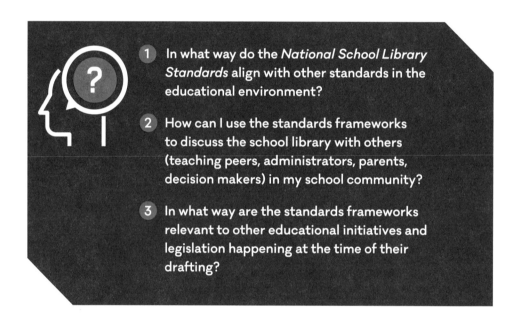

1 In what way do the *National School Library Standards* align with other standards in the educational environment?

2 How can I use the standards frameworks to discuss the school library with others (teaching peers, administrators, parents, decision makers) in my school community?

3 In what way are the standards frameworks relevant to other educational initiatives and legislation happening at the time of their drafting?

Appendices and Other Resources

This standards compendium concludes with appendices containing foundational documents: ALA's Library Bill of Rights, selected interpretations of the Library Bill of Rights, the Library Leadership and Management Association (LLAMA) Leadership Competencies, ALA's Code of Ethics, and selected AASL position statements. Another appendix is an overview of AASL's implementation plan to help you put the standards into action. Also included is a list of artifacts you could use as evidence of accomplishments—yours and learners'—in the school library, plus a brief historical timeline of the school library standards that preceded this new set of frameworks.

Following the appendices are other resources, including a glossary of terms used throughout this document, the list of works cited, a list of recommended reading to help build your knowledge base about the concepts and content in the standards, and the index.

Introduction to the Learner Standards

THE STANDARDS INCLUDED IN THE *AASL STANDARDS FRAMEWORK for Learners* acknowledge that people are learners throughout their lives. Administrators, school librarians, other educators, and all other members of the educational community continue to grow and learn as they progress throughout their careers and lives. Thus, the learner Competencies within the standards apply not only to learners in Pre-K–12 schools, but also to educators who pursue knowledge for lifelong personal and professional growth. Learner and the school librarian Competencies, as well as the school library Alignments, are presented in an integrated framework anchored by Shared Foundations and supported by Key Commitments.

The six Shared Foundations (Inquire, Include, Collaborate, Curate, Explore, and Engage) and their Key Commitments are the backbone of the AASL Standards. Learners who are empowered to deepen their own learning will

- acquire new knowledge by thinking critically and solving problems;
- operate in global society by interacting with and acknowledging the perspectives of others;
- work with others to achieve common goals;
- collect, organize, and share resources;
- harness curiosity and employ a growth mindset to explore and discover; and
- follow ethical and legal guidelines while engaging with information.

Each Shared Foundation is a one-word idea encompassing each standard.

INQUIRE

The skills needed to effectively Inquire power curiosity and questioning for learners of all ages. Although individuals may not always consciously reflect on their inquiry processes, the process of asking questions, gathering information, making sense of the information, making decisions, and sharing results is something we all do every day. Learners who harness their prior knowledge to bring new meaning to the answers to their questions take a first step toward

- addressing their knowledge gaps;
- building collective knowledge; and
- strengthening intellectual tools to sustain an inquiry process.

INCLUDE

When learners' community includes members with diverse experiences, they are aware of a range of viewpoints and anticipate the challenges often encountered in reaching consensus. Learners who include other perspectives in their understanding

- build balanced perspectives and develop skills that allow these learners to articulate ideas;
- develop comprehensive and authentic knowledge products;
- exhibit tolerance for differing viewpoints; and
- reflect on their perspectives and the perspectives of others.

Learners who master Include are productive when working with others.

COLLABORATE

Collaborative learning involves groups of learners working together to solve a problem, complete a task, or create a product (Smith and MacGregor 1992). When learners Collaborate they

- broaden their ideas and achieve common goals, often in new and innovative ways;
- think critically to solve problems they would not be able to solve independently;
- negotiate new and shared meanings;
- solicit and respond to feedback from others; and
- adapt their thinking to new ideas and situations.

CURATE

Curating resources involves the collection, organization, description, and sharing of resources to make meaning for the learner and others. Learners who Curate

- evaluate information;
- describe resources so that they may be found and understood by others;
- integrate new information into their existing knowledge;
- share knowledge with others; and
- integrate resources into larger learning networks.

EXPLORE

When learners Explore, they consider their existing knowledge, formulate authentic questions, experiment with physical and intellectual pursuits, collaboratively investigate answers, self-assess progress, and openly receive constructive feedback to strengthen their skills. As a result of investigating new ideas through authentic exploration learners can

- engage in learning in deeper ways;
- do more-complex thinking;
- conceptualize ideas; and
- understand issues in greater depth.

ENGAGE

Engagement is the degree of attention, curiosity, interest, optimism, and passion that learners show when they are learning or being taught (Abbott 2016). When learners Engage they

- develop dispositions that allow them to participate ethically and respectfully in communities of practice;
- produce materials based on valid information;
- act ethically and responsibility in their sharing of information; and
- extend learning by personalizing their use of information.

Conceptual Overview of the Learner Standards

The learner standards are organized in a hierarchical structure that parallels the school librarian standards (see figure 2.1). Understanding how the learner standards align with the school librarian and school library standards empowers school librarians to develop a comprehensive program of instruction and activities. Because the learner, school librarian, and school library standards mirror each other and are interlinked, they allow for school librarians to use them for various purposes, such as planning professional development that improves the program to enhance learner competency or personalizing learning experiences in several conceptual areas.

When novice school librarians—learners themselves—have completed pre-service preparation programs aligned to national standards, these new school librarians are expected to base instructional and collaborative efforts on their knowledge of learners and work to develop their teaching to engage learner interest and motivation.

The six one-word Shared Foundations (Inquire, Include, Collaborate, Curate, Explore, and Engage) are the education base that learners, school librarians, and school libraries share. The Key Commitment is the main objective behind each Shared Foundation. For example, the Key Commitment for Explore is "Discover

FIGURE 2.1
Flowchart for *AASL Standards Integrated Framework*.

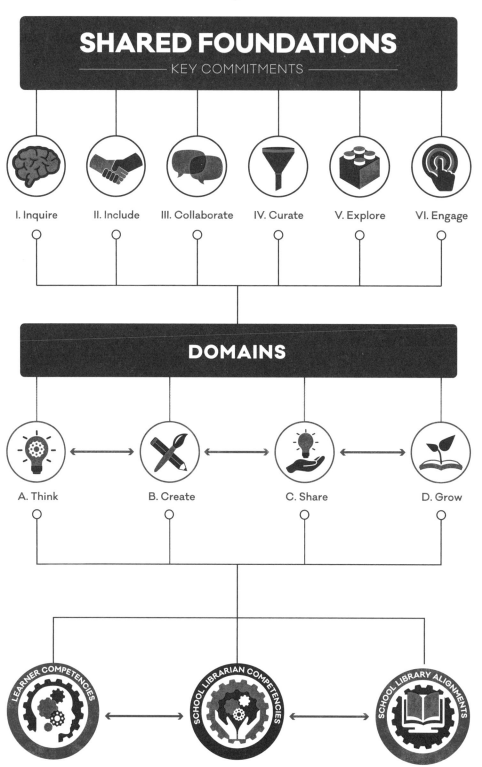

and innovate in a growth mindset developed through experience and reflection." Together, the Shared Foundation and Key Commitment provide a broad statement of the results of meeting the standards; school librarians and school library advocates can use these statements to communicate school library core values to various stakeholders.

Each Shared Foundation and Key Commitment is realized through Competencies that fall into four Domains: Think, Create, Share, and Grow. The Competencies apply to learners of all ages; the developmentally appropriate action taken to demonstrate the competency will depend on the grade level. Learners may build competency by progressing through the Domains, beginning with Think and culminating with Grow, or they may engage with the Domains most appropriate to their learning task.

Questions for the Reflective Practitioner

1. How has the structure of the AASL Standards frameworks altered the way I think about engaging with school library standards?

2. How can I most effectively use the *AASL Standards Framework for Learners* as I collaborate with my teaching peers?

3. What is the best way to use the *AASL Standards Framework for Learners* to guide my work with student learners?

Recommended Appendices

APPENDIX C. Annotated List of AASL Position Statements
APPENDIX C3. Position Statement: Instructional Role of the School Librarian
APPENDIX E3. Advocating for Intellectual Freedom
APPENDIX F. LLAMA's 14 Foundational Competencies

AASL Standards Framework
for Learners

SHARED FOUNDATION & KEY COMMITMENT	DOMAINS & COMPETENCIES			
	A. THINK	B. CREATE	C. SHARE	D. GROW
I. INQUIRE Build new knowledge by inquiring, thinking critically, identifying problems, and developing strategies for solving problems.	Learners display curiosity and initiative by: 1. Formulating questions about a personal interest or a curricular topic. 2. Recalling prior and background knowledge as context for new meaning.	Learners engage with new knowledge by following a process that includes: 1. Using evidence to investigate questions. 2. Devising and implementing a plan to fill knowledge gaps. 3. Generating products that illustrate learning.	Learners adapt, communicate, and exchange learning products with others in a cycle that includes: 1. Interacting with content presented by others. 2. Providing constructive feedback. 3. Acting on feedback to improve. 4. Sharing products with an authentic audience.	Learners participate in an ongoing inquiry-based process by: 1. Continually seeking knowledge. 2. Engaging in sustained inquiry. 3. Enacting new understanding through real-world connections. 4. Using reflection to guide informed decisions.

SHARED FOUNDATION & KEY COMMITMENT	DOMAINS & COMPETENCIES			
	A. THINK	B. CREATE	C. SHARE	D. GROW
II. INCLUDE Demonstrate an understanding of and commitment to inclusiveness and respect for diversity in the learning community.	Learners contribute a balanced perspective when participating in a learning community by: 1. Articulating an awareness of the contributions of a range of learners. 2. Adopting a discerning stance toward points of view and opinions expressed in information resources and learning products. 3. Describing their understanding of cultural relevancy and placement within the global learning community.	Learners adjust their awareness of the global learning community by: 1. Interacting with learners who reflect a range of perspectives. 2. Evaluating a variety of perspectives during learning activities. 3. Representing diverse perspectives during learning activities.	Learners exhibit empathy with and tolerance for diverse ideas by: 1. Engaging in informed conversation and active debate. 2. Contributing to discussions in which multiple viewpoints on a topic are expressed.	Learners demonstrate empathy and equity in knowledge building within the global learning community by: 1. Seeking interactions with a range of learners. 2. Demonstrating interest in other perspectives during learning activities. 3. Reflecting on their own place within the global learning community.

SHARED FOUNDATION & KEY COMMITMENT	DOMAINS & COMPETENCIES			
	A. THINK	B. CREATE	C. SHARE	D. GROW
III. COLLABORATE Work effectively with others to broaden perspectives and work toward common goals.	Learners identify collaborative opportunities by: 1. Demonstrating their desire to broaden and deepen understandings. 2. Developing new understandings through engagement in a learning group. 3. Deciding to solve problems informed by group interaction.	Learners participate in personal, social, and intellectual networks by: 1. Using a variety of communication tools and resources. 2. Establishing connections with other learners to build on their own prior knowledge and create new knowledge.	Learners work productively with others to solve problems by: 1. Soliciting and responding to feedback from others. 2. Involving diverse perspectives in their own inquiry processes.	Learners actively participate with others in learning situations by: 1. Actively contributing to group discussions. 2. Recognizing learning as a social responsibility.

SHARED FOUNDATION & KEY COMMITMENT	DOMAINS & COMPETENCIES			
	A. THINK	B. CREATE	C. SHARE	D. GROW
IV. CURATE Make meaning for oneself and others by collecting, organizing, and sharing resources of personal relevance.	Learners act on an information need by: 1. Determining the need to gather information. 2. Identifying possible sources of information. 3. Making critical choices about information sources to use.	Learners gather information appropriate to the task by: 1. Seeking a variety of sources. 2. Collecting information representing diverse perspectives. 3. Systematically questioning and assessing the validity and accuracy of information. 4. Organizing information by priority, topic, or other systematic scheme.	Learners exchange information resources within and beyond their learning community by: 1. Accessing and evaluating collaboratively constructed information sites. 2. Contributing to collaboratively constructed information sites by ethically using and reproducing others' work. 3. Joining with others to compare and contrast information derived from collaboratively constructed information sites.	Learners select and organize information for a variety of audiences by: 1. Performing ongoing analysis of and reflection on the quality, usefulness, and accuracy of curated resources. 2. Integrating and depicting in a conceptual knowledge network their understanding gained from resources. 3. Openly communicating curation processes for others to use, interpret, and validate.

SHARED FOUNDATION & KEY COMMITMENT	DOMAINS & COMPETENCIES			
	A. THINK	B. CREATE	C. SHARE	D. GROW
V. EXPLORE Discover and innovate in a growth mindset developed through experience and reflection.	Learners develop and satisfy personal curiosity by: 1. Reading widely and deeply in multiple formats and write and create for a variety of purposes. 2. Reflecting and questioning assumptions and possible misconceptions. 3. Engaging in inquiry-based processes for personal growth.	Learners construct new knowledge by: 1. Problem solving through cycles of design, implementation, and reflection. 2. Persisting through self-directed pursuits by tinkering and making.	Learners engage with the learning community by: 1. Expressing curiosity about a topic of personal interest or curricular relevance. 2. Co-constructing innovative means of investigation. 3. Collaboratively identifying innovative solutions to a challenge or problem.	Learners develop through experience and reflection by: 1. Iteratively responding to challenges. 2. Recognizing capabilities and skills that can be developed, improved, and expanded. 3. Open-mindedly accepting feedback for positive and constructive growth.

SHARED FOUNDATION & KEY COMMITMENT	DOMAINS & COMPETENCIES			
	A. THINK	B. CREATE	C. SHARE	D. GROW
VI. ENGAGE Demonstrate safe, legal, and ethical creating and sharing of knowledge products independently while engaging in a community of practice and an interconnected world.	Learners follow ethical and legal guidelines for gathering and using information by: 1. Responsibly applying information, technology, and media to learning. 2. Understanding the ethical use of information, technology, and media. 3. Evaluating information for accuracy, validity, social and cultural context, and appropriateness for need.	Learners use valid information and reasoned conclusions to make ethical decisions in the creation of knowledge by: 1. Ethically using and reproducing others' work. 2. Acknowledging authorship and demonstrating respect for the intellectual property of others. 3. Including elements in personal-knowledge products that allow others to credit content appropriately.	Learners responsibly, ethically, and legally share new information with a global community by: 1. Sharing information resources in accordance with modification, reuse, and remix policies. 2. Disseminating new knowledge through means appropriate for the intended audience.	Learners engage with information to extend personal learning by: 1. Personalizing their use of information and information technologies. 2. Reflecting on the process of ethical generation of knowledge. 3. Inspiring others to engage in safe, responsible, ethical, and legal information behaviors.

3

Introduction to the School Librarian Standards

SCHOOL LIBRARIANS RELY ON THEIR PROFESSIONAL STANDARDS TO provide direction and guidance in lesson planning, school library program development, curriculum-based unit creation, educator collaboration, pre-service school library education design, self-assessment, evaluation, and advocacy of the school library (AASL 2016a). Schools across the country have embraced the philosophy of employing skilled educators to prepare college- and career-ready learners who exemplify characteristics and skills that enable learners to participate in a changing global society. School librarians play a pivotal role in this re-envisioned learner-centered, relevant educational landscape.

The AASL Standards for school librarians consist of six one-word Shared Foundations, each of which is supported by a Key Commitment that explains more fully the intent of the Shared Foundation. Competencies for each Shared Foundation provide context for implementation under the Domains of Think, Create, Share, and Grow.

INQUIRE: Why would school librarians start with Inquire? For centuries, great thinkers have built new knowledge by inquiring, thinking critically, identifying problems, and developing strategies for solving problems. Questioning and curiosity are critical for learners of all ages. By facilitating the building of new knowledge through the process of inquiring, thinking critically, identifying problems, and developing strategies for solving problems, school librarians are conduits for Inquire.

INCLUDE: The fundamental concept Include addresses an understanding of and commitment to inclusiveness and respect for diversity in the learning community. School librarians are champions of these attributes, helping learners navigate varied perspectives and understand cultural relevancy. School librarians nurture productive debate and conversation by promoting the ideal of Include.

COLLABORATE: To collaborate with other educators and to teach learners to collaborate are dispositions integral to successful participation in our world community. In a society that values and strives for interconnectedness, learners require the abilities to participate in collaborative learning environments. School librarians are key to ensuring that learners gain the strategies necessary to work effectively with others to broaden perspectives and work toward common goals.

CURATE: School librarians recognize that learners now encounter more information every day than did learners in the past. Ensuring that learners can use information resources in deliberate and reflective ways is essential to deep inquiry learning. Learners must make meaning for themselves and others by collecting, organizing, and sharing resources of personal relevance. School librarians, masters at teaching learners to collect, organize, and share resources, help learners curate information in efficient and effective ways. School librarians must be well versed in the wealth of resources that complement both the curriculum and learners' interests, and model the curation techniques they teach.

 EXPLORE: Through exploration learners discover and innovate with a growth mindset developed through experience and reflection. School librarians are in a unique position to promote the growth mindset in all learners by providing opportunities for exploration, supporting persistence, and encouraging continuous reflective thinking. School librarians help learners view and practice learning as an iterative endeavor throughout which learners build stamina.

 ENGAGE: To flourish in our global society, maintaining engagement in their learning is a key practice of successful learners. School librarians support and promote learners' engagement and empowerment by modeling and explicitly teaching best practices in information and resource use. To engage in a global society as part of an interconnected learning community, learners must demonstrate safe, legal, and ethical creating and sharing of knowledge products.

Key Commitments and school librarian Competencies establish a comprehensive focus on the core concepts presented as Shared Foundations. As school librarians develop their competencies within the areas of Think, Create, Share, and Grow, a climate of intentional, innovative, and engaging learning is the result.

Conceptual Overview of the School Librarian Standards

By focusing on an environment in which learners and educators have unprecedented access to teaching and learning opportunities, school librarians create a mobile teaching and learning culture centered on innovation, collaboration, exploration, deep thinking, and creativity. School librarians are key to the success of this educational paradigm shift because they provide resources and instruction to all learners through an inquiry-based research model that supports questioning and the creation of new knowledge focused on learner interest and real-world problems.

This vision for teaching and learning is dependent on school librarians who embrace, lead, and model progressive pedagogies, including coteaching, personalized learning, and face-to-face and virtual active learning environments. To support learners' exploration, school librarians build virtual collections, encourage active collaborative learning, and create spaces and learning structures within flexible school library spaces. School librarians are master educators who provide leadership for a vision of learning centered on learner voice and choice.

School librarians catalyze change that creates college-, career-, and life-ready learners as well as passionate, innovative, and engaged citizens. These learners exhibit a growth mindset (Dweck 2007) and have the capacity to creatively solve complex and meaningful problems. To truly engage all learners in knowledge creation, school librarians immerse themselves in a systemic practice in which school librarians and other educators aim to naturally and routinely collaborate and coteach. School librarians guide this practice and bring teaching and learning to the core of the school library.

For school librarians the Shared Foundations represent the fundamental concepts crucial to an effective professional practice: Inquire, Include, Collaborate, Curate, Explore, and Engage. Although at times each might stand alone as an area of focus, the seamless integration of all six ensures that school librarians design, facilitate, and reflect on learners' growth experiences as productive, thoughtful, and ethical global citizens.

The Key Commitments explain more fully the ideas behind each of the Shared Foundations. For school librarians the Key Commitment provides a definition and focus within the Shared Foundation to establish professional mindsets for planning, collaboration, and learning in the school library.

School librarian Competencies intentionally parallel those of the learner, and emphasize the integrated nature of a comprehensive learning environment. As the school librarian implements the Competencies for professional practice, learners simultaneously work toward their own Competencies established in the learner standards. Similarly, novice school librarians, having completed pre-service preparation programs aligned to national standards, understand the Shared Foundations and Key Commitments, and demonstrate beginning competencies by applying the knowledge and skills necessary to achieve them.

The school librarian Competencies fall within four Domains—Think, Create, Share, and Grow; these Domains represent steps in a professional-growth process,

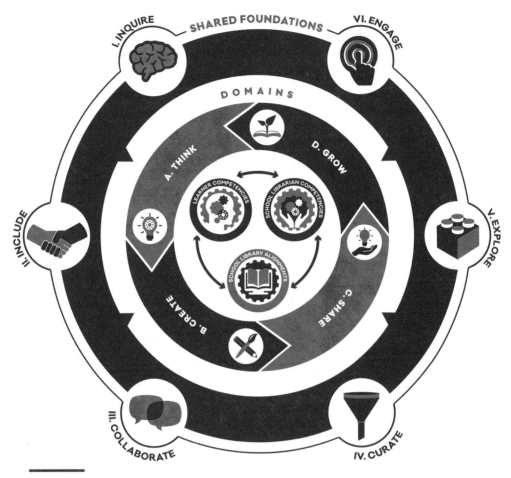

FIGURE 3.1
Chart illustrating the relationship of the parts within the standards structure.

flowing from thinking about knowledge needs to creating knowledge products, to sharing new knowledge, to reflecting on the learning process. Competencies in the Think Domain focus on the school librarian's role in encouraging learners to formulate questions and articulate viewpoints, scaffolding learning situations, modeling, guiding, and facilitating understanding. In the Create Domain, Competencies for the school librarian focus on designing opportunities for learners to create products that illustrate learning and foster collaboration in diverse settings. Share Competencies emphasize the importance of the school librarian's encouraging learners to responsibly share their innovative solutions to problems in multiple formats to appropriate audiences. Competencies within the Grow Domain focus on aspects of reflection, identifying future learning needs, and planning, as well as on promotion of the expansion of learning, recognizing the social context necessary for that learning to thrive.

Questions for the Reflective Practitioner

1. How do the AASL Standards frameworks challenge me to offer opportunities for innovation, collaboration, exploration, deep thinking, and creativity?

2. How will the *AASL Standards Framework for School Librarians* impact the way I think about teaching in my school library?

3. In what way can I use the *AASL Standards Framework for School Librarians* to support learners and develop an engaging learning environment?

Recommended Appendices

APPENDIX C. Annotated List of AASL Position Statements

APPENDIX C1. Position Statement: Definition of an Effective School Library Program

APPENDIX C3. Position Statement: Instructional Role of the School Librarian

APPENDIX C5. Position Statement: Role of the School Library Program

APPENDIX F. LLAMA's 14 Foundational Competencies

AASL Standards Framework
for School Librarians

SHARED FOUNDATION & KEY COMMITMENT	DOMAINS & COMPETENCIES			
	A. THINK	B. CREATE	C. SHARE	D. GROW
I. INQUIRE **Build new knowledge by inquiring, thinking critically, identifying problems, and developing strategies for solving problems.**	School librarians teach learners to display curiosity and initiative when seeking information by: 1. Encouraging learners to formulate questions about a personal interest or a curricular topic. 2. Activating learners' prior and background knowledge as context for constructing new meaning.	School librarians promote new knowledge generation by: 1. Ensuring that learners probe possible answers to questions. 2. Devising and implementing a plan to fill knowledge gaps. 3. Facilitating the development of products that illustrate learning.	School librarians guide learners to maintain focus throughout the inquiry process by: 1. Assisting in assessing the inquiry-based research process. 2. Providing opportunities for learners to share learning products and reflect on the learning process with others.	School librarians implement and model an inquiry-based process by: 1. Leading learners and staff through the research process. 2. Constructing tasks focused on learners' individual areas of interest. 3. Enabling learners to seek knowledge, create new knowledge, and make real-world connections for lifelong learning.

SHARED FOUNDATION & KEY COMMITMENT	DOMAINS & COMPETENCIES			
	A. THINK	B. CREATE	C. SHARE	D. GROW
II. INCLUDE Demonstrate an understanding of and commitment to inclusiveness and respect for diversity in the learning community.	School librarians direct learners to contribute a balanced perspective when participating in a learning community by: 1. Engaging learners to articulate an awareness of the contributions of a range of learners. 2. Guiding learners as they adopt a discerning stance toward points of view and opinions expressed in information resources and learning products. 3. Differentiating instruction to support learners' understanding of cultural relevancy and placement within the global learning community.	School librarians establish opportunities for learners to adjust their awareness of the global learning community by: 1. Providing opportunities for learners to interact with others who reflect a range of perspectives. 2. Devising learning activities that require learners to evaluate a variety of perspectives. 3. Designing opportunities that help learners to illustrate diverse viewpoints.	School librarians facilitate experiences in which learners exhibit empathy and tolerance for diverse ideas by: 1. Giving learners opportunities to engage in informed conversation and active debate. 2. Guiding learners to contribute to discussions in which multiple viewpoints on a topic are expressed.	School librarians explicitly lead learners to demonstrate empathy and equity in knowledge building within the global learning community by: 1. Creating an atmosphere in which learners feel empowered and interactions are learner-initiated. 2. Initiating opportunities that allow learners to demonstrate interest in other perspectives. 3. Showcasing learners' reflections on their place within the global learning community.

SHARED FOUNDATION & KEY COMMITMENT	DOMAINS & COMPETENCIES			
	A. THINK	B. CREATE	C. SHARE	D. GROW
III. COLLABO-RATE Work effectively with others to broaden perspectives and work toward common goals.	School librarians facilitate collaborative opportunities by: 1. Challenging learners to work with others to broaden and deepen understandings. 2. Scaffolding enactment of learning-group roles to enable the development of new understandings within a group. 3. Organizing learner groups for decision making and problem solving.	School librarians demonstrate the importance of personal, social, and intellectual networks by: 1. Modeling the use of a variety of communication tools and resources. 2. Cultivating networks that allow learners to build on their own prior knowledge and create new knowledge.	School librarians promote working productively with others to solve problems by: 1. Demonstrating how to solicit and respond to feedback from others. 2. Advocating and modeling respect for diverse perspectives to guide the inquiry process.	School librarians foster active participation in learning situations by: 1. Stimulating learners to actively contribute to group discussions. 2. Creating a learning environment in which learners understand that learning is a social responsibility.

SHARED FOUNDATION & KEY COMMITMENT	DOMAINS & COMPETENCIES			
	A. THINK	B. CREATE	C. SHARE	D. GROW
IV. CURATE Make meaning for oneself and others by collecting, organizing, and sharing resources of personal relevance.	School librarians challenge learners to act on an information need by: 1. Modeling the response to a need to gather and organize information. 2. Designing opportunities for learners to explore possible information sources. 3. Guiding learners to make critical choices about information sources to use.	School librarians promote information gathering appropriate to the task by: 1. Sharing a variety of sources. 2. Encouraging the use of information representing diverse perspectives. 3. Fostering the questioning and assessing of validity and accuracy of information. 4. Providing tools and strategies to organize information by priority, topic, or other systematic scheme.	School librarians contribute to and guide information resource exchange within and beyond the school learning community by: 1. Facilitating opportunities to access and evaluate collaboratively constructed information sites. 2. Devising pathways for learners to contribute to collaboratively constructed information sites by ethically using and reproducing others' work. 3. Directing learners to join others to compare and contrast information derived from collaboratively constructed information sites.	School librarians show learners how to select and organize information for a variety of audiences by: 1. Engaging learners in ongoing analysis of and reflection on the quality, usefulness, and accuracy of curated resources. 2. Formulating tasks that help learners to integrate and depict in a conceptual knowledge network learners' understanding gained from resources. 3. Making opportunities for learners to openly communicate curation processes for others to use, interpret, and validate.

SHARED FOUNDATION & KEY COMMITMENT	DOMAINS & COMPETENCIES			
	A. THINK	B. CREATE	C. SHARE	D. GROW
V. EXPLORE Discover and innovate in a growth mindset developed through experience and reflection.	School librarians foster learners' personal curiosity by: 1. Encouraging learners to read widely and deeply in multiple formats and write and create for a variety of purposes. 2. Challenging learners to reflect and question assumptions and possible misconceptions. 3. Enabling learners by helping them develop inquiry-based processes for personal growth.	School librarians stimulate learners to construct new knowledge by: 1. Teaching problem solving through cycles of design, implementation, and reflection. 2. Providing opportunities for tinkering and making. 3. Modeling persistence through self-directed tinkering and making.	School librarians prepare learners to engage with the learning community by: 1. Providing strategies for acting on curiosity about a topic of personal interest or curricular relevance. 2. Assisting learners to co-construct innovative means of investigation. 3. Structuring activities for learners to collaboratively identify innovative solutions to a challenge or problem.	School librarians help learners develop through experience and reflection by: 1. Scaffolding iterative challenge-response processes. 2. Helping learners to recognize capabilities and skills that can be developed, improved, and expanded. 3. Fostering an atmosphere in which constructive feedback is openly accepted for positive growth.

SHARED FOUNDATION & KEY COMMITMENT	DOMAINS & COMPETENCIES			
	A. THINK	B. CREATE	C. SHARE	D. GROW
VI. ENGAGE Demonstrate safe, legal, and ethical creating and sharing of knowledge products independently while engaging in a community of practice and an interconnected world.	School librarians promote ethical and legal guidelines for gathering and using information by: 1. Directing learners to responsibly use information, technology, and media for learning, and modeling this responsible use. 2. Modeling the understanding of ethical use of information, technology, and media. 3. Teaching learners how and why to evaluate information for accuracy, validity, social and cultural context, and appropriateness for need.	School librarians act as a resource for using valid information and reasoned conclusions to make ethical decisions in the creation of knowledge by: 1. Showing a variety of strategies to ethically use and reproduce others' work, and modeling this ethical use. 2. Requiring complete attribution to acknowledge authorship and demonstrate respect for the intellectual property of others. 3. Promoting the inclusion of elements in personal-knowledge products that allow others to credit content appropriately.	School librarians promote the responsible, ethical, and legal sharing of new information with a global community by: 1. Imparting strategies for sharing information resources in accordance with modification, reuse, and remix policies. 2. Guiding the dissemination of new knowledge through means appropriate for the intended audience.	School librarians support learners' engagement with information to extend personal learning by: 1. Structuring a learning environment for innovative use of information and information technologies. 2. Designing experiences that help learners communicate the value of the ethical creation of new knowledge and reflect on their process. 3. Championing and modeling safe, responsible, ethical, and legal information behaviors.

Introduction to the School Library Standards

AN EFFECTIVE SCHOOL LIBRARY PLAYS AN IMPORTANT ROLE IN PRE-
paring learners for life in an information-rich society. As defined by AASL, school
libraries are "dynamic learning environments that bridge the gap between access and
opportunity for all K–12 learners" (AASL 2016c, 1). Grounded in standards and best
practice, school libraries are an integral component of the educational landscape. The
school library provides an environment in which teaching and learning are the primary emphases. The school library provides a space and place for personalized learner
success; learners are encouraged to explore questions of personal and academic relevance. Under the direction of a qualified school librarian, school libraries are instrumental in fostering literacy and teaching inquiry skills to support lifelong learning.

 INQUIRE: Inquiry and investigation are at the core of the school
library. Through scaffolding the use of an inquiry-based model of
learning, the school library offers multiple opportunities for learners to integrate new and existing knowledge. School librarians
develop and facilitate learning activities that are academically rigorous, thought
provoking, and inquiry-based. Integrating a collaborative approach across a
variety of content areas, the school library promotes an inquiry process that
includes posing questions, finding answers, and developing critical-thinking
and communication skills through information exploration.

 INCLUDE: An effective school library will include resources, programs, and services that meet the needs of all learners; represents
various points of view on current and historical issues; and provides
support across a wide range of interest areas. The school library's
resources are diverse and inclusive, enabling learners to broaden their interests
and understanding through exposure to new authors, genres, multiple forms of
resources, and opportunities to recognize themselves as members of a global
learning community.

 COLLABORATE: An effective school library encourages broad-
ening personal knowledge and creating interconnected learning
opportunities through collaboration. Users of the school library
collaborate effectively, sharing ideas and information in a responsible and ethical manner. The school library encourages collaborative teaching
practices that integrate information-seeking practices through authentic real-
world applications. School librarians collaboratively partner with fellow educators to facilitate learning in the school library, classroom, and within a variety of
physical and virtual educational environments.

CURATE: The effective school library includes a professionally curated collection of resources selected based on their authority, currency, relevance, scope, and relationship to other items in the collection. Using this selection model, users of the school library are encouraged to examine the authority and bias of authors or producers of information when curating resources for personal and academic use. The school library includes opportunities for educators, including school librarians, to model and facilitate learners' own assessment of an information need and location of available information on a given topic as users determine the appropriateness of the information to meet a need. Additionally, the school library and its users may participate as a community to create and share new ideas, resources, products, and information, collecting resources of personal and academic relevance, and sharing these widely with a learning community.

 EXPLORE: An effective school library provides learners with a venue to explore questions that arise out of personalized learning opportunities and out of individual curiosity and interest. The school library focuses on the development of a culture of reading, supports reading for learning and personal enjoyment, and provides opportunities for learners to read for pleasure. To meet the needs of all learners, the school library provides a wide variety of resources in multiple formats. An effective school library is guided by a selection and evaluation plan for collection development; implementation of the plan provides the school community with a high-quality collection of reading materials in multiple formats. These materials reflect learners' personal interests and academic needs.

ENGAGE: Effective school libraries help learners engage with the principles of safe and effective information skills and provide opportunities for learners to develop competencies in a space that allows learners to share and disseminate information. With the vast amount of information available, it is critical that all users know how to find and evaluate information to ensure its reliability, and think critically and make informed decisions about the information they encounter. Ethical use of information is modeled and taught to ensure learners are proficient in creating and sharing new information with a larger community of learners.

As with the learner and school librarian standards, the six Shared Foundations and their Key Commitments provide the basis for the *AASL Standards Framework for School Libraries*. Alignment to each Shared Foundation provides a context for implementation of the standards under the four Domains of Think, Create, Share, and Grow. Using the framework with the Key Commitments, the Alignments outlining an effective school library guide practitioners in developing the requisite structure and dispositions to ensure success.

Conceptual Overview of the School Library Standards

Because the school library is situated at the building level, it is guided by policies and procedures defined by the school and school district as well as by state-level education policymakers (AASL n.d.2.). Discussions and decisions about policy may occur at those levels and impact the building-level program (see figure 4.1). An effective school library reflects and responds to this interconnectedness.

Learners require access to technology and online resources. Effective school libraries have adequate, up-to-date instructional and learning technologies. As part of the school library, the school librarian provides leadership and instruction to both educators and learners on how to use these information technologies constructively, ethically, and safely. To ensure learners are successful, it is essential for school librarians to have opportunities on a continuing basis to update their own knowledge about emerging and new technologies. They may then provide the support and training required to assist learners and staff on how to best use resources.

In an effective school library resources are available to all before, during, and after the school day. Scheduling of classes' use of the school library should allow flexible, open, unrestricted, and equitable access to collections and technology, and to the

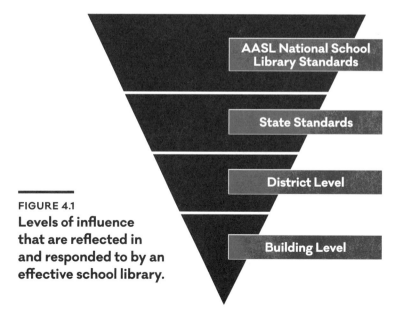

FIGURE 4.1
Levels of influence that are reflected in and responded to by an effective school library.

services of a certified school librarian. Scheduling should be thoughtfully designed to ensure learners have access to school library spaces and resources at the point of need for an integrated school library. Additionally, the school library is not confined to the physical school library space. Through the use of technology and online resources, the school library has the ability to provide continuous access to resources, whether in the school library, the classroom, the learner's home, or other remote locations.

The school library's value is demonstrated through the close alignment with the school librarian standards and the activities of a school librarian within the school community, such as representation on key decision-making committees. Representation on school-wide and district committees such as the curriculum, technology, and leadership committees that align with the school mission and strategic plan strengthens relationships for the school library and provides opportunities for library issues to be heard among decision makers.

Pre-service school librarians can also engage in meaningful and relevant activities that address the development and management of learner-centered school libraries and facilities. Providing opportunities for pre-service school librarians to get field experiences and clinical practice within a building setting, monitored and evaluated by a qualified on-site mentor and aligned to national standards, supports development of novice school librarians who can engage in meaningful and relevant activities that address the development and management of learner-centered school libraries and instruction.

Questions for the Reflective Practitioner

1 How do the structure and programming of the school library reflect and support the standards frameworks for learners and school librarians?

2 Other educational standards include mention of research or inquiry. Why is it necessary to have a set of standards unique to the school library profession?

3 How do the school library standards support and align with other initiatives in the school community?

Recommended Appendices

AASL Standards Framework
for School Libraries

SHARED FOUNDATION & KEY COMMITMENT	DOMAINS & ALIGNMENTS			
	A. THINK	B. CREATE	C. SHARE	D. GROW
I. INQUIRE Build new knowledge by inquiring, thinking critically, identifying problems, and developing strategies for solving problems.	The school library enables curiosity and initiative by: 1. Embedding the inquiry process within grade bands and within disciplines. 2. Using a systematic instructional-development and information-search process in working with other educators to improve integration of the process into curriculum.	The school library enables generation of new knowledge by: 1. Providing experiences with and access to resources, information, ideas, and technology for all learners in the school community. 2. Supporting flexible scheduling to provide learner and educator access to staff and resources at the point of need.	The school library provides learners opportunities to maintain focus throughout the inquiry process by: 1. Creating and maintaining a teaching and learning environment that is inviting, safe, adaptable, and conducive to learning. 2. Enabling equitable physical and intellectual access by providing barrier-free, universally designed environments. 3. Engaging with measurable learner outcomes and with data sources to improve resources, instruction, and services.	The school library ensures an inquiry-based process for learners by: 1. Establishing and supporting a learning environment that builds critical-thinking and inquiry dispositions for all learners. 2. Reinforcing the role of the school library, information, and technology resources in maximizing learning and institutional effectiveness.

SHARED FOUNDATION & KEY COMMITMENT	DOMAINS & ALIGNMENTS			
	A. THINK	B. CREATE	C. SHARE	D. GROW
II. INCLUDE Demonstrate an understanding of and commitment to inclusiveness and respect for diversity in the learning community.	The school library supports balanced perspectives through resources and learning opportunities by: 1. Providing challenging and authentic opportunities that address the needs of the broad range of learners. 2. Offering diverse learning experiences that allow for individual differences in learners. 3. Providing a comprehensive variety of resources.	The school library represents all members and their place in a global learning community by: 1. Establishing and maintaining a collection of reading and information materials in formats that support the diverse developmental, cultural, social, and linguistic needs of the range of learners and their communities. 2. Organizing facilities to enhance the use of and ensure equitable access to information resources and services for all learners. 3. Featuring learning opportunities that include diverse viewpoints.	The school library facilitates opportunities to experience diverse ideas by: 1. Implementing solutions that address physical, social, cultural, linguistic, and intellectual barriers to equitable access to resources and services. 2. Promoting the use of high-quality and high-interest literature in formats that reflect the diverse developmental, cultural, social, and linguistic needs of all learners and their communities. 3. Constructing a learning environment that fosters the sharing of a wide range of viewpoints and ideas.	The school library builds empathy and equity within the global learning community by: 1. Ensuring that all learning needs are met through access to information and ideas located in a diverse collection of sufficient size for the learner population and supported by reliable hardware and software. 2. Enabling equitable access to learning opportunities, academic and social support, and other resources necessary for learners' success. 3. Clearly and frequently articulating the school library's impact when communicating with administration, faculty, staff, learners, parents, and the community.

SHARED FOUNDATION & KEY COMMITMENT	DOMAINS & ALIGNMENTS			
	A. THINK	B. CREATE	C. SHARE	D. GROW
III. COLLABO-RATE Work effectively with others to broaden perspectives and work toward common goals.	The school library facilitates opportunities to integrate collaborative and shared learning by: 1. Partnering with other educators to scaffold learning and organize learner groups to broaden and deepen understanding. 2. Leading inquiry-based learning opportunities that enhance the information, media, visual, and technical literacies of all members of the school community.	The school library's policies ensure that school librarians are active participants in development, evaluation, and improvement of instructional and program resources with the school librarian by: 1. Consistently engaging with the school community to ensure that the school library resources, services, and standards align with the school's mission. 2. Participating in district, building, and department or grade-level curriculum development and assessment on a regular basis. 3. Including the school community in the development of school library policies and procedures.	The school library provides opportunities for school librarians to connect and work with the learning community by: 1. Facilitating diverse social and intellectual learner networks. 2. Designing and leading professional-development opportunities that reinforce the impact of the school library's resources, services, and programming on learners' academic learning and educators' effectiveness. 3. Promoting and modeling the importance of information-use skills by publicizing to learners, staff, and the community available services and resources; serving on school and district-wide committees; and engaging in community and professional activities.	The school library supports active learner participation by: 1. Creating and maintaining a learning environment that supports and stimulates discussion from all members of the school community. 2. Demonstrating and reinforcing the idea that information is a shared resource.

SHARED FOUNDATION & KEY COMMITMENT	DOMAINS & ALIGNMENTS			
	A. THINK	B. CREATE	C. SHARE	D. GROW
IV. CURATE Make meaning for oneself and others by collecting, organizing, and sharing resources of personal relevance.	The school library provides problem-based learning experiences and environments by: 1. Using resources and technology to foster inquiry and scaffold mastery of skills necessary for learning to progress. 2. Adopting a dynamic collection-development plan to ensure that adequate resources reflect current and in-depth knowledge. 3. Focusing on the effective use of a wide range of resources to foster information skills appropriate to content areas.	The school library promotes selection of appropriate resources and tools for information use by: 1. Demonstrating and documenting how resources and technology are used to address information needs. 2. Providing opportunities for all members of the school community to develop information and technology skills needed to promote the transfer of information-related problem-solving strategies across all disciplines. 3. Employing a dynamic collection policy that includes selection and retention criteria for all materials within the collection. 4. Implementing an administratively approved and endorsed policy that clearly addresses procedures for handling material challenges. 5. Designing and providing adequate, appropriate space for library resources, services, and activities.	The school library facilitates the contribution and exchange of information within and among learning communities by: 1. Providing an environment in which resources that support the school's curriculum and learning goals can be collaboratively selected and developed. 2. Including and tracking collection materials in a system that uses standardized approaches to description and location. 3. Establishing policies that promote effective acquisition, description, circulation, sharing, and access to resources within and beyond the school day. 4. Maintaining procedures that ensure user confidentiality and promote unimpeded access to materials by staff members and learners.	The school library engages the learning community in exploring resources by: 1. Describing, organizing, and promoting the collection for maximum and effective uses for multiple learning applications. 2. Maintaining a collection of sufficient breadth and currency to be pertinent to the school's program of studies. 3. Supporting access through a schedule that allows use by learners and staff at time of need. 4. Using local and external data to inform ongoing adjustments to the scope of the resource collection, and its audiences, formats, and applications

SHARED FOUNDATION & KEY COMMITMENT	DOMAINS & ALIGNMENTS			
	A. THINK	B. CREATE	C. SHARE	D. GROW
V. EXPLORE Discover and innovate in a growth mindset developed through experience and reflection.	The school library supports learners' personal curiosity by: 1. Providing resources and strategies for inquiry-based processes. 2. Fostering opportunities for learners to demonstrate personal curiosity and creation of knowledge through engaging with a wide variety of resources and technology.	The school library facilitates construction of new knowledge by: 1. Implementing technology as a tool or resource for learning. 2. Ensuring that multiple learning activities can occur in both physical and virtual spaces. 3. Establishing and maintaining a learning environment conducive to independent and collaborative exploration and problem solving.	The school library prepares learners to engage with a larger learning community by: 1. Modeling and promoting the use of personal and professional learning networks. 2. Encouraging families and other members of the community to participate in school library activities. 3. Building and advocating for strong relationships with stakeholders who recognize and support an effective school library.	The school library assists in the growth and development of learners by: 1. Leading other educators and learners to embrace a growth mindset through lifelong learning. 2. Anticipating learners' needs and adapting the learning environment in accordance with evidence-based best practices. 3. Embracing new skills, knowledge, and standards in the profession as they relate to teaching, learning, technology, and innovation.

SHARED FOUNDATION & KEY COMMITMENT	DOMAINS & ALIGNMENTS			
	A. THINK	**B. CREATE**	**C. SHARE**	**D. GROW**
VI. ENGAGE Demonstrate safe, legal, and ethical creating and sharing of knowledge products independently while engaging in a community of practice and an interconnected world.	The school library serves as a context in which the school librarian ensures that the school community is aware of the guidelines for safe, ethical, and legal use of information by: 1. Educating the school community on the ethical use of information and the intellectual property of others. 2. Designing instruction and delivery of services that support equitable access to information in an efficient and ethical manner by all members of the school community. 3. Embedding legal-, ethical-, and social-responsibility concepts into the inquiry and information-seeking processes.	The school library supports ethical processes for information seeking and use by: 1. Providing an environment in which all members of the school community can work together to develop, approve, and engage in clearly stated use policies to guide acceptable and ethical use of information, technology, and media. 2. Promoting the responsible use of ideas, information, media, and technology through compliance with copyright and intellectual-property policies developed by the school librarian in collaboration with all members of the school community.	The school library encourages participation in a diverse learning community to create and share information by: 1. Providing both online and physical spaces for the sharing and dissemination of ideas and information. 2. Providing a context in which the school librarian can model for learners, other educators, and administrators multiple strategies to locate, evaluate, and ethically use information for specific purposes.	The school library supports individual responsibility for information use by: 1. Providing an environment in which the school librarian can effectively develop, direct, and promote resources, services, policies, procedures, and programming aligned with current standards, ethical codes, and principles of the education and information professions. 2. Providing an engaging learning environment that supports innovative and ethical use of information and information technologies.

PART II

Standards
Integrated
Frameworks

5

Inquire

Build new knowledge by inquiring, thinking critically, identifying problems, and developing strategies for solving problems.

I. INQUIRE

VI. ENGAGE
Demonstrate safe, legal, and ethical creating and sharing of knowledge products independently while engaging in a community of practice and in an interconnected world.

V. EXPLORE
Discover and innovate in a growth mindset developed through experience and reflection.

DOMAINS

A. THINK
Inquire, think critically, and gain knowledge.

D. GROW
Pursue personal and aesthetic growth.

B. CREATE
Draw conclusions, make informed decisions, apply knowledge to new situations, and create new knowledge.

C. SHARE
Share knowledge and participate ethically and productively as members of our democratic society.

Demonstrate an understanding of and commitment to inclusiveness and respect for diversity in the learning community.

IV. CURATE

II. INCLUDE
Work effectively with others to broaden perspectives and work toward common goals.

III. COLLABORATE
Make meaning for oneself and others by collecting, organizing, and sharing resources of personal relevance.

KEY COMMITMENTS

SHARED FOUNDATIONS

67

Inquire

Domain	LEARNER DOMAINS AND COMPETENCIES	SCHOOL LIBRARIAN DOMAINS AND COMPETENCIES
A. Think	**Learners display curiosity and initiative by:** 1. Formulating questions about a personal interest or a curricular topic. 2. Recalling prior and background knowledge as context for new meaning.	**School librarians teach learners to display curiosity and initiative when seeking information by:** 1. Encouraging learners to formulate questions about a personal interest or a curricular topic. 2. Activating learners' prior and background knowledge as context for constructing new meaning.
B. Create	**Learners engage with new knowledge by following a process that includes:** 1. Using evidence to investigate questions. 2. Devising and implementing a plan to fill knowledge gaps. 3. Generating products that illustrate learning.	**School librarians promote new knowledge generation by:** 1. Ensuring that learners probe possible answers to questions. 2. Devising and implementing a plan to fill knowledge gaps. 3. Facilitating the development of products that illustrate learning.
C. Share	**Learners adapt, communicate, and exchange learning products with others in a cycle that includes:** 1. Interacting with content presented by others. 2. Providing constructive feedback. 3. Acting on feedback to improve. 4. Sharing products with an authentic audience.	**School librarians guide learners to maintain focus throughout the inquiry process by:** 1. Assisting in assessing the inquiry-based research process. 2. Providing opportunities for learners to share learning products and reflect on the learning process with others.
D. Grow	**Learners participate in an ongoing inquiry-based process by:** 1. Continually seeking knowledge. 2. Engaging in sustained inquiry. 3. Enacting new understanding through real-world connections. 4. Using reflection to guide informed decisions.	**School librarians implement and model an inquiry-based process by:** 1. Leading learners and staff through the research process. 2. Constructing tasks focused on learners' individual areas of interest. 3. Enabling learners to seek knowledge, create new knowledge, and make real-world connections for lifelong learning.

SCHOOL LIBRARY DOMAINS AND ALIGNMENTS	The school library facilitates the Key Commitment to and Competencies of INQUIRE	Domain
The school library enables curiosity and initiative by: 1. Embedding the inquiry process within grade bands and within disciplines. 2. Using a systematic instructional-development and information-search process in working with other educators to improve integration of the process into curriculum.		**A. Think**
The school library enables generation of new knowledge by: 1. Providing experiences with and access to resources, information, ideas, and technology for all learners in the school community. 2. Supporting flexible scheduling to provide learner and educator access to staff and resources at the point of need.		**B. Create**
The school library provides learners opportunities to maintain focus throughout the inquiry process by: 1. Creating and maintaining a teaching and learning environment that is inviting, safe, adaptable, and conducive to learning. 2. Enabling equitable physical and intellectual access by providing barrier-free, universally designed environments. 3. Engaging with measurable learner outcomes and with data sources to improve resources, instruction, and services.		**C. Share**
The school library ensures an inquiry-based process for learners by: 1. Establishing and supporting a learning environment that builds critical-thinking and inquiry dispositions for all learners. 2. Reinforcing the role of the school library, information, and technology resources in maximizing learning and institutional effectiveness.		**D. Grow**

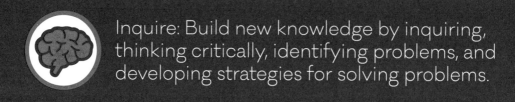

Inquire: Build new knowledge by inquiring, thinking critically, identifying problems, and developing strategies for solving problems.

INQUIRE LEARNER COMPETENCIES IN DEPTH

THINK: Learners build new knowledge through inquiry, critical thinking, and problem solving in a community in which learners help each other question and think. Successful learners develop the capacity to display curiosity and demonstrate initiative. Each learner should be given opportunities to invest his or her own thinking and inquiry in a topic of interest within the subject under study. In a safe, accepting learning environment in which questions are welcomed and encouraged, learners are empowered to display curiosity and build on prior and collective knowledge in new ways that bring meaning and background to their questions.

CREATE: Learners benefit from engaging in a structured inquiry-based research process in which they may struggle through questioning, reformulating, failing, rethinking problems, and deciding between solutions. This struggle will be evident in inquiry environments, regardless of whether learners are investigating a topic of personal interest or a specific curricular concept or topic. To create new knowledge, learners value and foster ideas, and devise and implement plans to address gaps in knowledge. Learners demonstrate their development of new knowledge by creating products while using a range of tools and resources.

SHARE: Learners share their newly acquired knowledge in a cyclical process of adapting, communicating, and exchanging products with their peers. In a safe, accepting, and open environment that supports personal growth, confidence, critical comment, and constructive praise, learners interact with and provide constructive feedback on many formats of other learners' content. The feedback process empowers each learner to grow and to improve his or her own learning and be accountable for knowledge products demonstrating that learning. The option to share learning products with an authentic audience affords learners unique viewpoints about their creations.

GROW: Learners grow each time they iteratively question, create, share, and reflect on new knowledge; natural curiosity is sparked by means of this sustained inquiry cycle. When learners have support and scaffolds to be persistent and resilient during inquiry, they develop processes that enable them to make real-world connections and reflect to guide informed decisions.

INQUIRE SCHOOL LIBRARIAN COMPETENCIES IN DEPTH

THINK: The school librarian is essential to inquiry-driven instructional frameworks. By promoting a culture of openness and acceptance, the school librarian captures learner interest with intellectually rich, appropriate, and rigorous ideas, and nurtures questioning behaviors. The school librarian scaffolds learners as they activate prior knowledge and make new connections. The school librarian supports the inquiry process by guiding other educators to an understanding of the power of learner-developed questions around personal interest or specific curricular topics or standards.

Inquiry pedagogy facilitates the questioning, helping learners master an iterative process that results in deeper, more-complex questions. The school librarian champions learner-led questioning, promotes exploration, and advocates for creation and sharing of new knowledge, while supporting learners' reflection on both product and process. The school librarian facilitates collaborative work groups in which multiple viewpoints and ideas are included in the inquiry process. By designing opportunities to share the benefits and products of inquiry learning with all stakeholders, including school administrators and parents, the school librarian becomes a valuable instructional leader and partner focused on engagement and deep authentic learning.

> Knowledge emerges only through invention and re-invention, through the restless, impatient, continuing, hopeful inquiry human beings pursue in the world, with the world, and with each other.
> —PAOLO FRIERE (1993)

CREATE: An effective school librarian is a specialist in research-based inquiry processes in which learners exercise voice and choice. To support learners' creativity, the school librarian assists learners to identify knowledge gaps and provides supports and resources to address those disparities. Helping learners generate products that illustrate their knowledge requires a school librarian to be conversant in a wide variety of information resources and multiple literacies as well as to provide an environment that fosters learner exploration and experimentation. The school librarian engages in ongoing professional learning relating to technologies for creation, making, and publishing.

SHARE: To assist learners to critically reflect on their own and others' learning processes and products, school librarians help learners feel confident and encourage their persistence throughout inquiry. The school librarian provides collaborative encounters that promote constructive, honest, and reflective feedback as well as unique, authentic opportunities to share learning. Learners benefit from presenting their learning products to broad audiences within and beyond the immediate learning community. In creating a community of mentors who support school-wide inquiry, the school librarian fosters global, real-world connections through which learners can acquire and share knowledge.

GROW: The school librarian empowers learners to create new knowledge in an inquiry-based research process aligned to each learner's interests. The school librarian continually fosters a school-wide atmosphere that promotes a growth mindset by teaching and valuing persistence—even when faced with obstacles. A growth mindset enables all learners to seek knowledge, create new meaning, and make real-world connections for lifelong learning. The school librarian also models the behaviors being encouraged in learners.

INQUIRE SCHOOL LIBRARY ALIGNMENTS IN DEPTH

THINK: The school library establishes an inquiry culture that permeates all facets of learners' lives by engaging learner curiosity and bolstering learners' initiative. A systematic research-based inquiry process supports learners across all grade bands and roles, and in all disciplines. The inquiry-based research process is embedded in collaborative instructional partnerships in which curriculum, standards, and all literacy skills are seamlessly intertwined. The outcome is a rich collaborative atmosphere that provides learners and educators with meaningful cotaught experiences. This inquiry atmosphere creates unique synergies throughout the school, with the school library as the learning catalyst.

CREATE: The school library fosters knowledge creation by supporting age-appropriate learning experiences. This support includes providing digital and print information formats, mentors and experts, ideas, and technologies. The school library furthers learners' information-seeking and creative endeavors in an atmosphere that enables learners to wonder, explore, innovate, question, dabble, fail, invent, and reinvent. The library's physical space is conducive to learners' inquiry efforts because areas for collaboration and creation are provided. This learning environment necessitates a flexible schedule that ensures that learners and educators have access to both school library staff and resources at their point of need.

SHARE: The school library supports school librarians as they guide learners to maintain focus throughout the inquiry process. The inviting, flexible, and safe school library helps learners develop important dispositions, including acceptance, encouragement, and understanding. Learners develop trust and thrive in an effective school library that gives them freedom to move through the inquiry process in a barrier-free, universally designed environment that allows equitable physical and intellectual access.

School librarians tailor learning outcomes to standards and all learner levels, and communicate these targets clearly in the school library space. With clear statements of expectations, learners confidently share knowledge products and work in teams to design evaluation protocols that include data gathering and outcome measurement related to those products. Learners are aware of their roles in assessing their inquiry products and processes. By implementing collaborative formative assessment approaches in the school library, evidence-based practice becomes a norm for effective inquiry. School librarians use these practices to improve the school library and communicate to others ways in which the school library is improving.

GROW: Systematic and deliberate inquiry builds critical-thinking dispositions throughout the school learning community. In an effective school library, school librarians innovate, implement, and model an inquiry-based process for learners. So that learners and other educators in the school see the inquiry process presented in authentic ways, inquiry demonstrations may occur in a faculty meeting, in a non-traditional classroom, or with a small subgroup of learners. Continuous modeling and implementation reinforces the role of the school library and its resources in maximizing learning, creating new knowledge and institutional effectiveness.

RECOMMENDED APPENDICES

APPENDIX C. Annotated List of AASL Position Statements

APPENDIX E. Interpretations of the Library Bill of Rights

APPENDIX E2. Access to Resources and Services in the School
Library Program

APPENDIX E3. Advocating for Intellectual Freedom

APPENDIX H. Evidence of Accomplishment

APPENDIX I. Useful Verbs

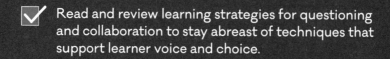

INQUIRE Best Practices

- ☑ Read and review learning strategies for questioning and collaboration to stay abreast of techniques that support learner voice and choice.

- ☑ Select and trust in a systematic inquiry process that supports true inquiry—not basic reporting. The process should be research-based, focused on learner-developed questions, and embrace exploration, innovation, creativity, invention, reflection, and revision.

- ☑ Find a willing collaborator to implement your inquiry-based process.

- ☑ Share learner outcomes and reflections with other educators and your principal to get other educators interested in your inquiry process.

- ☑ Listen and acquire ideas for where and with whom to start teaching the inquiry process. Educators who enjoy their work will readily share passions for curriculum, standards, learners, and preferred resources.

- ☑ Engage in professional learning by reading library- and education-related social media posts, articles, and books as well as attending webinars, workshops, and conferences. Seek sources that will help you gain new ideas for ways learners can demonstrate their learning and explore technologies and activities for multiple literacies.

- ☑ Encourage learners to consider a variety of products to use as they demonstrate their learning.

6

Include

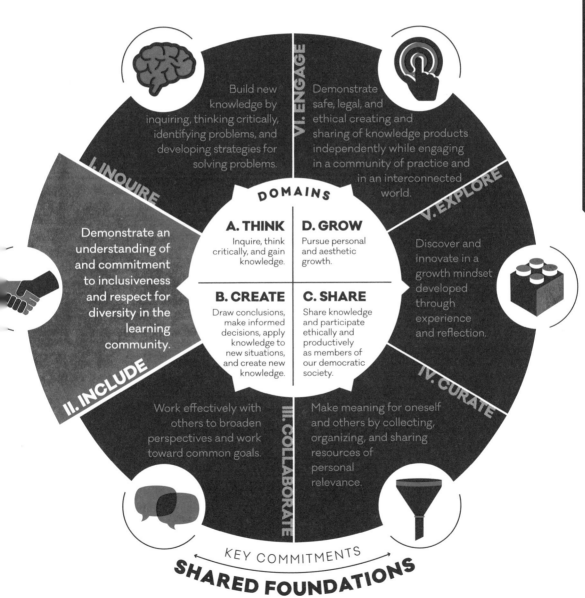

VI. ENGAGE

Build new knowledge by inquiring, thinking critically, identifying problems, and developing strategies for solving problems.

Demonstrate safe, legal, and ethical creating and sharing of knowledge products independently while engaging in a community of practice and in an interconnected world.

I. INQUIRE

Demonstrate an understanding of and commitment to inclusiveness and respect for diversity in the learning community.

II. INCLUDE

V. EXPLORE

Discover and innovate in a growth mindset developed through experience and reflection.

DOMAINS

A. THINK
Inquire, think critically, and gain knowledge.

D. GROW
Pursue personal and aesthetic growth.

B. CREATE
Draw conclusions, make informed decisions, apply knowledge to new situations, and create new knowledge.

C. SHARE
Share knowledge and participate ethically and productively as members of our democratic society.

III. COLLABORATE

Work effectively with others to broaden perspectives and work toward common goals.

IV. CURATE

Make meaning for oneself and others by collecting, organizing, and sharing resources of personal relevance.

KEY COMMITMENTS

SHARED FOUNDATIONS

SHARED FOUNDATION II.

Include

Domain	LEARNER DOMAINS AND COMPETENCIES	SCHOOL LIBRARIAN DOMAINS AND COMPETENCIES
A. Think	Learners contribute a balanced perspective when participating in a learning community by: 1. Articulating an awareness of the contributions of a range of learners. 2. Adopting a discerning stance toward points of view and opinions expressed in information resources and learning products. 3. Describing their understanding of cultural relevancy and placement within the global learning community.	School librarians direct learners to contribute a balanced perspective when participating in a learning community by: 1. Engaging learners to articulate an awareness of the contributions of a range of learners. 2. Guiding learners as they adopt a discerning stance toward points of view and opinions expressed in information resources and learning products. 3. Differentiating instruction to support learners' understanding of cultural relevancy and placement within the global learning community.
B. Create	Learners adjust their awareness of the global learning community by: 1. Interacting with learners who reflect a range of perspectives. 2. Evaluating a variety of perspectives during learning activities. 3. Representing diverse perspectives during learning activities.	School librarians establish opportunities for learners to adjust their awareness of the global learning community by: 1. Providing opportunities for learners to interact with others who reflect a range of perspectives. 2. Devising learning activities that require learners to evaluate a variety of perspectives. 3. Designing opportunities that help learners to illustrate diverse viewpoints.
C. Share	Learners exhibit empathy with and tolerance for diverse ideas by: 1. Engaging in informed conversation and active debate. 2. Contributing to discussions in which multiple viewpoints on a topic are expressed.	School librarians facilitate experiences in which learners exhibit empathy and tolerance for diverse ideas by: 1. Giving learners opportunities to engage in informed conversation and active debate. 2. Guiding learners to contribute to discussions in which multiple viewpoints on a topic are expressed.
D. Grow	Learners demonstrate empathy and equity in knowledge building within the global learning community by: 1. Seeking interactions with a range of learners. 2. Demonstrating interest in other perspectives during learning activities. 3. Reflecting on their own place within the global learning community.	School librarians explicitly lead learners to demonstrate empathy and equity in knowledge building within the global learning community by: 1. Creating an atmosphere in which learners feel empowered and interactions are learner-initiated. 2. Initiating opportunities that allow learners to demonstrate interest in other perspectives. 3. Showcasing learners' reflections on their place within the global learning community.

SCHOOL LIBRARY DOMAINS AND ALIGNMENTS	The school library facilitates the Key Commitment to and Competencies of INCLUDE	Domain
The school library supports balanced perspectives through resources and learning opportunities by: 1. Providing challenging and authentic opportunities that address the needs of the broad range of learners. 2. Offering diverse learning experiences that allow for individual differences in learners. 3. Providing a comprehensive variety of resources.		**A. Think**
The school library represents all members and their place in a global learning community by: 1. Establishing and maintaining a collection of reading and information materials in formats that support the diverse developmental, cultural, social, and linguistic needs of the range of learners and their communities. 2. Organizing facilities to enhance the use of and ensure equitable access to information resources and services for all learners. 3. Featuring learning opportunities that include diverse viewpoints.		**B. Create**
The school library facilitates opportunities to experience diverse ideas by: 1. Implementing solutions that address physical, social, cultural, linguistic, and intellectual barriers to equitable access to resources and services. 2. Promoting the use of high-quality and high-interest literature in formats that reflect the diverse developmental, cultural, social, and linguistic needs of all learners and their communities. 3. Constructing a learning environment that fosters the sharing of a wide range of viewpoints and ideas.		**C. Share**
The school library builds empathy and equity within the global learning community by: 1. Ensuring that all learning needs are met through access to information and ideas located in a diverse collection of sufficient size for the learner population and supported by reliable hardware and software. 2. Enabling equitable access to learning opportunities, academic and social support, and other resources necessary for learners' success. 3. Clearly and frequently articulating the school library's impact when communicating with administration, faculty, staff, learners, parents, and the community.		**D. Grow**

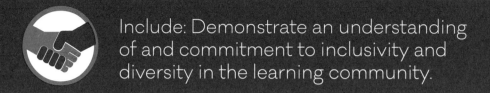

Include: Demonstrate an understanding of and commitment to inclusivity and diversity in the learning community.

INCLUDE LEARNER COMPETENCIES IN DEPTH

THINK: Our global society requires empathetic learners and thinkers who can contribute to systems, processes, work, and conversations in a variety of contexts. Learners who practice discernment in their research and interactions foster collaborative opportunities for individual and collective growth. When learners recognize they have different perspectives on a topic, they can begin to seek understanding of different viewpoints and to consider how that understanding can affect their own views. Learners contribute a balanced perspective in learning communities by acknowledging the contributions of others, regardless of backgrounds and experiences, and by listening closely and thoughtfully. Not everything a learner hears will be accurate or beneficial, so honing critical and analytical skills is crucial to growth as an informed global citizen. When learners articulate the cultural relevancy of varying viewpoints and perspectives, and appreciate others' unique contributions, they better understand their own placement within larger learning communities.

CREATE: When learners create in the school library, they interact with a range of learners with a variety of learning styles, ability levels, or interest levels. To produce comprehensive, authentic products valuable to a variety of audiences, during the process of co-creating knowledge learners continuously evaluate their creative processes and seek to understand others' thinking and contributions. Learning activities that include participants' expression of diverse perspectives foster deep thinking and relevant results.

SHARE: The process of investigating an idea or concept beyond the immediate environment or comfort level develops empathetic learners. When learners listen to others with the goal of understanding discussions and debates, learners develop vital skills for future interactions. Sharing thoughts and ideas with others who express contrasting viewpoints and practicing tolerance for differing perspectives helps learners to demonstrate empathy. Learners who communicate informed ideas to diverse audiences with multiple viewpoints build a foundation for future informed action.

GROW: As learners facilitate empathetic and equitable conversations with peers, they begin to translate informed ideas into appropriate action and improve conditions in their immediate surroundings and larger communities. That process starts with the learner showing interest in others' perspectives, reflecting on the unique viewpoints shared by peers, and taking learning further by reflecting on questions such as: How can I include others in my learning? Who can offer a new perspective on this concept or idea? What is my role now that I have an informed viewpoint? How has my own thinking changed or improved from my interaction with others and their differing opinions and insights?

INCLUDE SCHOOL LIBRARIAN COMPETENCIES IN DEPTH

THINK: School librarians contribute balanced perspectives in a learning community by empowering learners to articulate an awareness of all learners' contributions and by facilitating learners' opportunities to adopt discerning stances. School librarians also provide differentiated learning experiences to support learners' understanding of cultural relevancy and their placement within the global learning community. By providing learners access to a diverse collection of resources, school librarians provide a foundational step toward helping learners respect and appreciate the contributions of others. To foster learners developing a commitment to inclusivity and diversity, school librarians recognize the unique experiences each learner brings to a conversation or project and encourage learners to share insights and perspectives.

CREATE: To ensure that learners are aware of the global learning community, school librarians structure opportunities—for themselves and for their learners—to interact with others who reflect a range of perspectives, devise learning activities that require learners to evaluate a variety of perspectives, and design opportunities that help learners to illustrate diverse viewpoints. School librarians connect learners with varying life experiences for collaborative

> Not having heard something is not as good as having heard it; having heard it is not as good as having seen it; having seen it is not as good as knowing it; knowing it is not as good as putting it into practice.
>
> **—XUN KUANG (KNOBLOCK 1994)**

interactions and provide access to resources that encourage and enable learners to demonstrate their awareness of multiple points of view on issues. Access for learners to information, opinions, and experiences of those beyond the immediate community is an important step in developing awareness of the global learning community.

SHARE: School librarians facilitate experiences in which learners exhibit empathy and tolerance for diverse ideas by developing learners who engage in informed conversation, debate, and persuasion and by guiding learners to contribute to discussions in which multiple viewpoints on a topic are expressed. By modeling and facilitating questioning techniques and group discussion strategies, school librarians give learners opportunities to develop the types of skills they need to participate fully in a diverse community. School librarians encourage learners to express their knowledge and experiences through a variety of formats and in ways that are respectful to the viewpoints of others.

GROW: School librarians explicitly lead learners to demonstrate empathy and equity in knowledge building. By innovating opportunities for learners to demonstrate interest in others' perspectives, school librarians empower learners to reflect on and showcase a range of learners' places in a global learning community. School librarians recognize the unique contributions all learners bring to the school community and encourage them to acknowledge, appreciate, and celebrate differences and similarities through learner-led projects, displays, and initiatives.

INCLUDE SCHOOL LIBRARY ALIGNMENTS IN DEPTH

THINK: The school library encourages balanced perspectives by providing challenging and authentic opportunities to address the needs of the broad range of learners, offering diverse learning experiences that allow for learners' individual differences, and providing current, high-quality fiction and informational texts in a variety of formats. Ensuring equity in the school library begins with an ongoing reflective analysis of the school library's existing digital and print collection, outreach programs, and user services to assess diversity, how well the school community's needs and desires are met, and the extent to which learning opportunities include the global community.

CREATE: The school library ensures that all school community members are represented and aware of their place in a learning community by promoting print and digital materials that support diverse developmental, cultural, social, and linguistic needs; organizing school library facilities to ensure that all learners have equitable access to information resources and services; and developing learning opportunities that include a range of viewpoints. The school library includes processes to capture learner, staff, and community feedback to ensure that the collection, communications, and displays accurately depict and represent the diversity of a global learning community.

SHARE: The school library facilitates opportunities to experience diverse ideas by addressing physical, social, cultural, linguistic, and intellectual barriers to communication tools, resources, and services; promoting learner interactions informed by high-quality digital and print texts that reflect diverse interests, developmental, cultural, social, linguistic, and community needs and values; and providing a learning environment in which learners exchange a wide range of viewpoints and ideas. The school library crafts opportunities for learners, educators, and community members to fully participate in one-on-one, small-group, and large-group learning activities, enrichment programs, and other opportunities. The school library honors all school community members through displays and resources that celebrate a variety of needs and interests. Challenges to materials are addressed through established, detailed, and approved processes that uphold the American Library Association's Library Bill of Rights.

GROW: The school library builds empathy and equity by encouraging members of the learning community to access information and ideas in a current, multi-format resource collection and by providing communication opportunities and academic and social support. The school library's impact on learning success is articulated in a manner that is clearly understood by administrators, faculty, staff, learners, parents, and the community. The school library makes use of ongoing reflection data to strengthen resources, improve instruction, and meet the diverse needs of the school community. The school library includes opportunities to showcase programmatic and learner success through regular communication with school and district leadership.

RECOMMENDED APPENDICES

INCLUDE Best Practices

- ☑ Provide up-to-date print and digital collections that reflect the diversity of the larger global community.

- ☑ Ensure that displays and communications focus on resources in multiple formats that reflect a variety of viewpoints, cultures, and experiences.

- ☑ Use furniture that is adjustable and moveable to meet the needs of all individuals, as well as small and large groups. Arrange materials and equipment so they can be easily accessed by all learners.

- ☑ Ensure that groups of learners include people with a range of learning styles, experiences, and abilities; model discussion techniques and strategies to engage all participants.

- ☑ Invite learning community members to participate in conversations and projects that reflect diverse perspectives and seek input from learners and staff to inform selection of materials.

- ☑ Provide programs that appeal to a variety of audiences and interests.

- ☑ Promote the American Library Association's Library Bill of Rights and the concept of intellectual freedom.

- ☑ Establish policies to address challenges to materials, including digital content and technology.

7

Collaborate

VI. ENGAGE

Build new knowledge by inquiring, thinking critically, identifying problems, and developing strategies for solving problems.

Demonstrate safe, legal, and ethical creating and sharing of knowledge products independently while engaging in a community of practice and in an interconnected world.

I. INQUIRE

Demonstrate an understanding of and commitment to inclusiveness and respect for diversity in the learning community.

V. EXPLORE

Discover and innovate in a growth mindset developed through experience and reflection.

DOMAINS

A. THINK
Inquire, think critically, and gain knowledge.

D. GROW
Pursue personal and aesthetic growth.

B. CREATE
Draw conclusions, make informed decisions, apply knowledge to new situations, and create new knowledge.

C. SHARE
Share knowledge and participate ethically and productively as members of our democratic society.

II. INCLUDE

Work effectively with others to broaden per-spectives and work toward common goals.

III. COLLABORATE

IV. CURATE

Make meaning for oneself and others by collecting, organizing, and sharing resources of personal relevance.

KEY COMMITMENTS
SHARED FOUNDATIONS

Collaborate

Domain	LEARNER DOMAINS AND COMPETENCIES	SCHOOL LIBRARIAN DOMAINS AND COMPETENCIES
A. Think	**Learners identify collaborative opportunities by:** 1. Demonstrating their desire to broaden and deepen understandings. 2. Developing new understandings through engagement in a learning group. 3. Deciding to solve problems informed by group interaction.	**School librarians facilitate collaborative opportunities by:** 1. Challenging learners to work with others to broaden and deepen understandings. 2. Scaffolding enactment of learning-group roles to enable the development of new understandings within a group. 3. Organizing learner groups for decision making and problem solving.
B. Create	**Learners participate in personal, social, and intellectual networks by:** 1. Using a variety of communication tools and resources. 2. Establishing connections with other learners to build on their own prior knowledge and create new knowledge.	**School librarians demonstrate the importance of personal, social, and intellectual networks by:** 1. Modeling the use of a variety of communication tools and resources. 2. Cultivating networks that allow learners to build on their own prior knowledge and create new knowledge.
C. Share	**Learners work productively with others to solve problems by:** 1. Soliciting and responding to feedback from others. 2. Involving diverse perspectives in their own inquiry processes.	**School librarians promote working productively with others to solve problems by:** 1. Demonstrating how to solicit and respond to feedback from others. 2. Advocating and modeling respect for diverse perspectives to guide the inquiry process.
D. Grow	**Learners actively participate with others in learning situations by:** 1. Actively contributing to group discussions. 2. Recognizing learning as a social responsibility.	**School librarians foster active participation in learning situations by:** 1. Stimulating learners to actively contribute to group discussions. 2. Creating a learning environment in which learners understand that learning is a social responsibility.

KEY COMMITMENT
**Work effectively with others
to broaden perspectives and
work toward common goals.**

SCHOOL LIBRARY DOMAINS AND ALIGNMENTS	The school library facilitates the Key Commitment to and Competencies of COLLABORATE	Domain
The school library facilitates opportunities to integrate collaborative and shared learning by: 1. Partnering with other educators to scaffold learning and organize learner groups to broaden and deepen understanding. 2. Leading inquiry-based learning opportunities that enhance the information, media, visual, and technical literacies of all members of the school community.		**A. Think**
The school library's policies ensure that school librarians are active participants in development, evaluation, and improvement of instructional and program resources with the school librarian by: 1. Consistently engaging with the school community to ensure that the school library resources, services, and standards align with the school's mission. 2. Participating in district, building, and department or grade-level curriculum development and assessment on a regular basis. 3. Including the school community in the development of school library policies and procedures.		**B. Create**
The school library provides opportunities for school librarians to connect and work with the learning community by: 1. Facilitating diverse social and intellectual learner networks. 2. Designing and leading professional-development opportunities that reinforce the impact of the school library's resources, services, and programming on learners' academic learning and educators' effectiveness. 3. Promoting and modeling the importance of information-use skills by publicizing to learners, staff, and the community available services and resources; serving on school and district-wide committees; and engaging in community and professional activities.		**C. Share**
The school library supports active learner participation by: 1. Creating and maintaining a learning environment that supports and stimulates discussion from all members of the school community. 2. Demonstrating and reinforcing the idea that information is a shared resource.		**D. Grow**

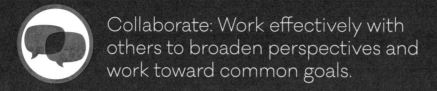

Collaborate: Work effectively with others to broaden perspectives and work toward common goals.

COLLABORATE LEARNER COMPETENCIES IN DEPTH

THINK: Learning is a social process. When learners work together in group- and team-based situations, they are able to solve problems together that they would not be able to solve independently. Being able to identify opportunities for collaboration and use those opportunities to broaden and deepen understanding, develop new understanding, and make decisions to solve problems is critical to effective collaboration and learner growth. In collaboration, learners consider and incorporate new information into their existing knowledge base and belief systems. Collaboration affords learners the opportunity to challenge their own assumptions through discussion with others. They think critically as they comment, elaborate in response to questions, and question other learners. Being confronted with diverse viewpoints and alternative interpretations of a situation or problem improves critical-thinking and problem-solving strategies.

CREATE: In our increasingly diverse society, effective communication is essential to productive collaboration. Learners who practice effective communication techniques can also develop effective collaboration skills, including working effectively within diverse teams, making compromises, establishing common goals, and sharing responsibility for collaborative work. Effective collaboration in personal, social, and intellectual networks requires the use of a variety of communication tools and resources, and results in establishing connections with other learners to build on learners' prior knowledge and create new knowledge. When collaborating, learners communicate by articulating thoughts and ideas using oral, written, and nonverbal forms of communication for a range of purposes (e.g., inform, instruct, motivate, or persuade) throughout the collaboration. Good communication involves a complex set of skills that can result in the development of mutual understandings through the processes of listening effectively, explaining one's ideas, and negotiating new and shared meanings. Through this process of communication, learners decipher information, access new knowledge, and integrate new ideas into their existing perspectives.

SHARE: Successful problem solving in our modern society requires us to work effectively and creatively with technology, with vast amounts of information, and with other learners from diverse backgrounds. To effectively solve problems, learners must be open to soliciting and responding to feedback from others, involving diverse perspectives in their own inquiry processes, exercising flexibility, and demonstrating a willingness to make compromises to accomplish a shared goal. Learners solicit information and feedback from others by identifying questions that will clarify points of view and lead to better solutions.

> Most great learning happens in groups. Collaboration is the stuff of growth.
> —SIR KEN ROBINSON (2010)

They solve different kinds of problems in both conventional and innovative ways by working with others and integrating the perspectives of others into their own inquiry process. Productive and effective problem solving is accomplished through acknowledging, analyzing, interpreting, and integrating the ideas of others as part of the greater whole.

GROW: Collaborative efforts create more-holistic results than individual efforts alone, as each learner in the collaborative groups brings his or her knowledge, perspectives, and experiences to the group. In effective teams every member values the individual contributions of each team member. By working collaboratively, groups can generate more knowledge than can individuals working alone. Therefore, collaboration is a key ingredient in our global and technological society. Learners working in collaborative teams recognize and assume shared responsibility for collaborative work. To achieve shared goals, learners make compromises, demonstrate the ability to adapt to new ideas and situations, and actively contribute to group discussions. When learners actively participate in collaboration, the group is more likely to be effective, and individual learners develop better communication skills and discipline-specific language.

COLLABORATE SCHOOL LIBRARIAN COMPETENCIES IN DEPTH

THINK: School librarians facilitate collaborative opportunities when they challenge learners to work with others to broaden and deepen understanding, scaffold roles to enable the development of new understandings within a learning group, and organize learner groups for decision making and problem solving. School librarians can challenge learners to work together by creating opportunities for collaboration through school library programs and instruction, thereby helping learners to enhance their problem-solving and critical-thinking skills. School librarians structure learner groups to maximize their effectiveness in various ways, including establishing the size of groups, assigning or helping learners to assign group roles and norms of behavior, and helping learners to build trust through open communication and the quick resolution of problems. School librarians also scaffold roles and responsibilities of group members by initially assigning group roles, norms, and goals and allowing groups to make more independent decisions as their teamwork skills develop over time.

CREATE: School librarians demonstrate the importance of personal, social, and intellectual networks by modeling the use of a variety of communication tools and resources, and cultivating networks that allow learners to build on and create new knowledge. School librarians model by demonstrating relevant and authentic examples of communication and use of collaboration tools and resources that learners can apply to their learning situations. Modeling provides a scaffolding structure whereby learners observe how to accomplish a task before trying it on their own. Seeing the task performed shows them a variety of skills and tools they can apply in future investigations. School librarians also cultivate networks by bringing together learners of diverse backgrounds and experience in the sharing of common goals and interests, enabling learners to build on their existing knowledge and create new knowledge through shared experiences and collaborative learning.

SHARE: School librarians promote working productively with others to solve problems by demonstrating how to solicit and respond to feedback from others, and advocating and modeling respect for diverse perspectives to guide the inquiry process. Modeling and demonstrating go beyond merely providing examples; during modeling and demonstrating the school librarian performs an authentic learning task and then provides learners with guided practice to facilitate the growth of trust between learners and promote open communication in collaborative groups. School librarians help learners gain the communication skills necessary to present their own ideas, defend their positions, be active listeners, negotiate disagreements, and be self-reflective about the learning process. School librarians advocate respect for diverse perspectives by helping learners develop the skills of compromising, relieving tension, generating options, and seeking out alternative perspectives. Collaborative learning relies on learners' respect and appreciation for one another's viewpoints. School librarians foster tolerance by exposing learners to examples in the real world and literature, as well as modeling acceptance of others.

GROW: School librarians foster active participation in learning situations by stimulating learners to actively contribute to group discussion and creating a learning environment in which learners understand that learning is a social responsibility. School librarians help stimulate learners to actively contribute to group discussion by presenting learners with relevant engaging problems and posing questions requiring critical thinking. Learners successfully contribute to group discussions when they are taught how to listen, how to ask good questions, and how to negotiate. Learning is a social process. School librarians assist learners in developing responsibility for shared learning goals and understanding how working together results in deeper understanding.

COLLABORATE SCHOOL LIBRARY ALIGNMENTS IN DEPTH

THINK: Within the school library inquiry-based information-literacy instruction is designed, delivered, and assessed to enhance the information, media, visual, and technical literacies of learners. In doing so, the school library helps the school achieve curricular goals and meet learners' personalized learning needs. School librarians are instructional partners and collaborators with other educators in the school library, classroom, and other learning spaces. School librarians work with educators to scaffold learning by structuring learner groups to maximize their effectiveness. School librarians and educators also work together to scaffold roles and responsibilities of group members by initially assigning group roles, norms, and goals, and allowing groups to make more independent decisions as their teamwork skills develop over time. School librarians provide instruction independently and in collaboration with educators to meet the learning needs of all learners, including other educators and administrators, so learners can develop information skills for success in academics, career, and community.

CREATE: School libraries are an integral and integrated part of a school community. To ensure that instruction and activities in the school library are aligned with the school's mission and needs, school librarians communicate and collaborate with learners, educators, administrators, and community members to effectively align the resources, services, and standards of the school library with the school's mission. As part of this process, school librarians collaborate with representatives of the school community in the development of school library policies and procedures, creating effective school libraries, policies, and procedures that reflect the needs of the school community. School librarians also participate in building, district, and department or grade-level curriculum development and assessment on a regular basis. This participation assists in the integration of the school library with broader curricular goals and assists educators in integrating information-literacy instruction into discipline-specific content.

SHARE: The school library serves as a bridge between discrete disciplines and departments within a school community. By facilitating the connection of diverse social and intellectual networks of learners, the school library provides opportunities for educators to connect and work together within the learning community. An effective school library results in learners' increased academic achievement and improved educator effectiveness. These improvements result when the school librarian designs and leads professional-development opportunities that articulate the positive impact of the school library's resources, services, and programming. By publicizing available services and resources to learners, staff, and the community, the school library also promotes and models the importance of information literacy in education and in life outside school. As part of the broader school community, and in an effort to promote and model effective information-literacy practices, the school librarian also serves on school and district-wide committees and participates in community projects.

GROW: To support active participation by learners, the school library, under the leadership of the school librarian, creates a learning environment that supports and stimulates discussion from all members of the school community. The school library provides a welcoming environment and facilitates programs that support inclusivity and diversity, encouraging participation by providing opportunities for sharing and collaboration by all members of the school community. The school library policies and the school librarian's practices acknowledge that information is a shared resource, support equity of access, and encourage sharing of information to the benefit of all. The school library policies and practices enable making connections to other libraries and programs to maximize resources available to the school community.

RECOMMENDED APPENDICES

APPENDIX C. Annotated List of AASL Position Statements

APPENDIX C3. Position Statement: Instructional Role of the School Librarian

APPENDIX C5. Position Statement: Role of the School Library Program

APPENDIX E. Interpretations of the Library Bill of Rights

APPENDIX E2. Access to Resources and Services in the School Library Program

APPENDIX F. LLAMA's 14 Foundational Competencies

APPENDIX H. Evidence of Accomplishment

APPENDIX I. Useful Verbs

COLLABORATE Best Practices

 Scaffold the work of learner teams by providing explicit direction (such as questions to consider) at the beginning of their work and slowly allow groups to take on more decision making over the course of the project and in future projects.

 Ensure that each group includes a mix of talents, experiences, learning styles, and ideas when grouping learners. Members of mixed-aptitude groups often learn more from one another than members of groups in which all learners have the same skills and ideas.

 Get to know your colleagues as people before attempting to convince them to collaborate. Personal relationships build trust and are more long lasting than purely work relationships. People with whom you already have a friendly rapport will be more likely to work with you on an instructional project. The easiest way to get to know the other educators in your building is to eat lunch with them. You can also attend department or grade-level meetings; at first just listen, over time bring relevant resources to share.

 Share with educators the ways in which you collaborate in your next monthly, quarterly, or annual report. Showing administrators and the broader school community a collaboration rubric that shows how you collaborated with educators can help tell the story of exactly how you and the school library impact learning.

8

Curate

VI. ENGAGE
Demonstrate safe, legal, and ethical creating and sharing of knowledge products independently while engaging in a community of practice and in an interconnected world.

I. INQUIRE
Build new knowledge by inquiring, thinking critically, identifying problems, and developing strategies for solving problems.

V. EXPLORE
Discover and innovate in a growth mindset developed through experience and reflection.

II. INCLUDE
Demonstrate an understanding of and commitment to inclusiveness and respect for diversity in the learning community.

IV. CURATE
Make meaning for oneself and others by collecting, organizing, and sharing resources of personal relevance.

III. COLLABORATE
Work effectively with others to broaden perspectives and work toward common goals.

DOMAINS

A. THINK
Inquire, think critically, and gain knowledge.

D. GROW
Pursue personal and aesthetic growth.

B. CREATE
Draw conclusions, make informed decisions, apply knowledge to new situations, and create new knowledge.

C. SHARE
Share knowledge and participate ethically and productively as members of our democratic society.

KEY COMMITMENTS

SHARED FOUNDATIONS

93

SHARED FOUNDATION IV.

Curate

KEY COMMITMENT
Make meaning for oneself and others by collecting, organizing, and sharing resources of personal relevance.

Domain	LEARNER DOMAINS AND COMPETENCIES	SCHOOL LIBRARIAN DOMAINS AND COMPETENCIES
A. Think	Learners act on an information need by: 1. Determining the need to gather information. 2. Identifying possible sources of information. 3. Making critical choices about information sources to use.	School librarians challenge learners to act on an information need by: 1. Modeling the response to a need to gather and organize information. 2. Designing opportunities for learners to explore possible information sources. 3. Guiding learners to make critical choices about information sources to use.
B. Create	Learners gather information appropriate to the task by: 1. Seeking a variety of sources. 2. Collecting information representing diverse perspectives. 3. Systematically questioning and assessing the validity and accuracy of information. 4. Organizing information by priority, topic, or other systematic scheme.	School librarians promote information gathering appropriate to the task by: 1. Sharing a variety of sources. 2. Encouraging the use of information representing diverse perspectives. 3. Fostering the questioning and assessing of validity and accuracy of information. 4. Providing tools and strategies to organize information by priority, topic, or other systematic scheme.
C. Share	Learners exchange information resources within and beyond their learning community by: 1. Accessing and evaluating collaboratively constructed information sites. 2. Contributing to collaboratively constructed information sites by ethically using and reproducing others' work. 3. Joining with others to compare and contrast information derived from collaboratively constructed information sites.	School librarians contribute to and guide information resource exchange within and beyond the school learning community by: 1. Facilitating opportunities to access and evaluate collaboratively constructed information sites. 2. Devising pathways for learners to contribute to collaboratively constructed information sites by ethically using and reproducing others' work. 3. Directing learners to join others to compare and contrast information derived from collaboratively constructed information sites.
D. Grow	Learners select and organize information for a variety of audiences by: 1. Performing ongoing analysis of and reflection on the quality, usefulness, and accuracy of curated resources. 2. Integrating and depicting in a conceptual knowledge network their understanding gained from resources. 3. Openly communicating curation processes for others to use, interpret, and validate.	School librarians show learners how to select and organize information for a variety of audiences by: 1. Engaging learners in ongoing analysis of and reflection on the quality, usefulness, and accuracy of curated resources. 2. Formulating tasks that help learners to integrate and depict in a conceptual knowledge network learners' understanding gained from resources. 3. Making opportunities for learners to openly communicate curation processes for others to use, interpret, and validate.

SCHOOL LIBRARY DOMAINS AND ALIGNMENTS	The school library facilitates the Key Commitment to and Competencies of CURATE	Domain
The school library provides problem-based learning experiences and environments by: 1. Using resources and technology to foster inquiry and scaffold mastery of skills necessary for learning to progress. 2. Adopting a dynamic collection-development plan to ensure that adequate resources reflect current and in-depth knowledge. 3. Focusing on the effective use of a wide range of resources to foster information skills appropriate to content areas.		**A. Think**
The school library promotes selection of appropriate resources and tools for information use by: 1. Demonstrating and documenting how resources and technology are used to address information needs. 2. Providing opportunities for all members of the school community to develop information and technology skills needed to promote the transfer of information-related problem-solving strategies across all disciplines. 3. Employing a dynamic collection policy that includes selection and retention criteria for all materials within the collection. 4. Implementing an administratively approved and endorsed policy that clearly addresses procedures for handling material challenges. 5. Designing and providing adequate, appropriate space for school library resources, services, and activities.		**B. Create**
The school library facilitates the contribution and exchange of information within and among learning communities by: 1. Providing an environment in which resources that support the school's curriculum and learning goals can be collaboratively selected and developed. 2. Including and tracking collection materials in a system that uses standardized approaches to description and location. 3. Establishing policies that promote effective acquisition, description, circulation, sharing, and access to resources within and beyond the school day. 4. Maintaining procedures that ensure user confidentiality and promote unimpeded access to materials by staff members and learners.		**C. Share**
The school library engages the learning community in exploring resources by: 1. Describing, organizing, and promoting the collection for maximum and effective uses for multiple learning applications. 2. Maintaining a collection of sufficient breadth and currency to be pertinent to the school's program of studies. 3. Supporting access through a schedule that allows use by learners and staff at time of need. 4. Using local and external data to inform ongoing adjustments to the scope of the resource collection, and its audiences, formats, and applications.		**D. Grow**

Curate: Make meaning for oneself and others by collecting, organizing, and sharing resources of personal relevance.

CURATE LEARNER COMPETENCIES IN DEPTH

THINK: Effective use of ideas and information comes as a result of finding, evaluating, and selecting resources appropriate to a given task. In inquiry-driven learning, learners must first recognize a need for information. A critical examination of available resources allows the learner to assess the different types of resources that best meet the information need. To use information most effectively, learners must evaluate and assess information accuracy, validity, completeness, and bias, and then use informed judgment to accept, replace, or reject information that meets a particular learning need.

In school libraries, information is increasingly available in a variety of formats. Learners must identify all possible sources of information: traditional print resources as well as digital formats. Only after considering all information sources can learners narrow their information selection to those resources that best meet the given task. They then make critical choices to best match the information sources with the task.

CREATE: In an increasingly global society information is represented through diverse, often varying perspectives. Learners use a variety of resources, covering multiple perspectives, to explore an information need, and then explore the authority and validity of information presented. Learners must actively seek diverse perspectives in the resources they select for their information needs. By integrating their own previous knowledge with information from a variety of sources they create new meaning and knowledge products while acknowledging authorship and demonstrating respect for the intellectual property of others. It is this newly found meaning that is then organized into a logical sequence for practical application.

SHARE: Learners select and share resources that further their own knowledge on a given topic. Learners may collaborate with others, either in person or with a larger learning community through technology, to integrate their own knowledge with the information of others. When working with others, learners learn to respect the ideas and backgrounds of others. This new shared understanding, based on information and ideas from group members, can then be presented in an appropriate format that is both informative and meaningful to a larger community.

When sharing their ideas, learners select an appropriate format for presenting information based on the information itself, the audience, and the nature of the information problem. The presentation may be in a collaboratively constructed site.

GROW: Learners select resources appropriate to a given task and assess them to meet evaluation criteria. Ongoing analysis of these selected resources and their continued relevance to a given task is required. Not only must individual resources be examined, but also their relationship to other resources must be considered. This includes consideration of format as well as content.

As learners gain knowledge from resources, they integrate new knowledge into their conceptual network and are able to illustrate new understandings in an openly curated collection accessible to other learners and available for other learners' comment and use.

CURATE SCHOOL LIBRARIAN COMPETENCIES IN DEPTH

THINK: Assisting all learners to become effective users of ideas and information is one of the primary roles of the school librarian. Learners in the school library evaluate information critically to determine the usefulness of information to a given task. School librarians must model this behavior and guide the information-selection process to develop discerning young information users who look beyond easily found information sources and explore other sources that may be better for the learners' purposes. The school librarian demonstrates for learners and others in the school community strategies for locating, accessing, and evaluating information located in and available through the school library and elsewhere.

CREATE: The school librarian serves as a resource for others in the school community, demonstrating the skill of selecting, gathering, describing, and organizing a variety of vetted resources that may be used for a specific task. When working with individual users or assisting the learning community to gather or curate resources, the school librarian addresses the need to independently consider validity and accuracy of information and fosters the disposition to question information's reliability. Learners should be encouraged to seek multiple perspectives in the resources they consider and to acknowledge authorship and demonstrate respect for the intellectual property of others.

> It's just as valuable to curate content as it is to create it.
> —GUY KAWASAKI (2015)

The learning community is introduced to strategies and tools to effectively organize and manage those resources selected for various tasks and interests. The school librarian frequently provides instruction in how to organize information found within resources. Additionally, the school librarian employs these same practices when developing and organizing the resource collection for the school library as a whole.

SHARE: The school librarian facilitates opportunities for learners and other users to expand their learning community through the social and intellectual exchange of information by providing access to learning networks within and beyond the school. Introducing learners to controlled, authoritative sites, such as databases and subscription sites, introduces access to curated resources that have been selected, described, and organized for a specific purpose. Modeling the use of these sites, school librarians assist users to build their personal resource repositories and share resources with proper attribution. Learners may then work to build their personal or collaboratively constructed sites for which they must discern if the information they are including is most appropriate for the given task or intended purpose and audience.

GROW: The school librarian's role in maintaining a quality selection of curated resources in a variety of formats is essential. Engaging all users in the ongoing analysis of resources that best align with content curricula, personal learning needs, and interests ensures that selected information meets the requirements of the intended tasks. School librarians work with users to select information that will be most useful, describe and organize that information, and use appropriate tools and strategies to share that information with others. School librarians then organize information to ensure users can access the information. Displaying resources curated by topic provides a model for all users. Learners and other school library users are then able to create information resource collections for personal use or sharing that are personally and academically relevant, and communicate curation processes for others to use.

CURATE SCHOOL LIBRARY ALIGNMENTS IN DEPTH

THINK: The collection is at the center of the school library, and expert curation, conducted by a qualified school librarian, is essential to ensuring that the collection meets the needs of learners and educators. The school library provides a collection of resources and materials in all formats. The school library has an established, widely available collection-development plan, which the school librarian follows. This plan should begin with an assessment of user needs. In addition, the plan should be in alignment with the demonstrated needs of the community. Resources in the collection should frequently be reviewed for scope, age, and condition in accordance with the plan's provisions for weeding and removal of physical items that are out of date, infrequently used, and excessively worn. Links to digital items must be monitored to ensure the links are still valid and that the content is still authoritative.

CREATE: Selection and curation of quality resources that are appropriate to the task, as well as to the school audience, are important components of the school librarian's role. Scope, accuracy, currency, cost, and relevance to collection and curriculum should all be considered when resources are selected for inclusion. Policy manuals that address and guide selection policy should be created to guide collection-development efforts of the school library.

Learners and other users within the school community want to find and use information in an authentic manner, simulating their real-world practice. Selecting and using information resources that are relevant to their information needs and personal interest allow this type of independent information use. The creation of user supports that act as tutorials for independent research skills and other information-seeking activities facilitate users' seeking ways to incorporate resources collection into practice, including use of social media sites. These tutorials may then be published for shared use within the school learning community.

Policies used to guide materials challenges should include descriptions of steps to follow and copies of forms so that the process is transparent, objective, and easy to follow. The process should reinforce the fact that final decisions about the collection's contents reside with the school librarian; the policy should be approved by appropriate school and/or district administrators.

Policies may also be needed to guide use of the school library space by outside organizations or district committees. These policies should account for after-hours security, furniture arrangement, and other concerns relating to hosting meetings.

SHARE: A school library collection reflects the school's community, supports the school's mission and curriculum and is built with input from all stakeholders. A core value shared in the school library profession is equitable, confidential access to resources for all patrons. Access to materials at the time of need is best practice in the school library. This access is ensured through the use of systems that enable users to independently locate materials as well as systems that allow for confidential and secure tracking of materials. Digital resources within the collection should be accessible to users at all times. This 24-7 access ensures the greatest potential for use by most learners. Therefore, a well-developed school library website provides digital access to digital resources. Curation of resources shared through a school-based site developed and maintained by a certified school librarian ensures continuity of resources shared. Social media links on the website allow users to identify and suggest needed sources, engage with digital content, and request further assistance. Increased communication with stakeholders providing updates about school library resources and their potential uses to educators and learners is an additional advantage of a website of well-curated resources maintained by the school librarian. These affordances are maintained and communicated through current, comprehensive policies that describe and address all aspects of collection development and curation.

GROW: Thoughtful organization of a school library is an essential component of an effective school library. The collection should be described for ease of location and allow for learners to provide their feedback about their experiences with particular sources and suggest additional descriptors that will enable them to effectively locate materials. The school library collection should align with current school curriculum. School library resources that support integration of school library instruction and classroom content allow for the strongest collaborative relationships within the larger learning community.

Access to the collection is best met at the time of need. Ensuring the collection is physically and intellectually accessible is critical for making the collection personally relevant to all users. Scheduling practices should allow maximum access to the school library collection before, during, and after school. When learners and other community users share ownership of the school library and the resources available for use, the collection becomes more relevant to all users. The school librarian ensures that mechanisms are in place for the collection's users to provide suggestions for new materials and to provide feedback on existing materials. Others in the school should be involved in the collection and organization of school library resources. An advisory board composed of multiple stakeholder groups such as learners, parents, classroom educators, and administrators can provide input on collection priorities.

RECOMMENDED APPENDICES

APPENDIX E. Interpretations of the Library Bill of Rights

APPENDIX E1. Access for Children and Young Adults to Nonprint Materials

APPENDIX E2. Access to Resources and Services in the School Library Program

APPENDIX E3. Advocating for Intellectual Freedom

APPENDIX E4. Challenged Resources

APPENDIX E5. Diversity in Collection Development

APPENDIX E6. Internet Filtering

APPENDIX E7. Privacy

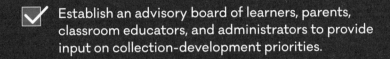

CURATE Best Practices

☑ Establish an advisory board of learners, parents, classroom educators, and administrators to provide input on collection-development priorities.

☑ Create and frequently revise a collection policy that addresses selection and retention criteria for all formats. Include a section about handling materials challenges. Be sure your administrators and school board review and sign the policy and know where it is located.

☑ Frequently review the collection's contents for scope, age, and condition. Remove physical items that are out of date, infrequently used, and excessively worn. Be sure that links to digital items are still valid and that the content is still factually valid.

☑ Create mechanisms for your collection's users to provide suggestions for new materials and provide feedback on existing materials.

☑ Ensure that your online public access catalog and collection of digital resources are available 24–7 so that users can identify and suggest needed sources, engage with digital content, and request further assistance.

☑ Provide classroom educators and learners with frequent updates about school library resources and their potential uses.

☑ Create and share self-guided user supports for independent research skills and other information-seeking activities.

(continued on page 102)

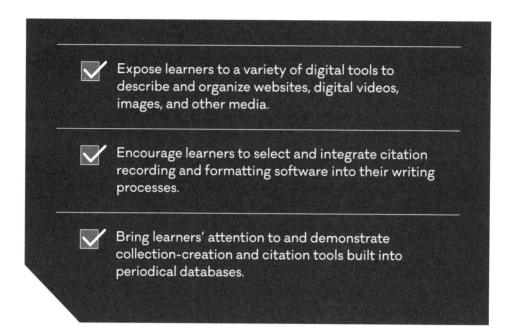

☑ Expose learners to a variety of digital tools to describe and organize websites, digital videos, images, and other media.

☑ Encourage learners to select and integrate citation recording and formatting software into their writing processes.

☑ Bring learners' attention to and demonstrate collection-creation and citation tools built into periodical databases.

9

Explore

VI. ENGAGE
Build new knowledge by inquiring, thinking critically, identifying problems, and developing strategies for solving problems.

Demonstrate safe, legal, and ethical creating and sharing of knowledge products independently while engaging in a community of practice and in an interconnected world.

I. INQUIRE
Demonstrate an understanding of and commitment to inclusiveness and respect for diversity in the learning community.

V. EXPLORE
Discover and innovate in a growth mindset developed through experience and reflection.

DOMAINS

A. THINK
Inquire, think critically, and gain knowledge.

D. GROW
Pursue personal and aesthetic growth.

B. CREATE
Draw conclusions, make informed decisions, apply knowledge to new situations, and create new knowledge.

C. SHARE
Share knowledge and participate ethically and productively as members of our democratic society.

II. INCLUDE
Work effectively with others to broaden perspectives and work toward common goals.

III. COLLABORATE

IV. CURATE
Make meaning for oneself and others by collecting, organizing, and sharing resources of personal relevance.

KEY COMMITMENTS

SHARED FOUNDATIONS

103

Explore

Domain	LEARNER DOMAINS AND COMPETENCIES	SCHOOL LIBRARIAN DOMAINS AND COMPETENCIES
A. Think	**Learners develop and satisfy personal curiosity by:** 1. Reading widely and deeply in multiple formats and write and create for a variety of purposes. 2. Reflecting and questioning assumptions and possible misconceptions. 3. Engaging in inquiry-based processes for personal growth.	**School librarians foster learners' personal curiosity by:** 1. Encouraging learners to read widely and deeply in multiple formats and write and create for a variety of purposes. 2. Challenging learners to reflect and question assumptions and possible misconceptions. 3. Enabling learners by helping them develop inquiry-based processes for personal growth.
B. Create	**Learners construct new knowledge by:** 1. Problem solving through cycles of design, implementation, and reflection. 2. Persisting through self-directed pursuits by tinkering and making.	**School librarians stimulate learners to construct new knowledge by:** 1. Teaching problem solving through cycles of design, implementation, and reflection. 2. Providing opportunities for tinkering and making. 3. Modeling persistence through self-directed tinkering and making.
C. Share	**Learners engage with the learning community by:** 1. Expressing curiosity about a topic of personal interest or curricular relevance. 2. Co-constructing innovative means of investigation. 3. Collaboratively identifying innovative solutions to a challenge or problem.	**School librarians prepare learners to engage with the learning community by:** 1. Providing strategies for acting on curiosity about a topic of personal interest or curricular relevance. 2. Assisting learners to co-construct innovative means of investigation. 3. Structuring activities for learners to collaboratively identify innovative solutions to a challenge or problem.
D. Grow	**Learners develop through experience and reflection by:** 1. Iteratively responding to challenges. 2. Recognizing capabilities and skills that can be developed, improved, and expanded. 3. Open-mindedly accepting feedback for positive and constructive growth.	**School librarians help learners develop through experience and reflection by:** 1. Scaffolding iterative challenge-response processes. 2. Helping learners to recognize capabilities and skills that can be developed, improved, and expanded. 3. Fostering an atmosphere in which constructive feedback is openly accepted for positive growth.

SCHOOL LIBRARY DOMAINS AND ALIGNMENTS	The school library facilitates the Key Commitment to and Competencies of EXPLORE	Domain
The school library supports learners' personal curiosity by: 1. Providing resources and strategies for inquiry-based processes. 2. Fostering opportunities for learners to demonstrate personal curiosity and creation of knowledge through engaging with a wide variety of resources and technology.		**A. Think**
The school library facilitates construction of new knowledge by: 1. Implementing technology as a tool or resource for learning. 2. Ensuring that multiple learning activities can occur in both physical and virtual spaces. 3. Establishing and maintaining a learning environment conducive to independent and collaborative exploration and problem solving.		**B. Create**
The school library prepares learners to engage with a larger learning community by: 1. Modeling and promoting the use of personal and professional learning networks. 2. Encouraging families and other members of the community to participate in school library activities. 3. Building and advocating for strong relationships with stakeholders who recognize and support an effective school library.		**C. Share**
The school library assists in the growth and development of learners by: 1. Leading other educators and learners to embrace a growth mindset through lifelong learning. 2. Anticipating learners' needs and adapting the learning environment in accordance with evidence-based best practices. 3. Embracing new skills, knowledge, and standards in the profession as they relate to teaching, learning, technology, and innovation.		**D. Grow**

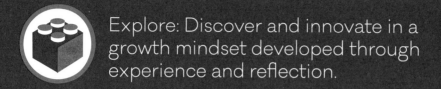

Explore: Discover and innovate in a growth mindset developed through experience and reflection.

EXPLORE LEARNER COMPETENCIES IN DEPTH

THINK: Learners' curiosity is piqued when they are given opportunities to exercise choice as they read widely and deeply in multiple formats and write for a variety of purposes. This reading and writing for personal growth can be structured during class time with the support of the school librarian, based on discipline-specific topics or through exploration of the collection and physical space that fosters open-ended curiosity stimulated by personal interests. Learners need to easily access digital resources remotely 24–7 and physically in the learning space at time of need. After reflecting on their own knowledge assumptions and misconceptions, learners are able to formulate authentic questions to guide their exploration of information resources to find answers and create new knowledge.

CREATE: Learners construct new knowledge when they demonstrate persistence by solving problems through cycles of design, implementation, and reflection. This process includes creating questions of personal interest, using a diverse array of resources to find possible answers, and reflecting on information found. Based on their reflection, learners may develop more questions or identify a need for further information to develop solutions. Learners also benefit from opportunities to cultivate creative pursuits by making and experimenting with hands-on activities within the library space. These creative pursuits may be the basis for an authentic learning product or a means to exhibit personal interest.

SHARE: Learners become part of and engage with the larger learning community by expressing curiosity about topics of curricular relevance or personal interest. When learners are given the opportunity to collaboratively brainstorm various investigation strategies and develop innovative solutions for critical problem-solving tasks, they are deeply engaged in the learning process and make productive use of instructional time. As members of a learning community, learners share ideas face to face and through physical and virtual knowledge products; they also participate in a connected learning network. Learners recognize their social responsibilities in a group by actively and collaboratively identifying solutions to challenges and problems.

GROW: Learners advance by tackling challenges that build skill through multiple opportunities to engage in problem-solving and critical-thinking processes. When they self-assess and open-mindedly receive constructive feedback, learners develop by recognizing skills that should be strengthened. To grow, learners use self-assessment and peer feedback provided through formative and summative activities, including written or oral self-reflections conducted as formal or informal opportunities.

EXPLORE SCHOOL LIBRARIAN COMPETENCIES IN DEPTH

THINK: Drawing on a well-developed collection of digital and print resources accessible to learners through physical and 24–7 virtual presences, school librarians design and foster conversations and activities that challenge learners to question assumptions and misconceptions about topics of personal interest or curricular relevance. These opportunities may be informal conversations guided by participants' prior knowledge and interests or structured discussions with prompts that encourage learners to build on prior knowledge and experience by exploring new questions and developing new insights. By extending an interest-driven inquiry-based research process through defined activities or self-directed explorations encouraged by the school library's design and arrangement, the school librarian enables learners to use school library resources for investigating personal information needs.

> A mind stretched by a new idea or sensation never shrinks back to its former dimensions.
>
> **—OLIVER WENDELL HOLMES SR.**
> **(1858)**

CREATE: School librarians identify and pose authentic, real-world problems to spark learners' new knowledge pursuits through critical thinking and problem solving. Employing lessons that use cycles of designing questions, implementing a research plan, and reflecting on found information, school librarians enable learners to realize the flow and effectiveness of exploring ideas through an inquiry-based process. School librarians develop active and engaging opportunities, often hands-on and visual, for learners to build persistence by making knowledge products that demonstrate knowledge related to a personal interest or curricular topic.

SHARE: To prepare learners to engage with the larger learning community, school librarians build, maintain, and promote personal and professional learning networks. In structured lessons and informal conversations, school librarians model curiosity by helping learners to seek answers to authentic personal questions. By assisting learners to brainstorm strategies to investigate and find answers, school librarians promote an environment of curiosity and ongoing learning. School librarians encourage learners to exchange ideas by working collaboratively to articulate questions and test possible solutions to authentic challenges.

GROW: In an atmosphere of mutual respect and sharing, reflection and feedback are key parts of an ongoing learning process; school librarians create opportunities for learners to strengthen skills through oral or written reflection and peer feedback. School librarians provide opportunities for formative and summative assessment, including formal or informal reflection. These opportunities allow learners to identify directions for further investigation.

EXPLORE SCHOOL LIBRARY ALIGNMENTS IN DEPTH

THINK: The school library makes resources accessible in a variety of formats that represent learners' interests and developmental levels. The school library provides access to resources that allow the school librarian to structure inquiry-driven authentic activities in response to learner choice. To communicate the value of acting upon personal interest, school librarians enable learners to incorporate available technology and tools into learning activities.

CREATE: Within the school library, the school librarian works with appropriate stakeholders to ensure that learners have access to devices and applications that best support all learners' abilities to demonstrate learning. The school librarian establishes, maintains, and leads a school library that includes physical and virtual presences that enable continuous learning in and beyond school. To meet multiple learners' needs, the school librarian ensures that the physical space within the learning environment simultaneously allows for collaborative problem solving, independent research, and exploration areas.

SHARE: The school librarian solicits stakeholder input regarding the school library through formal surveys, interactive communication tools, informal conversations, and family participation. The school librarian publicizes and advocates for the school library by inviting stakeholders to visit and observe, encouraging broad representation in decisions about the school library, and presenting data that illustrate the school library's impact. Examples of data include school library user surveys, school library materials usage statistics, pre- and post-intervention achievement scores, and displays of authentic products resulting from processes being taught in the school library.

GROW: The school library provides a context in which the school librarian models lifelong learning by sharing resources and interacting in conversations about the school library's mission and goals, resources, practices, and impact on the learning environment. The school librarian is aware of and researches trends and best practice to improve the school library and shares this information with stakeholders. The school librarian takes educated risks to improve the school library by trying new technologies and honing new skills and knowledge to benefit learners and themselves.

RECOMMENDED APPENDICES

APPENDIX C. Annotated List of AASL Position Statements

APPENDIX E. Interpretations of the Library Bill of Rights

APPENDIX E1. Access for Children and Young Adults to Nonprint Materials

APPENDIX E3. Advocating for Intellectual Freedom

APPENDIX E6. Internet Filtering

APPENDIX F. LLAMA's 14 Foundational Competencies

EXPLORE Best Practices

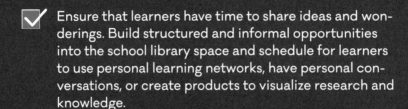 Ensure that learners have time to share ideas and won-
derings. Build structured and informal opportunities
into the school library space and schedule for learners
to use personal learning networks, have personal conversations, or create products to visualize research and
knowledge.

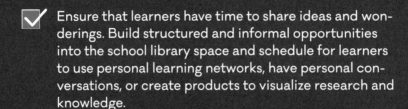 Make sure the school library space includes conversa-
tion areas containing comfortable seating as well as
books and magazines that spark and support exploration of personal interests.

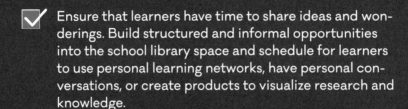 Create physical and/or virtual "gallery" space within
the school library where learners can share creative
products that illustrate their personal interests. If possible, this space should be frequently updated and images
of the products curated. Provide means for participants' comments and input.

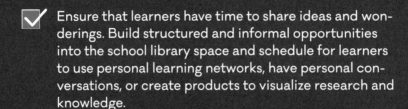 Choose furniture and physical structures for the
school library space that are moveable and able to be
arranged for independent research and reflection as
well as for collaborative work and easy access to the
collection.

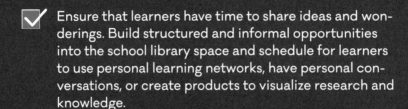 To encourage choice, reflection, and authentic learn-
ing in the school library, establish formal and informal
mechanisms for learners to share their suggestions
for and engage with information resources, devices,
applications, activities, and other supports for personal
curiosity. These mechanisms range from a simple suggestion box or blog to visits to the cafeteria or activity
areas to personally solicit input on learner needs.

10

Engage

VI. ENGAGE

Demonstrate safe, legal, and ethical creating and sharing of knowledge products independently while engaging in a community of practice and in an interconnected world.

I. INQUIRE

Build new knowledge by inquiring, thinking critically, identifying problems, and developing strategies for solving problems.

DOMAINS

A. THINK
Inquire, think critically, and gain knowledge.

D. GROW
Pursue personal and aesthetic growth.

B. CREATE
Draw conclusions, make informed decisions, apply knowledge to new situations, and create new knowledge.

C. SHARE
Share knowledge and participate ethically and productively as members of our democratic society.

V. EXPLORE

Discover and innovate in a growth mindset developed through experience and reflection.

IV. CURATE

Make meaning for oneself and others by collecting, organizing, and sharing resources of personal relevance.

III. COLLABORATE

Work effectively with others to broaden perspectives and work toward common goals.

II. INCLUDE

Demonstrate an understanding of and commitment to inclusiveness and respect for diversity in the learning community.

KEY COMMITMENTS

SHARED FOUNDATIONS

Engage

Domain	LEARNER DOMAINS AND COMPETENCIES	SCHOOL LIBRARIAN DOMAINS AND COMPETENCIES
A. Think	**Learners follow ethical and legal guidelines for gathering and using information by:** 1. Responsibly applying information, technology, and media to learning. 2. Understanding the ethical use of information, technology, and media. 3. Evaluating information for accuracy, validity, social and cultural context, and appropriateness for need.	**School librarians promote ethical and legal guidelines for gathering and using information by:** 1. Directing learners to responsibly use information, technology, and media for learning, and modeling this responsible use. 2. Modeling the understanding of ethical use of information, technology, and media. 3. Teaching learners how and why to evaluate information for accuracy, validity, social and cultural context, and appropriateness for need.
B. Create	**Learners use valid information and reasoned conclusions to make ethical decisions in the creation of knowledge by:** 1. Ethically using and reproducing others' work. 2. Acknowledging authorship and demonstrating respect for the intellectual property of others. 3. Including elements in personal-knowledge products that allow others to credit content appropriately.	**School librarians act as a resource for using valid information and reasoned conclusions to make ethical decisions in the creation of knowledge by:** 1. Showing a variety of strategies to ethically use and reproduce others' work, and modeling this ethical use. 2. Requiring complete attribution to acknowledge authorship and demonstrate respect for the intellectual property of others. 3. Promoting the inclusion of elements in personal-knowledge products that allow others to credit content appropriately.
C. Share	**Learners responsibly, ethically, and legally share new information with a global community by:** 1. Sharing information resources in accordance with modification, reuse, and remix policies. 2. Disseminating new knowledge through means appropriate for the intended audience.	**School librarians promote the responsible, ethical, and legal sharing of new information with a global community by:** 1. Imparting strategies for sharing information resources in accordance with modification, reuse, and remix policies. 2. Guiding the dissemination of new knowledge through means appropriate for the intended audience.
D. Grow	**Learners engage with information to extend personal learning by:** 1. Personalizing their use of information and information technologies. 2. Reflecting on the process of ethical generation of knowledge. 3. Inspiring others to engage in safe, responsible, ethical, and legal information behaviors.	**School librarians support learners' engagement with information to extend personal learning by:** 1. Structuring a learning environment for innovative use of information and information technologies. 2. Designing experiences that help learners communicate the value of the ethical creation of knowledge and reflect on their process. 3. Championing and modeling safe, responsible, ethical, and legal information behaviors.

Demonstrate safe, legal, and ethical creating and sharing of knowledge products independently while engaging in a community of practice and an interconnected world.

SCHOOL LIBRARY DOMAINS AND ALIGNMENTS	The school library facilitates the Key Commitment to and Competencies of ENGAGE	Domain
The school library serves as a context in which the school librarian ensures that the school community is aware of the guidelines for safe, ethical, and legal use of information by: 1. Educating the school community on the ethical use of information and the intellectual property of others. 2. Designing instruction and delivery of services that support equitable access to information in an efficient and ethical manner by all members of the school community. 3. Embedding legal-, ethical-, and social-responsibility concepts into the inquiry and information-seeking processes.		**A. Think**
The school library supports ethical processes for information seeking and use by: 1. Providing an environment in which all members of the school community can work together to develop, approve, and engage in clearly stated use policies to guide acceptable and ethical use of information, technology, and media. 2. Promoting the responsible use of ideas, information, media, and technology through compliance with copyright and intellectual-property policies developed by the school librarian in collaboration with all members of the school community.		**B. Create**
The school library encourages participation in a diverse learning community to create and share information by: 1. Providing both online and physical spaces for the sharing and dissemination of ideas and information. 2. Providing a context in which the school librarian can model for learners, other educators, and administrators multiple strategies to locate, evaluate, and ethically use information for specific purposes.		**C. Share**
The school library supports individual responsibility for information use by: 1. Providing an environment in which the school librarian can effectively develop, direct, and promote resources, services, policies, procedures, and programming aligned with current standards, ethical codes, and principles of the education and information professions. 2. Providing an engaging learning environment that supports innovative and ethical use of information and information technologies.		**D. Grow**

Engage: Demonstrate safe, legal, and ethical creating and sharing of knowledge products independently while engaging in a community of practice and an interconnected world.

ENGAGE LEARNER COMPETENCIES IN DEPTH

THINK: Successful learners adapt quickly to an ever-changing society that has shifted from industrial, to knowledge-based, to conceptual. Learners live in and will compete in a global community; therefore, their success depends on adding flexible skills to their repertoire. This success includes the ability to work independently and in collaboration with others to use information to develop social and situational literacies. Learners need to actively and effectively contribute to communities of practice and engage in shared learning opportunities that allow them to responsibly use information and technology to delve deeply into areas of interest, passion, or concern. By ethically using media and critically evaluating information for a given need or social and cultural context, learners effectively contribute to inquiry, collaborations, and learning practices.

CREATE: Through multiple literacies as well as critical and creative thinking, respectful interactive communication, and problem solving, learners generate a wide range of evidence that documents and demonstrates what they have learned and contributed to personal and collaborative situations. In producing learning products, learners use valid information, ethical decisions, reasoned conclusions, and a variety of techniques to create content, derive knowledge, and seek alternatives to works they do not have permission to use. When reproducing the work of others, learners use complete attribution to acknowledge authorship and respect for the intellectual property of others. Learners also include elements in their own personal knowledge products that allow others to appropriately credit the content.

SHARE: As learners develop skills and embrace new collaborative experiences that enhance and expand their awareness and capabilities, they also share and contribute information, knowledge, and "voice" within and across communities of practice. Learners display resilience, curiosity, motivation, and enthusiasm as active contributors to discussions and other collaborative efforts. In exchanging new information, content, or derivatives with an interconnected global community, learners act according to accepted norms, practices, and policies related to responsible, ethical, and legal modification and reuse of the intellectual property of others. Learners recognize the need to be culturally and linguistically sensitive by distributing new knowledge and information through appropriate means for target populations and audiences.

GROW: Learners blend skills, knowledge, dispositions, and competencies related to the ethical use and exchange of ideas and information when they extend learning by personalizing their use of information and information technologies; creating and sharing new knowledge; reflecting on their learning processes; and seeking to inspire others to engage in responsible information behaviors. These actions empower learners by providing growth opportunities within their community of practice and beyond.

ENGAGE SCHOOL LIBRARIAN COMPETENCIES IN DEPTH

THINK: School librarians follow professional norms to support every learner's academic success and well-being. School librarians encourage learners to be active participants and take responsibility for their own learning by exploring a wide variety of resources with a critical stance. School librarians acknowledge and base instructional and program decisions on current standards, codes, and principles of the education and information professions. School librarians thoroughly understand and model social, ethical, and legal implications of information access, services, and technologies. They empower all members of the learning community to be responsible consumers and producers of ideas and information

> Example isn't another way to teach, it is the only way to teach.
>
> —ALBERT EINSTEIN (HERMANNS 1983)

when the librarians articulate, communicate, and demonstrate digital citizenship responsibilities regarding intellectual freedom, intellectual property, the right to privacy, educational fair use, and security, and teach and model appropriate use of creative commons and public domain resources.

CREATE: School librarians direct and promote effective school libraries having resources, services, policies, and procedures that are clearly aligned with the school's mission and that support the ethical principles and current standards of the education and information services professions. School librarians create a flexible learning environment and provide a variety of opportunities for learning, opportunities that are conducive to active participation, inquiry and resource-based instructional practices. School librarians model and promote efficient and ethical information behaviors by providing authentic and relevant learning experiences for all members of the school community. School librarians ensure that instructional endeavors are designed, taught, cotaught, and assessed according to the principles of copyright, plagiarism avoidance, intellectual property, privacy protection, and civil discourse. The school librarian works with all members of the school community to develop, implement, and follow clearly stated policies for ethical information use. Included are policies for responsible use of technology and information. All such policies will have been approved by the school and district.

SHARE: School librarians design programs, services, and instruction that support equitable, efficient, and ethical information access by learners and other members of their school and community. They embed concepts related to legal, ethical, and social responsibility in the information-seeking, inquiry, and research processes. School librarians prepare learners to engage with the learning community by developing and using multiple strategies for learners, other educators, and administrators to locate, evaluate, synthesize and use information for personal, curricular, or professional interests.

GROW: School libraries are uniquely at intersections of the curriculum, and school librarians address all forms of inquiry and technology integration through scaffolded and iterative processes that promote safe, legal, and ethical pursuit of knowledge. School librarians contribute to curriculum mastery; college, career, and community readiness; and ongoing personal learning by providing opportunities for a variety of authentic, social, and collaborative learning experiences in which individual capabilities and skills are developed, improved, and expanded through continuous feedback, civil discourse, and participation. These actions empower school librarians by providing growth opportunities within their community of practice and beyond.

ENGAGE SCHOOL LIBRARY ALIGNMENTS IN DEPTH

THINK: School libraries provide equitable access to ongoing opportunities for learners to become effective, thoughtful, responsible, and ethical users and creators of ideas and information. When school libraries are strategically planned and provide instruction designed to guide learners through a complex information and digital landscape, they impart ethical use principles as well as the ability to locate, evaluate, create, synthesize, and present information for career, college, and community readiness. Through modeling, demonstration, and support, school librarians guide learners to practice appropriate behavior while actively using social media, learning management systems, online resources, and tools for authentic learning.

CREATE: Instruction and other activities in school libraries emphasize and model the ethical use of resources and reinforce ongoing collaborative instructional efforts for all learners. Recognizing that technology makes it easier to create, access, duplicate, and share information as well as recognizing the need for learners to understand the use of copyrighted material and intellectual property, school librarians advocate for administration-adopted policies, collaboratively created by members of the school community, to address such areas as selection and reconsideration of school library resources, responding to plagiarism, maintaining confidentiality of learners' school library records, and responsible, legal, and ethical use of information resources. School library policies are reviewed and updated on a regular basis.

SHARE: School library policies, procedures, and processes must ensure that educators, learners, and parents have multiple means and opportunities to become aware of accepted policies and practices. Instruction, effective signage, and regular communications should be used to reinforce policies with the learning community. Additionally, efforts to help learners recognize that they are members and participants in the wider scholarly community should be ongoing. Learners need to understand licensing and how they can use it to define authorized sharing, reusing, remixing, and building on their own creative works; learners must also understand ethical guidelines to build upon the work of creators of other licensed materials. These understandings help learners to respect the work of others and give credit to sources that they use in generating content. Instruction in school libraries must provide multiple opportunities for learners to practice and use citation, and provide instruction regarding plagiarism and the benefits of citing sources that have been used. Additionally, the school librarian addresses appropriate guidelines for conducting and representing oneself in online communications, from social networks to e-mail. School libraries should provide opportunities for all learners to practice netiquette in a variety of digital forums and communities.

GROW: The school library provides a context in which the school librarian demonstrates and supports ethical behavior, and promotes the principles of intellectual freedom, information access, privacy, and proprietary rights. As part of the school library's dedication to ethical behavior, the school librarian also models and promotes the highest standards of conduct, ethics, and integrity in the use of all types of resources. School librarians selectively curate and provide learners with collections of vetted digital and online resources while simultaneously working with learners to ensure that they are able to independently evaluate resources and make responsible and ethical decisions regarding use of these resources.

RECOMMENDED APPENDICES

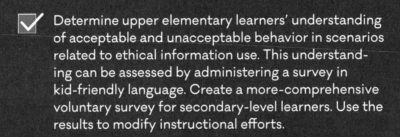

ENGAGE Best Practices

☑ Determine upper elementary learners' understanding of acceptable and unacceptable behavior in scenarios related to ethical information use. This understanding can be assessed by administering a survey in kid-friendly language. Create a more-comprehensive voluntary survey for secondary-level learners. Use the results to modify instructional efforts.

☑ Develop a similar voluntary survey for educators. For each learner behavior addressed by the survey, include a question eliciting the educator's perception of how often learners have engaged in that behavior, and a second question asking how often the educator has had to confront a learner about the same behavior. Use the results to develop collaborative instructional units that address areas in which learners need to develop their understanding.

☑ Invite stakeholders (learners, parents, educators, administrators, school librarians, elected officials) to examine current local policies related to selection and reconsideration of school library resources; confidentiality of learners' school library records; and the responsible, legal, and ethical use of information resources,

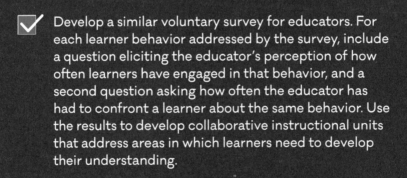

including how to respond to plagiarism. Discuss how to align local policies and best practices to guidelines created by various state and national organizations. Convene this group regularly to refresh, revise, and modify policies when appropriate.

 Read examples of policies regarding selection and reconsideration of school library resources; confidentiality of learners' school library records; and the responsible, legal, and ethical use of information resources. (Examples are often published by the state school library organization and the state and national departments of education.)

 Allow learners to select technology tools and strategies to personalize their knowledge sharing. For example, some learners may choose to produce a short video while other learners may create an infographic.

PART III

Assessment and Evaluation

Meeting the AASL Standards

MEASURING SUCCESS

Overview

THE AASL STANDARDS ARE DESIGNED TO SUPPORT LEARNERS AND school librarians to achieve competency within a Domain. As skilled professionals, school librarians engage in learning as they undertake their work.

A continuous process of improvement depends on measuring growth over time through assessments that are designed prior to the learning experience and that take into account prior learning. Interim assessments serve to give learners—including school librarians—formative feedback that allows them to adjust and improve during the course of the learning experience. Finally, learners culminate their experiences with a product that signifies and represents the Competencies that have been developed.

Competency-Based Learning

WHY THE FOCUS ON COMPETENCY-BASED LEARNING?

Unlike earlier AASL learning standards, this set of standards is built around competencies rather than learning outcomes. Learners' mastery is framed in terms of measurable competencies to ensure that users of AASL's standards

- put the learner at the center, focus on growth, and acknowledge that various learners are intelligent in different ways;
- enable learners to progress based on stages of mastery and, at every step of the way, to have appropriate supports;
- enable learner voice, choice, and agency; and
- employ a pedagogical philosophy, assessment techniques, and reporting systems that build upon and leverage learning.

Competencies and learning outcomes are two related educational terms; their use can sometimes create confusion. Competencies and outcomes can be written to describe the learning gained by learners in individual courses (course outcomes) or for the program as a whole (program outcomes), but the competencies and outcomes are reached at different levels. This document uses the working definitions that follow.

OUTCOME

Broadly defined, a learning outcome is something that a learner is able to do at the end of a learning experience. In the context of learning standards, an outcome is a very specific statement that describes exactly what a learner will be able to do in some measurable way. More than one measurable outcome may be defined for a given competency. A learning outcome is written so that it can be measured or assessed. Because an outcome focuses on what the learner is able to do at the end of a learning experience, learning outcomes are the basis for an assessment program that focuses on what a learner can or should be able to do, upon completion of either a course or a program.

COMPETENCY

Competencies commonly define the applied skills and knowledge that enable learners to successfully perform in professional, educational, and other life contexts. In the context of learning standards, a competency is a general statement that describes the desired knowledge, skills, and behaviors of a learner completing an educational experience. Competencies are defined in terms of a "package" of observable behaviors and, therefore, can be assessed or measured (Gosselin 2016).

In a competency-driven environment:

1. A beginner closely follows prescribed steps to complete a task; a competent learner can personalize actions through recognition of unique aspects of a learning activity. This ability is acquired through experience.

2. A beginner perceives all elements of a learning activity as equally relevant; a competent learner can discern among the elements to identify the most significant aspects of an activity.

3. A beginner functions as an observer; a competent learner functions as an involved participant who articulates group needs and engages others.

Competence is not developed as an all-or-nothing phenomenon; gaining competence is both progressive and personalizable. Learners advance through several stages as they achieve competence; achieved competencies are the building blocks of mastery.

TABLE 11.1
Stages of competency.

STAGE	CHARACTERISTICS
Beginner	Learner has no experience and usually has difficulty with this skill or behavior; requires basic information and direction, and close supervision.
Developing	Learner has limited experience and may continue to have some difficulty with skill or behavior; requires coaching, reinforcement, and close supervision.
Advancing	Learner has additional experience and often performs skills or behaviors effectively in common situations; requires continued coaching/reinforcement and supervision.
Competent	Learner almost always performs skills or behaviors effectively; may require assistance in unusual circumstances.

As learners and school librarians improve through competency-building activities, keep in mind that:

- Participants develop competence in different skills at different rates.
- Learners demonstrate their level of competence at specific assessed milestone points.
- School librarians should identify milestones for timely acquisition of competence.
- School librarians should define specific competencies to be acquired during specific time periods (units, semesters, academic years).
- Pre- and post-learning evaluations of competence can be used to demonstrate progress.

As figure 11.1 suggests, as learners and school librarians progress toward competency, they engage in an improvement cycle that is informed by assessment. Each assessment cycle builds toward mastery; as learners become more competent and move closer to mastery, they personalize their use of information and tools (Rosenberg 2012).

FIGURE 11.1
Competency assessment cycle.

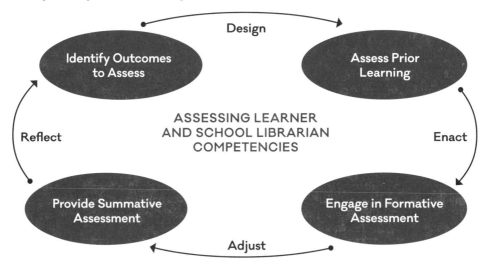

Evaluation of a Responsive School Library

The school library is an environment for learners and school librarians to develop competence and achieve mastery relating to educational content and tools. The evaluation process for school libraries mirrors that of the assessment processes for learners and school librarians.

The goal of evaluating the school library is to measure the extent to which the school library is aligned with the school's goals related to providing intellectual and technological resources that enable the school community to engage effectively in learning experiences.

To evaluate a school library, school librarians and other school library stakeholders

1. define outcomes to assess;
2. gather baseline information;
3. design and enact an improvement activity;
4. formatively assess progress;

5. adjust the improvement plan as needed; and

6. conclude the process with documentation, reflection, and a plan for further improvement.

In Part III, this introductory chapter is followed by chapters devoted to concepts and strategies for assessing learners and school librarians in the context of the AASL Standards. In the final chapter of this section, we provide approaches to enable school librarians to evaluate their school libraries, create a plan for ongoing improvement, and document success.

RECOMMENDED APPENDICES

APPENDIX C. Annotated List of AASL Position Statements

APPENDIX F. LLAMA's 14 Foundational Competencies

APPENDIX I. Useful Verbs

12

Measuring Learner Growth

Assessment in a Competency-Based Environment

MANY SCHOOLS, DISTRICTS, AND STATE-LEVEL EDUCATION DEPART-
ments are moving to competency-based education. Competency-based education
(CBE) differs from standards-based education in that the ultimate goal of CBE is
mastery with time as the variable. Learners advance in their coursework only when
mastery has been achieved. Learners understand where they are and what the next
step is in their education journey; they get the instructional support they need to
succeed, even if achieving success takes several tries.

Like standards-based education, competency-based education uses a common
set of standards. Typically, standards and competencies do not have a one-to-one
correspondence. A standard is what a learner needs to be able to know and do to be
successful in college and career. A competency requires that learners develop skills
and acquire subject-specific information, make meaning of the information, and
also transfer their insights and skills from one academic subject to another. Competencies should also focus on the application and creation of knowledge—in contrast
to the memorization of information—and the development of both skills and dispositions. Competencies are more granular than standards, with a standard consisting
of several competencies together; competencies are part of explicit, measurable,
and transferable learning objectives.

Personalization of learning is a major component of competency-based education.
Since learners learn at their own pace, they must have timely and differentiated support based on their individual needs. School librarians support personalized learning
by matching resources to individual learners' needs and to the educators' needs for
differentiation. Databases that include read-aloud features or translation, for example, provide individual help to a struggling reader or English language learner who
needs content but is not ready to read the content independently in English.

School librarians provide resources, instruction, and opportunities that enable
learners to thrive in a competency-based education system. Effectively addressing
the standards means learners are exposed to ideas and able to practice skills that
allow them to inquire, include, collaborate, curate, explore, and engage with learning, one another, and their communities. Through effective instruction, learners
develop the skills and dispositions that make them ready for their futures.

Knowing whether learners are ready for the next stage of learning requires effective assessment. Assessment should be a meaningful and positive learning experience for learners. To facilitate long-term retention and transfer of learning across
disciplines, competency-based assessments measure the application of skills in
authentic settings. Traditional assessments, such as those with multiple-choice

questions that focus on recall, are not sufficient to measure a competency. Instead, performance tasks that use artifacts and scenarios that simulate real-world challenges should be designed.

There are a variety of approaches to learner assessment. Each method brings its own unique benefits. Deciding which assessments are best for learners can be a challenge. Effective teaching means assessing learners' prior learning, applying formative assessment to identify how learners are progressing throughout the learning process, and facilitating summative assessment to determine learners' mastery of a topic or skill. (For more on the different types of assessment, see the next chapter.)

The remainder of this chapter will provide tips and suggestions for assessing prior learning, creating a formative assessment task, and designing summative assessments for learners.

Using these strategies, in combination with knowledge and understanding of learning theory, child development, and the need for digital-age learning experiences provided through school librarians' pre-service preparation programs, novice school librarians are also able to assess student progress and learning in collaboration with members of the learning community to ensure alignment of that learning with academic standards within and across grade levels.

Pre-Assessment

Pretests or pre-assessments allow the school librarian to determine if the content in the lesson or unit has already been mastered. If all learners understand the concepts, then the lesson can be skipped. If only a few learners need the content, instruction can be personalized to bring those learners up to speed. However, if the majority of learners are struggling, the lesson or unit can proceed as planned.

A pretest can be as simple as a one-question poll at the start of a lesson to check for understanding or as complex as an assessment at the beginning of the year to determine what concepts can be skipped and what ideas need to be reinforced. It is good practice to explain the purpose of the assessment to reduce anxiety and encourage learners to do their best.

By comparing pre-assessments with summative assessments, school librarians can view a comparison of what learners have learned. In this situation, assessment tasks or questions can be the same or comparable so a direct comparison can be made.

FIGURE 12.1

Flowchart for creating formative assessment.

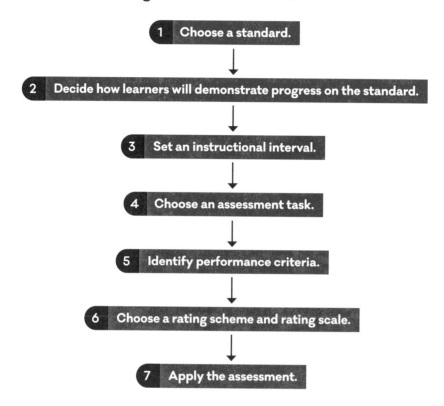

Creating a Formative Assessment Task

One process for determining assessment needs and selecting the most appropriate method for measuring learners' progress includes six steps, which are described below using an example from Standard IV, Curate. This standard's Key Commitment calls for learners to "make meaning for oneself and others by collecting, organizing, and sharing resources of personal relevance."

STEP 1. Choose a standard and Competency. Decide on the specific Competency within the standard to address. When and how you address each Competency will depend on your school, district, or state curriculum. Work with other educators to determine how their content standards align the school library with the broader school curriculum.

STEP 2. Decide how learners will demonstrate progress on the Competency. Next, decide what learners will do to demonstrate their progress on a Competency related to the selected standard. This demonstration will look different depending on the grade and abilities of the learner. For example, the first Competency in the Create Domain (IV. B.1.) states: "Learners gather information appropriate to the task by: 1) Seeking a variety of sources." A learner in grades K–2 may demonstrate this Competency by using two or three books instead of just one in an information-seeking task, while older learners may be expected to use more sources and more types of sources—reference books, nonfiction books, websites, and several other types of sources—for that same task.

STEP 3. Set an instructional interval and milestones. Because learners do not master a competency in a single day or through a single activity, measure growth along the way to evaluate progress. This process involves setting milestones at regular intervals. Milestones might consist of yearly academic goals such as grade-level expectations, or goals tied to school-calendar intervals such as a semester, quarter, month, or even week goals. These milestones mark the instructional interval's conclusion, such as the end of a four-week research project. Instructional intervals are typically based on state, district, or local curriculum and courses.

STEP 4. Choose an assessment task. After choosing a specific learner Competency and specifying the time interval over which the goal will be mastered, the next step is to design or locate an appropriate learning activity that can serve as a formative assessment; such an activity is often called an "assessment task." Many assessment tasks have been developed by other educators and made available in educational clearinghouses and open education resource (OER) repositories.

Your choice of assessment task will be driven by the target Competency. Some assessment tasks are better suited to independent work, some to group work, and some may suit both types of competencies.

For example:

> The first Competency in Curate's Share Domain (IV.C.1.) is: "Learners exchange information resources within and beyond their learning community by: 1) Accessing and evaluating collaboratively constructed information sites." This Competency could be demonstrated by an individual learner who, after evaluating the accuracy and currency of information on a collaboratively constructed information site (e.g., Wikipedia) presents various opinions and positions when reporting on a controversial issue.

In Curate's Share Domain the third Competency (IV.C.III.) is: "Learners exchange information resources within and beyond their learning community by: 3) Joining with others to compare and contrast information derived from collaboratively constructed information sites." This Competency can be developed and demonstrated in a group setting.

Best Apps and Websites for Teaching and Learning

SELECTION FOR INCLUSION in Best Apps for Teaching and Learning is a recognition honoring mobile applications of exceptional value to inquiry-based teaching and learning as embodied in the AASL Standards for learners and the profession. Websites, tools, and resources recognized as Best Websites for Teaching and Learning foster the qualities of innovation, creativity, active participation, and collaboration. They are free websites that are user friendly and encourage a community of learners to explore and discover.

Updated annually, the "Best Lists" are based on feedback and nominations from AASL members. The new lists are released each June. School librarians can nominate their most-used apps and websites at <www.ala.org/aasl/standards/best>.

The second Curate Competency within the Share Domain (IV.C.2.) could be achieved independently or collaboratively: "Learners exchange information resources within and beyond their learning community by: 2) Contributing to collaboratively constructed information sites by ethically using and reproducing others' work."

STEP 5. Identify performance criteria. After an assessment task has been selected, identify the desired criteria for performance on the task. In other words, what will successful task performance look like? For example, if your assessment for Curate's Create Domain third Competency (IV.B.3.) ("Learners gather information appropriate to the task by: 3) Systematically questioning and assessing the validity and accuracy of information") requires learners to choose the best of several resources to answer questions about the state animal, success will depend on learners' abilities to use a set of evaluation criteria to explain why one source was better than others.

STEP 6. Choose a rating scheme and rating scale. Rating schemes and scales can vary in length and complexity, depending on what they will be used to assess. Several types of rating schemes and scales are discussed in the next section of this chapter.

For all rating schemes, providing detailed competency descriptions that use language and terminology familiar to learners is essential.

Regardless of the rating scheme chosen, a rating scale must also be selected. You may be able to use a universal rating scale to evaluate all competencies. However, typically different rating scales are used for different types of competencies, depending on how the rating information will be used.

Another consideration when choosing a rating scale is the level of granularity you need in the ratings. The rating scale used can be as simple as "Demonstrated/Not Demonstrated" or can include several levels of performance:

"5 - Outstanding; 4 - Excellent; 3 - Proficient; 2 - Developing; 1 - Beginning."

Possible Formative Assessment Tasks

1. Completing exit slips
2. Answering oral questions
3. Taking quizzes
4. Completing worksheets
5. Creating or filling in graphic organizers
6. Doing authentic tasks
7. Providing short responses to prompts
8. Creating products (artifacts)

Rating Schemes and Scales for Formative Assessments

SHORT AND SIMPLE

A short, simple rating scheme provides a definition of a competency and invites school librarians and classroom educators to choose a rating that characterizes the level of performance demonstrated by the learner. Simple rating schemes also sometimes invite school librarians and educators to provide comments about their rating or the learner's performance. These schemes are typically used for assessing very specific competencies that a learner either demonstrates or does not.

Figure12.2 illustrates a simple rating scheme and four-level performance scale.

FIGURE 12.2

Example of short, simple formative assessment rating scheme and scale.

BIBLIOGRAPHY	RATING
A bibliography that demonstrates a sufficient amount of research to answer a question includes credible sources that reflect a diversity of perspectives and sources, are formatted properly in the assigned bibliographic style, and provide information that helps contribute to the arguments in the thesis and present a supportive body of evidence.	**4**–Excellent **3**–Proficient **2**–Developing **1**–Beginning

Benefits

- Can be quick and easy for school librarians and educators to complete.
- Good for assessing a competency for which various levels of performance are possible.
- Allows learners to reflect upon the learning artifact's completeness prior to assessment.
- Gives everyone a general sense of a learner's performance level.
- Gives the school librarians and other educators the "big picture" on performance.

Cautions

- Does not give learners detailed feedback on what they need to improve unless the school librarian and/or other educator provides detailed comments.
- Makes consistent evaluations difficult because only high-level descriptions of ratings are used.

DETAILED RATING SCHEME

A detailed rating scheme includes not only a general description of a competency but also details the various levels of demonstration (see figure 12.3). School librarians rate a learner by choosing the description that best describes the learner's behavior, and can also usually provide additional comments. This rating scheme is ideal for evaluating leadership competencies and group participation. With this scheme, specific areas for improvement are identified for learners.

FIGURE 12.3

Example of a detailed rating scheme and scale.

BIBLIOGRAPHY	RATING
A bibliography that demonstrates a sufficient amount of research to answer a question includes credible sources that reflect a diversity of perspectives and sources, are formatted properly in the assigned bibliographic style, and provide information that helps contribute to the arguments in the thesis and present a supportive body of evidence.	**4–Excellent:** The bibliography is properly formatted. It contains sources that are all credible, reflect a diversity of perspectives and sources, and are sufficient to present a body of evidence. **3–Proficient:** The bibliography is properly formatted. It contains sources that are almost all credible, reflect a diversity of perspectives, and are almost sufficient to present a body of evidence. **2–Developing:** The bibliography is formatted but contains some errors. It contains sources that are mostly credible and reflect some diversity of perspectives. The sources are not enough to provide a supportive body of evidence. **1–Beginning:** The bibliography is not properly formatted. It contains sources that are not credible and do not reflect differing perspectives. The sources are not enough to present a supportive body of evidence.

Benefits

- Facilitates consistent ratings because assessment is based on specific behavior descriptions.
- Gives learners clear information about how they are performing. Because learners can see descriptions of higher levels of performance, they know what and how to improve.

Cautions

- Can make the assessment rubric very long.
- Consumes educators' time to write the detailed descriptions of the various levels of demonstration.
- Can cause "information overload," resulting in educators and learners not reading the descriptions carefully or completely.
- May cause confusion (because of level of detail) about what must be fixed and what is already OK.

MATRIX RATING SCHEME

Educators need to capture additional performance data to evaluate learners in a cotaught and peer-assessed environment. Educators first identify the level of performance required for a particular competency, share these levels with learners to guide them as they prepare their knowledge products, and then let peers or co-teachers rate the learner's performance using those same levels. A matrix format (see figure 12.4) is an effective method to rate competencies.

FIGURE 12.4

Example of a matrix rating scheme.

CRITERIA	BEGINNING	DEVELOPING	PROFICIENT	EXCELLENT
Diversity of Sources	Fewer than three types of sources are included in the bibliography or list of works cited.	At least three types of sources are included in the bibliography or list of works cited.	At least four types of sources, including primary sources, are included in the bibliography or list of works cited.	At least five types of sources, including primary sources, are included in the bibliography or list of works cited.
Credibility of Sources	Few resources are credible.	At least half of the resources are credible.	Almost all the resources are credible.	All of the resources are credible.
Quality of Research	Few resources help answer the research question and present a supportive body of evidence.	At least half of the resources help answer the research question and present a supportive body of evidence.	Almost all of the resources help answer the research question and present a supportive body of evidence.	All of the resources help answer the research question and present a supportive body of evidence.
Citation Format	Fewer than half of the citations are properly formatted. The bibliography is not properly formatted.	At least half of the citations are properly formatted. The bibliography is formatted with some minor errors.	Almost all of the citations are properly formatted. The bibliography is properly formatted.	All of the citations are properly formatted. The bibliography is properly formatted.

Benefits
- Provides quick way to gather details of the assessment.
- Facilitates data-gathering for a large number of competencies.
- Gives school librarians, other educators, and learners lots of detail about performance.

Cautions
- Potential for improvement depends on the extent of detailed, actionable feedback.

Applying the Assessment

OVERVIEW
Once designed, an assessment can be applied in one of several ways. Learners can self-evaluate, assess each other, be graded by the school librarian or other educator, or a combination of these methods can be used.

LEARNER SELF-ASSESSMENT
Regular use of self-assessment allows learners to develop reflective practice, self-monitoring, and self-directed learning. Learners who self-assess develop skills that are transferable to college, career, and life. Learners who can see their own growth toward a learning outcome will have a greater sense of satisfaction and take more personal responsibility for their own learning than will learners who perceive their educators as being in charge of learning.

For effective self-assessment, it is important to spend time showing learners how to complete evaluation rubrics as well as explaining the expectations and criteria for the task. Allowing learners to assist in developing the assessment criteria can aid in learner ownership and buy-in. However, it is important to differentiate between self-assessment and self-grading. School librarians and other educators must be clear about their intentions; they must clearly communicate to learners who is ultimately in charge of the grade for the assignment.

Self-assessment can be implemented with a rating scale or with simple reflective questions such as "What went well with this assignment? What is weak about this assignment?" Combining both approaches can also help the instructor understand learners' thinking; this understanding can lead to more-effective feedback and instruction.

LEARNER PEER ASSESSMENT

Peer assessment can empower learners to take responsibility for their own learning, enable them to learn the skills of assessment, enhance learners' understanding through the process of evaluating the work of others, and motivate learners to engage more deeply with the instructional material.

As with self-assessment, it is important when implementing peer assessment to spend time introducing the rubrics to ensure learners understand how to apply them properly. Educators must make sure learners know the reason for the peer review and the expectations for engaging in the peer review process. The school

Assessment of Learner in Action: Example Scenario

Step 1 **Choose a standard.** For this example we will look at Include's Think Domain, second Competency (II.A.2.) "Learners contribute a balanced perspective when participating in a learning community by 2) Adopting a discerning stance toward point of view and opinions expressed in information resources and learning products."

Step 2 **Decide how learners will demonstrate progress on the standard.** Now that we have identified the standard to be assessed, we need to determine what we want to see learners do to demonstrate they have made progress toward this competency. This demonstration may look very different depending on the age of the learners. A high school learner might be expected to identify purpose, opinion, and bias in a variety of sources. In contrast, an

elementary school learner may be expected to be able to identify fact versus opinion. For this example, let's assume our learners are in upper elementary.

Step 3 **Set an instructional interval.** Teaching learners how to distinguish between fact and opinion will definitely require more than one class period, and this skill will be something they will practice with increasing complexity as time goes on. However, for this initial lesson on the topic, the instructional intervention could be anywhere from a few days to one week.

Step 4 **Choose an assessment task.** Assessments can be formative or summative. For this example, we will assume that the assessment will be formative. There are many possibilities for formative assessments, and librarian or classroom educator can model effective assessment through the constructive feedback they give learners on their work and by giving feedback on learners' feedback to each other. Showing learners examples of feedback of varying levels of quality and then discussing which are the most useful can help learners understand expectations for peer assessment.

Peer feedback can be applied in various ways; however, it is most likely to be effective in small groups of learners so they can explain and discuss their feedback with one another. Alternatively, learners can be asked to evaluate one another's work anonymously.

each has its benefits. Since our expectation for our elementary learners is to distinguish between fact and opinion, we might ask them to read a short article and highlight facts in one color and opinions in another color. Depending on the needs of the class, and the school librarian's and classroom educator's preference and time, every learner might read the same article, or each might find an article based on personal interest.

Step 5 **Identify performance criteria.** What will it look like when learners have done well on this task? In this example, good performance will mean that a learner has highlighted all the facts in one color and all the opinions in another color.

Step 6 **Choose a rating scheme and rating scale.** Because each learner doing this task either demonstrates the competency or does not, a short, simple rating scheme can be applied here. The results of the assessment can be examined for the whole class to determine an overall skill level and whether additional teaching or further practice is needed by the whole class or only by some learners.

Step 7 **Apply the assessment.** Should self-assessment, peer-assessment, school librarian assessment, or a combination be used? For this example, learners would benefit from assessing each other. This peer-assessment will provide learners with extra practice on the identified competency and also help them develop the skills to effectively assess others. It is important that learners understand who will do final grading: the school librarian, another educator, or peers.

Creating a Summative Assessment Task

PURPOSE

Because competency-based learning focuses on mastery of skills, summative assessment gives school librarians and learners the opportunity and ability to assess competencies at the end of the instructional interval. The competencies being assessed could be product- or process-based, depending on the chosen standard. A collaboratively created timeline for learners to master both school library and content-area competencies will drive the type of summative assessment to use. For school librarians, summative assessment documents the extent to which learners are developing Competencies across Domains and have acquired the desired knowledge. To create a complete picture of competency mastery, summative assessment includes assessment of process knowledge as well as content knowledge.

Choosing a summative assessment to use depends on the time available to collect data and work samples from the learners. If the school librarian sees a class consistently, then journals or portfolios may be a viable option for summative assessment. For a class that visits the school library only for particular units of study, learners and educators may be best served if reports, work products, presentations, or end-of-unit tests are used for summative assessment.

PORTFOLIOS

Portfolios provide an option for summative assessment by collecting learners' work samples (digital or print), as well as for formative assessments by the school librarian and another educator, and formative self-assessments by learners. This combination of learner work and learner assessment provides a comprehensive overview of competency mastery. In addition to using widely available tools for website creation and learning management, school librarians can show learners how to create digital portfolios using several popular applications.

Benefits

- Allows learners to collect work in one location.
- Integrates work products and assessments for prior, formative, and summative assessment.
- Documents learners' development over time.
- Takes advantage of digital and print collection options.

Cautions

- Requires investment of time by learners, school librarians, and other educators for portfolio creation and assessment.

- Requires investment of time by school librarians and other educators to decide upon the portfolio's purpose as well as which products learners should collect.
- May require more time than is available to manage portfolio creation and archiving for a large number of learners.

JOURNALS AND LOGS

Journals or learning logs are another summative assessment option. These written artifacts can be used at all levels and allow learners to keep together in one location informal observations, formal records, and assessments given by the school librarian and classroom educator. If school librarians keep learners' journals in the school library or accessible online, these logs will always be available for learners' reflections on learning activities in the school library.

Benefits

- Gives learners ownership of the work, causing them to feel more invested in what they put into their journals.
- Makes learners' ideas, illustrations, and reflections accessible to learners, school librarians, and other educators in one place.
- Can be used with all grade levels.

Cautions

- Can cause resistance among learners who do not want to record their ideas, especially if writing notes by hand is required.
- Requires time and effort to manage and archive digital journals.
- Supports individualized work better than collaborative activities.

JOURNALS AND LEARNING logs are based in the tradition of science notebooking, in which scientists record their ideas, observations, theories, and experiments. Science notebooks commonly include drawings, photos, and other illustrations in addition to text. Many scientists keep notebooks for their entire careers, providing chronicles of decades of research, learning, and knowledge growth. Learners can derive the same benefits from keeping learning journals and logs.

REFLECTIVE PAPER

Having learners write a short essay or report at the end of a research unit may document the synthesis of new information. With part of the essay or report focusing on the process of learning and another part focusing on content learned, learners convey new knowledge of the topic while reflecting on the steps taken to obtain the information.

Benefits

- Employs skills familiar to learners accustomed to writing essays or reports.
- Supports learners' analyzing their learning processes while sharing new content knowledge.
- Allows learners to work collaboratively to produce the essay or report.

Cautions

- May not be a creative representation of what was learned.
- Does not provide an opportunity for improvement because essays and reports are closed ended.

PRODUCT OR PRESENTATION

Having learners create a product or presentation at the end of a unit of study can serve as a summative assessment strategy. The presentation or product could be creation of a website, preparation and delivery of an informative speech, or construction of a 3-D poster; the ideas are endless. The purpose of the presentation or product is to let learners choose a tool to show the incorporation of new and prior knowledge in a visual, audial, or tactile representation. Preparation of an end-of-unit artifact also allows the learner to reflect on and reinforce the research process developed during the unit of study.

Benefits

- Gives learners a creative opportunity to convey both process and content knowledge.
- Gives learners a choice of how to present information.

Cautions

- Will bore learners if all are assigned the same presentation tool.
- Does not document improvement over time.
- Does not provide a path to improvement.

Conclusion

In this chapter, we reviewed the competency-based education (CBE) assessment cycle for learners. In a competency framework like the *AASL Standards Framework for Learners*, assessment is a key tool for helping learners achieve mastery through personalized learning experiences and for providing school librarians and other educators with guidance for instructional differentiation. The CBE assessment cycle begins with a prior learning assessment (PLA), which will indicate learners' levels of familiarity with the topic under study and the degree to which learners have mastered the knowledge, skills, and abilities to demonstrate knowledge. As learners progress through learning tasks, they engage in an ongoing process of formative assessment that helps them chart their progress toward mastery. Learners culminate the learning event by creating and sharing products with peers, school librarians, other educators, and other stakeholders.

Questions for the Reflective Practitioner

1. Which components of the AASL Standards frameworks might best be shared with my school community (peer educators, administrators, parent groups) so others understand how learners can grow in the school library?

2. In what ways do the AASL Standards frameworks lend themselves to both formative and summative assessments?

3. How can I best integrate the *AASL Standards Framework for Learners* with other content areas and demonstrate an impact on student learning through the lessons I teach with my peer educators?

RECOMMENDED APPENDICES

APPENDIX C. Annotated List of AASL Position Statements

APPENDIX C3. Position Statement: Instructional Role of the School Librarian

APPENDIX C5. Position Statement: Role of the School Library Program

APPENDIX H. Evidence of Accomplishment

APPENDIX I. Useful Verbs

13

Measuring School Librarian Growth

Dimensions of Professional Activity

OVERVIEW

Lifelong learning, a process of continuous improvement, permeates every aspect of an effective school library. Looking at the dimensions of professional activity through the lens of the Shared Foundations (Inquire, Include, Collaborate, Curate, Explore, and Engage) provides school librarians with a framework for reflection and self-assessment to achieve personal professional growth that supports empowerment of learners and of the school librarian. Shared Foundations are woven throughout the standards and provide both a theoretical and actionable framework that elevates the unique and important work of the school librarian to the center of learning. These Shared Foundations are inspired by and promote pedagogical shifts in teaching and learning.

INQUIRE

Effective school librarians actively engage in professional learning. Adopting a growth mindset and a receptive attitude is necessary for effective practice as a school librarian. Self-reflection, a fundamental aspect of a school librarian's Inquire framework, stimulates school librarians to seek, embrace, and create new ideas about teaching, learning, and school librarianship. One critical component of Inquire when applied to professional activities in the Domains Think, Create, Share, and Grow is the opportunity to share with colleagues reflections and ideas related to learning and best school library practice.

INCLUDE

School librarians have a pivotal role in facilitating opportunities for learners to understand and participate in activities that honor diversity and embrace inclusion. It is imperative that the school librarian be well-versed in a variety of perspectives and strategies that foster inclusion. School librarians' celebration of the diversity and commonality of humankind helps learners contextualize the ideal of inclusion.

COLLABORATE

Collaboration is integral to school librarians' work as educators. Being skilled in collaboration and practicing coteaching positively affect learners' learning. The old adage, "Two heads are better than one," applies here. Having a wide repertoire of collaborative planning strategies helps foster this disposition throughout the school community. Seeking out other educators and discussing ideas and information with them serves as an exemplar of collaboration that elevates all members of the faculty.

CURATE

Curation, an area of expertise for school librarians, supports self-growth and is critical in creating a knowledge base and cultivating best practices in the area of school librarianship. Curating as an endeavor to personalize professional learning is at the root of creating a thriving and effective school library. Seeking out research and scholarly information about school librarianship, teaching, and learning helps school librarians formulate ideas and make connections that enhance their practice.

EXPLORE

School librarians encourage learners' exploration and innovation at all levels in all curricular areas and in areas of personal interest. School librarians are adept at supporting learners when they fail and encouraging them to modify their processes and persevere to improve their learning. As learners themselves, school librarians must participate in learning activities without fear of failure. School librarians, like all learners, must be free to try new ideas and reinvent ideas. It is acceptable to not know everything. The journey—the process used to gain knowledge—is paramount and must be systematic, responsive, and comfortable.

ENGAGE

Engaging with the learning community as a learner allows the school librarian to practice and model continual, sustainable behaviors related to searching for, assessing, curating, and using information. As school librarians learn themselves, their innovative uses of information and technologies are an important contribution to a flourishing school culture. The school librarian's modeling and explicitly communicating the value of the ethical use of information and creation of knowledge—as well as reflecting on the process—make success with these complex tasks attainable for all learners.

Domains of Professional Competence

Four Domains provide an overview of areas considered important in an evaluation of a school librarian: Think, Create, Share, and Grow. These four Domains parallel the categories also used in the standards for learners and for school libraries, thus providing the basis of a coherent system for measurements of effectiveness and growth.

THINK

Think focuses on the school librarian's skills in helping learners activate prior and background knowledge as a context for new meaning; facilitating, organizing, and scaffolding learner groups; and challenging learners to inquire about the world around them and to recognize the contributions and perspectives of other learners. This Domain also addresses the school librarian's ability to teach learners how and why to evaluate information and use it ethically.

CREATE

Create focuses on the school librarian's skills in assisting learners through a process of creating products to demonstrate learning. In this Domain, school librarians model use of a variety of communication tools and resources, and work to ensure that learners interact with diverse groups and consider a variety of viewpoints as they build on and create new knowledge to share with a wide audience. Create also includes providing learners with tools and strategies to organize information systematically, and the school librarian's curation of resources to meet the needs of the school community. Efforts to create an engaging atmosphere that fosters exploration and pursuit of personal interests can be measured within this Domain.

SHARE

Share focuses on the school librarian's skills in teaching and modeling the ethical use of information in the creation of products. Within this Domain are also the elements of fostering collaborative opportunities for learners to gather information and use it ethically, and to share problem-solving strategies and solutions. The Domain also includes the aspects of guiding learners to contribute to discussions with diverse partners while respecting diverse perspectives.

GROW

Grow focuses on the school librarian's skills in leading learners to reflect on processes, interactions, and products as part of a collaborative learning culture locally and globally. Part of this Domain includes the school librarian's ability to recognize and acknowledge learner skills that can be developed, improved, expanded, and shared, including innovative use of information and technology. This Domain also includes the school librarian's responsibilities to enable equitable access to learning opportunities and resources necessary for learners' success.

Formative Assessment

PURPOSE

In the past, school library instruction was often delivered according to a one-size-fits-all model. Isolated lessons taught to the whole class were commonly conducted with no assessment of an individual learner's mastery of the concept being taught. Happily for us and our learners, this approach is no longer common. School librarians want to know exactly what their learners know and how to help them learn. Formative assessment provides school librarians with feedback about their instruction; this feedback allows them to fine-tune their practice in real time to ensure and personalize learning for all learners. Formative assessment permits school librarians to make adjustments, tweaking their practice at every juncture of a lesson. Formative assessments help ensure that all learners are mastering the concepts and content being taught. The power of formative assessment is amplified when school librarians and other educators collaboratively use the assessments systematically and continually to improve teaching and learning. Formative assessment must be a foundational part of a school librarian's toolkit.

The use of formative assessments as a tool in evaluation of school librarians' work is critical as school librarians and their administrators engage in consistent and continual conversation about honing the work of the school librarian within the goals of the school community. It is important that administrators use walk-throughs to formatively assess school librarians. In addition, it is essential that school librarians share with their evaluating administrators the learners' and school librarians' own responses to measures of formative assessment.

SCHOOL LIBRARIANS USING FORMATIVE ASSESSMENT FOR ADAPTING INSTRUCTION

As described in the previous chapter in the context of assessing learners' progress, formative assessments can take many forms from very simple to complex and can occur at any point in the lesson or unit cycle. These learning checks serve as gauges for learners' understanding. The timing is dependent on what the school librarian or classroom educator wants to know about the learning and effectiveness of the teaching. Using an assessment during the teaching of a particularly complex concept allows an educator to determine what the next instructional task should be and for which learners: reteach everyone, provide additional instruction for a subset of the learners, move forward, or jump ahead. This opportunity for educators to adjust instruction applies to all learners from the youngest to adults.

Sharing with learners the evidence of learning provides opportunities for conversations around learners' thinking and perceptions. A simple example might look like this. If half of the learners identify one answer to a question about a concept and half identify a different answer, the school librarian can begin a dialogue about why one group answered one way and the other answered another way. Learners and the school librarian will learn from such a discussion. In this instance, learners who answered incorrectly can figure out what they misunderstood. The school librarian can identify what needs to be retaught.

Formative assessments can be as simple as asking learners if they understand. While this practice can be useful for many things, it does not ensure the school librarian that every learner has mastered the concept being taught. As described in the previous chapter, there are many ways to capture evidence of learning incrementally throughout the learning process. This evidence might include artifacts such as photos, videos, checklists, surveys, quick writes, exit tickets, or drawings. These artifacts provide great insights into learner perception and understanding, and allow the school librarian to change instruction and teaching strategies on the fly. Using formative assessments to tailor learning strategies in real time based on each learner's needs fosters differentiation for all learners.

Using the evidence of learning to give descriptive feedback to a learner is an important part of teaching and learning. At times, an open-ended question in response to a learner's formative assessment can help a learner rethink his or her response to learning. Sometimes the learner's answer reveals a need for more-explicit teaching.

LEADING FORMATIVE ASSESSMENT OF SCHOOL LIBRARIAN'S WORK

Formative assessments serve as a growth path for school librarians and provide opportunities for dialogue between the administrator and the school librarian.

A starting point would be an initial dialogue early in the year when the administrator and school librarian discuss the school library standards in the context of the school's mission. Throughout the year, school librarians should engage their evaluator in ongoing conversations about practice, process, challenges, and successes. Formative evaluation should be an iterative process that provides opportunities for checkpoints throughout the year, allowing the school librarian to listen, reflect, and, if necessary, respond to the feedback provided, and then modify practice as appropriate.

During observations and subsequent conversations with the administrator, school librarians should ask questions that are open ended. School librarians should also be prepared to provide background on their teaching choices, including concepts taught, strategies used, activities led, etc. These conversations are opportunities to ask for suggestions. Instead of asking "Did you think this lesson went well?" a school librarian might ask, "In what ways do you think I could better engage learners in my lesson?" Regular sharing of information and data, including anecdotes and statistics, can provide administrators with a snapshot of continual progress toward established goals for learners, the school librarian, and the school library.

Summative Evaluation

Summative evaluations of school librarians' work are holistic and combine evidence gathered over the course of a year or longer (the summative cycle). Although summative evaluations often include some subjectivity, objective sources of evidence to support a rating are critical to the process. Sources of evidence to support ratings can include observations, print and/or digital samples of learners' work, print and/or digital samples of school library programming materials (including photos, videos, and other media), and learner and staff feedback as well as statistics and data about use and impact of the school library, its resources, and the school librarian.

SEE APPENDIX H: Evidence of Accomplishment for examples of the kinds of materials and activities that can be used to illustrate your practice.

Using *AASL Standards Framework for School Librarians* to Conduct Professional Evaluation

OVERVIEW

When evaluators of school librarians use the *AASL Standards Framework for School Librarians,* those evaluators focus on specific Competencies that are part of each of the four Domains: Think, Create, Share, and Grow. A sample of an excerpt from a rubric is provided in figure 13.1. This sample includes descriptors for each of four performance levels: Foundational, Developing, Mastery, and Exemplary. Evidence to support each rating is essential, but evaluators should be aware that not all Competencies are easily observable. To determine an appropriate rating for each Competency in rubrics locally developed, school librarians must be part of conversations with evaluators.

EXAMPLE OF A RUBRIC SECTION

Figure 13.1 is an example of a section of a rubric based on the Inquire foundation's Think Domain.

SHARED FOUNDATION: INQUIRE

KEY COMMITMENT: Build new knowledge by inquiring, thinking critically, identifying problems, and developing strategies for solving problems.

SCHOOL LIBRARIAN	FOUNDATIONAL	DEVELOPING	MASTERY	EXEMPLARY
A. THINK: School librarians teach learners to display curiosity and initiative when seeking information by: 1. Encouraging learners to formulate questions about a personal interest or a curricular topic. 2. Activating learners' prior and background knowledge as context for constructing new meaning.	**School librarian provides learners with topics to research.**	**School librarian encourages learners to develop questions about specified topics for the purpose of research.**	**School librarian supports learners in developing their own questions to explore topics of personal interest.**	**School librarian models the process of formulating questions of personal interest and facilitates question development and inquiry by learners.**

FIGURE 13.1

Example of a section of a rubric based on a portion of the *AASL Standards Framework for School Librarians*.

As of 2017, the Charlotte Danielson Framework and the Marzano Focused Teacher Evaluation Model have been used as the basis for certified staff evaluations in a number of states (Danielson Group 2013; Carbaugh 2017). Each of these professional evaluation frameworks focuses on similar aspects of professional growth toward effectiveness and aligns well with the school librarian standards presented in this AASL resource. Emphases in each include: a focus on student engagement, professional practices for ongoing growth, and highly effective instructional strategies. The AASL school librarian standards more specifically address particular aspects of school librarianship that are unique to the role, and with this new framework, directly correlate those school librarian standards with learner standards and school library standards. These standards are unique to school librarianship and provide additional support to already established or adopted evaluation instruments currently in place in school districts and states. Some evaluation instruments are specifically for school librarians and address competencies required for effectiveness. Other instruments are more generic and designed for certified teachers.

In the subsections below, the Shared Foundation Inquire has been aligned with the Danielson framework and Marzano model. Creating this type of an alignment for all the Shared Foundations will be an important exercise for school librarians in each district to do. After these correlations have been made, it is critical that school librarians have ongoing dialogue with the evaluating administrator about how the *AASL Standards Framework for School Librarians* aligns with the district evaluation document used for school librarians.

DANIELSON AND AASL STANDARDS CROSSWALK

The Framework for Library Media Specialists presented in *Enhancing Professional Practice: A Framework for Teaching* (Danielson 2007) is used in many states as a tool (or the basis for a tool) for measuring a school librarian's effectiveness. The *AASL Standards Framework for School Librarians* consists of four Domains, as does the Danielson Framework for Library Media Specialists, although the titles and content of the Domains are different in the two documents. However, the two documents can be used in tandem to create a full picture of school librarian effectiveness within a school.

As a formative tool, the *AASL Standards Framework for School Librarians* can be used side by side with the Danielson Framework for Library Media Specialists to reflect on current practices and to determine areas for potential growth.

By providing more-detailed school librarian-specific descriptors about the role, the *AASL Standards Framework for School Librarians* can be used for summative assessment to support a school, district, or state assessment based on the Danielson framework. As evaluators review evidence to support ratings in a Danielson-based summative assessment tool, a school librarian can share additional information and self-reflections around the Competencies included in the *AASL Standards Framework for School Librarians*.

The chart in figure 13.2 provides a crosswalk example to demonstrate the correlation between Danielson's Framework for Library Media Specialists (as adapted by Londonderry (NH) School District for AASL's Learning4Life initiative) and the *AASL Standards Framework for School Librarians*.

> . . . it is critical that school librarians have ongoing dialogue with the evaluating administrator about how the *AASL Standards Framework for School Librarians* aligns with the district evaluation document used for school librarians.

FIGURE 13.2

Crosswalk example demonstrating correlation between Danielson's Framework for Library Media Specialists as adapted by Londonderry (NH) School District for AASL's Learning4Life initiative (AASL 2009a) and the *AASL Standards Framework for School Librarians.*

AASL STANDARDS FRAMEWORK FOR SCHOOL LIBRARIANS	DANIELSON FRAMEWORK DOMAINS/COMPONENTS
KEY FOUNDATION: INQUIRE **A. Think: School librarians teach learners to display curiosity and initiative when seeking information by:** 1. Encouraging learners to formulate questions about a personal interest or a curricular topic. 2. Activating learners' prior and background knowledge as context for constructing new meaning. **B. Create: School librarians promote new knowledge generation by:** 1. Ensuring that learners probe possible answers to questions. 2. Devising and implementing a plan to fill knowledge gaps. 3. Facilitating the development of products that illustrate learning. **C. Share: School librarians guide learners to maintain focus throughout the inquiry process by:** 1. Assisting in assessing the inquiry-based research process. 2. Providing opportunities for learners to share learning products and reflect on the learning process with others. **D. Grow: School librarians implement and model an inquiry-based process by:** 1. Leading learners and staff through the research process. 2. Constructing tasks focused on learners' individual areas of interest. 3. Enabling learners to seek knowledge, create new knowledge, and make real-world connections for lifelong learning.	**DOMAIN 1: PLANNING AND PREPARATION** **Component 1A: Demonstrating Knowledge of Content Curriculum and Process** **Elements:** • Knowledge of curriculum • Knowledge of information, media, and digital literacy • Knowledge of the research process **Distinguished**—School librarian displays extensive knowledge of the curriculum, resources, various literacies, and the research process, and is able to develop meaningful connections. **DOMAIN 3: INSTRUCTION** **Component 3b: Using Questioning and Research Techniques** **Elements:** • Quality of questions • Research techniques • Student inquiry **Distinguished**—School librarian nearly always uses open-ended and probing questions to guide students' inquiry and to help students to think critically as they formulate pertinent questions about their research topics. Students are able to refine their research techniques and strategies and extend their own learning through the research process.

MARZANO AND AASL STANDARDS CROSSWALK

The Marzano Focused Teacher Evaluation Model (Carbaugh 2017) is used in many states as a tool (or the basis of a tool) for measuring an educator's effectiveness. Teaching and coteaching are central to the role of a school librarian who is engaged in all aspects of learning. Because school librarians are educators and instructional leaders, the Marzano evaluation for a certified teacher is recommended for use in school librarian evaluation rather than the document for non-instructional certified personnel.

The chart in figure 13.3 depicts the crosswalk between the *AASL Standards Framework for School Librarians* and the Marzano Focused Teacher Evaluation Elements. This crosswalk should be used as a starting point for school librarians and their evaluators; it does not encompass all aspects of the work of a school librarian and can be tailored to meet local circumstances. As the school administrator does a walkthrough in a school library, the school librarian may or may not be engaged in the activities outlined below. During a pre-evaluation conference, the school librarian and administrator can discuss the elements to be evaluated during the scheduled observation.

FIGURE 13.3

Crosswalk between the *AASL Standards Framework for School Librarians* and the Marzano Focused Teacher Evaluation Elements (Carbaugh 2017).

INQUIRE

AASL STANDARDS FRAMEWORK FOR SCHOOL LIBRARIANS	MARZANO FOCUSED TEACHER EVALUATION ELEMENTS
A. Think: School librarians teach learners to display curiosity and initiative when seeking information by: 1. Encouraging learners to formulate questions about a personal interest or a curricular topic.	**Standards-Based Instruction** • Using Questions to Help Students Elaborate on Content • Helping Students Practice Skills, Strategies, and Processes **Conditions for Learning** • Using Engagement Strategies • Establishing and Maintaining Effective Relationships in a Student-Centered Classroom **Professional Responsibilities** • Maintaining Expertise in Content and Pedagogy

(continued on page 158)

AASL STANDARDS FRAMEWORK FOR SCHOOL LIBRARIANS	MARZANO FOCUSED TEACHER EVALUATION ELEMENTS
A. Think: School librarians teach learners to display curiosity and initiative when seeking information by: 2. Activating learners' prior and background knowledge as context for new meaning.	**Standards-Based Planning** • Aligning Resources to Standard(s) **Standards-Based Instruction** • Identifying Critical Content from the Standards • Previewing New Content • Helping Students Process New Content **Professional Responsibilities** • Maintaining Expertise in Content and Pedagogy
B. Create: School librarians promote new knowledge generation by: 1. Ensuring that learners probe questions.	**Standards-Based Planning** • Aligning Resources to Standard(s) **Standards-Based Instruction** • Previewing New Content • Helping Students Process New Content • Using Questions to Help Students Elaborate on Content • Reviewing Content • Helping Students Examine Similarities and Differences • Helping Students Examine Their Reasoning • Helping Students Revise Knowledge • Helping Students Engage in Cognitively Complex Tasks **Conditions for Learning** • Using Engagement Strategies

AASL STANDARDS FRAMEWORK FOR SCHOOL LIBRARIANS	MARZANO FOCUSED TEACHER EVALUATION ELEMENTS
B. Create: School librarians promote new knowledge generation by: 2. Devising and implementing a plan to fill knowledge gaps.	**Standards-Based Instruction** • Identifying Critical Content from the Standards • Previewing New Content • Helping Students Process New Content • Using Questions to Help Students Elaborate on Content • Reviewing Content • Helping Students Examine Similarities and Differences • Helping Students Examine Their Reasoning • Helping Students Revise Knowledge • Helping Students Engage in Cognitively Complex Tasks **Conditions for Learning** • Organizing Students to Interact with Content • Using Engagement Strategies • Communicating High Expectations for Each Student to Close the Achievement Gap **Professional Responsibilities** • Maintaining Expertise in Content and Pedagogy • Promoting Teacher Leadership and Collaboration
B. Create: School librarians promote new knowledge generation by: 3. Facilitating the development of products that illustrate learning.	**Standards-Based Planning** • Aligning Resources to Standard(s) **Standards-Based Instruction** • Helping Students Revise Knowledge • Helping Students Engage in Cognitively Complex Tasks **Conditions for Learning** • Using Formative Assessment to Track Progress • Organizing Students to Interact with Content • Using Engagement Strategies • Establishing and Maintaining Effective Relationships in a Student-Centered Classroom • Communicating High Expectations for Each Student to Close the Achievement Gap **Professional Responsibilities** • Maintaining Expertise in Content and Pedagogy • Promoting Teacher Leadership and Collaboration

(continued on page 160)

AASL STANDARDS FRAMEWORK FOR SCHOOL LIBRARIANS	MARZANO FOCUSED TEACHER EVALUATION ELEMENTS
C. Share: School librarians guide learners to maintain focus throughout the inquiry process by: 1. Assisting in assessing the inquiry-based research process	**Standards-Based Instruction** • Helping Students Engage in Cognitively Complex Tasks **Conditions for Learning** • Using Formative Assessment to Track Progress • Providing Feedback and Celebrating Progress **Professional Responsibilities** • Maintaining Expertise in Content and Pedagogy
C. Share: School librarians guide learners to maintain focus throughout the inquiry process by: 2. Providing opportunities for learners to share learning products and reflect on the learning process with others.	**Standards-Based Instruction** • Helping Students Engage in Cognitively Complex Tasks **Conditions for Learning** • Providing Feedback and Celebrating Progress **Professional Responsibilities** • Maintaining Expertise in Content and Pedagogy • Promoting Teacher Leadership and Collaboration
D. Grow: School librarians implement and model an inquiry-based process by: 1. Leading learners and staff through the research process.	**Standards-Based Instruction** • Identifying Critical Content from the Standards • Previewing New Content • Helping Students Process New Content • Using Questions to Help Students Elaborate on Content • Reviewing Content • Helping Students Engage in Cognitively Complex Tasks **Conditions for Learning** • Organizing Students to Interact with Content • Using Engagement Strategies • Establishing and Maintaining Effective Relationships in a Student-Centered Classroom • Communicating High Expectations for Each Student to Close the Achievement Gap **Professional Responsibilities** • Maintaining Expertise in Content and Pedagogy

AASL STANDARDS FRAMEWORK FOR SCHOOL LIBRARIANS	MARZANO FOCUSED TEACHER EVALUATION ELEMENTS
D. Grow: School librarians implement and model an inquiry-based process by: 2. Constructing tasks focused on learners' individual areas of interest.	**Standards-Based Instruction** • Helping Students Engage in Cognitively Complex Tasks **Conditions for Learning** • Organizing Students to Interact with Content • Using Engagement Strategies • Establishing and Maintaining Effective Relationships in a Student-Centered Classroom • Communicating High Expectations for Each Student to Close the Achievement Gap **Professional Responsibilities** • Maintaining Expertise in Content and Pedagogy
D. Grow: School librarians implement and model an inquiry-based process by: 3. Enabling learners to seek knowledge, create new knowledge, and make real-world connections for lifelong learning.	**Standards-Based Instruction** • Previewing New Content • Helping Students Process New Content • Using Questions to Help Students Elaborate on Content • Helping Students Examine Similarities and Differences • Helping Students Examine Their Reasoning • Helping Students Revise Knowledge • Helping Students Engage in Cognitively Complex Tasks **Conditions for Learning** • Using Engagement Strategies • Communicating High Expectations for Each Student to Close the Achievement Gap **Professional Responsibilities** • Maintaining Expertise in Content and Pedagogy

Crosswalking Educator Evaluation Forms to School Librarian Standards

WHY CREATE A CROSSWALK?

The *AASL Standards Integrated Framework* provides a guide for exemplary school libraries and highly effective school librarians. A school librarian who compares the *AASL Standards Framework for School Librarians* with the district's current educator evaluation form has an opportunity to strengthen his or her practice and to engage the evaluator in dialogue about the school librarian's work, its value, and

Crosswalking Teacher Evaluations to School Librarian Standards

1 Know
Read your local evaluation document and the *AASL Standards Framework for School Librarians* carefully.

2 View and Compare
Take a look at your local evaluation standards side-by-side with the *AASL Standards Framework for School Librarians*.

3 Format
Determine a format for your crosswalk that best suits your needs and those of your evaluator.

4 Make It Real
Your crosswalk will be most useful for your administrator if you provide examples of how the school library standards look in action and how what the administrator sees aligns with the elements of the local evaluation standards.

the value of the school library. A crosswalk will inform the school librarian's growth plan and make it personalized.

KNOW

The first step in the crosswalking process is to closely read the district's evaluation document and the *AASL Standards Framework for School Librarians*. Familiarity with the district's evaluation instrument and with the AASL Standards will enable the school librarian to recognize and consider the links and gaps between the two documents.

VIEW AND COMPARE

Looking at the district's evaluation standards side by side with the *AASL Standards Framework for School Librarians* is useful. Comparing hard copies of both facilitates highlighting and annotating as similarities and differences are identified.

After this comparison has been completed, finding a school librarian colleague with whom to compare notes can be useful. Using a collaborative online document to do the comparison can facilitate the work.

FORMAT

During the comparison, it's a good idea to think about how to present findings in a format that best suits both the evaluator and the school librarian. A side-by-side arrangement like those in this chapter is the most typical.

MAKE IT REAL

The crosswalk will be most useful for an administrator if it includes examples of how the school library standards look in action and how what the administrator sees in the school library aligns with the elements of the local evaluation standards for educators.

The chart in figure 13.4 is a sample section of a crosswalk with examples of the standard in practice.

FIGURE 13.4

Sample section of a crosswalk with examples of the standard in practice.

INQUIRE

AASL STANDARDS FRAMEWORK FOR SCHOOL LIBRARIANS	MARZANO FOCUSED TEACHER EVALUATION ELEMENTS (CARBAUGH 2017)	EXAMPLES OF STANDARDS IN PRACTICE
B. Create: School librarians promote new knowledge generation by: 1. Ensuring that learners probe possible answers to questions.	**Standards-Based Planning** • Aligning Resources to Standard(s) **Standards-Based Instruction** • Previewing New Content • Helping Students Process New Content • Using Questions to Help Students Elaborate on Content • Reviewing Content • Helping Students Examine Similarities and Differences • Helping Students Examine Their Reasoning • Helping Students Revise Knowledge • Helping Students Engage in Cognitively Complex Tasks **Conditions for Learning** • Using Engagement Strategies	**School librarian and educator will provide new knowledge through the use of multimedia. This could be a short video or a song with lyrics specifically related to the content.** **The school librarian and educator:** • Work collaboratively to group learners and guide them by providing a series of prompts that elicit questions. • Lead learners in a process to record questions in a collaborative space. • Direct learners to find and look at questions similar to theirs and make a determination about whether their question needs to be modified. • Guide learners through process to adjust their question. • Organize learners to share questions.

WHY DEVELOP A GROWTH PLAN?

The *AASL Standards Integrated Framework* presents the ideal for a quality school library supported by an effective school librarian. Potential areas for growth that individuals can self-identify within the school librarian standards offer an opportunity for school librarians to expand their knowledge and practices and to model the type of lifelong learning school librarians promote for learners.

REFLECT

The first step in determining an area for growth is a self-reflection process. A school librarian reads the standards, and then, using the performance ratings provided in the locally developed rubric, rates his or her own performance based on reflection on experiences and current practices.

DETERMINE AREA FOR GROWTH

The next step is prioritizing areas of growth so that the school librarian can focus on one or two that are most essential for the current school year. Although ideally school librarians always grow in all areas of the standards, focusing on one or two areas can be the best approach to ensure growth toward exemplary practices.

Developing a Growth Plan

Reflect

The first step in determining an area for growth is a self-reflection process.

Determine Area for Growth

The next step is prioritizing areas of growth to focus on one or two most essential for the current school year.

Develop a Goal

School librarians can consider a S.M.A.R.T. goal process as a model when developing goals based on their self-reflection: Specific, Measurable, Achievable, Realistic, Timely (Braxton 2003).

Assess Progress

Ongoing assessment of progress toward the goal is critical to growth.

Measure Growth

By the end of the school year (or semester), growth can be determined by looking back at the progress assessments throughout the year and by comparing present actions, attitudes, or knowledge with those at the beginning of the year.

DEVELOP AT LEAST ONE GOAL

After determining at least one area for growth, school librarians can consider a S.M.A.R.T. goal process as a model when developing goals based on their self-reflections: Specific, Measurable, Achievable, Realistic, Timely (Braxton 2003). A specific goal is based on a Competency within the *AASL Standards Framework for School Librarians*. A measurable goal is one that can be assessed with quantitative or qualitative data—or both. An achievable goal is one that is narrow enough to be accomplished (i.e., based on a Competency within the standards rather than on a top-level Key Commitment). A realistic goal is one that can be accomplished given the current circumstances of the school library (budget, staff, schedule, etc.). A timely goal is one that can be accomplished within a set time period (one semester, one school year) and is relevant to the current school library priorities. Figure 13.5 provides an overview of S.M.A.R.T Goals definitions.

ASSESS PROGRESS

Ongoing assessment of progress toward the goal is critical to growth. Self-reflection is part of that assessment process, but periodic "pulse checks" that provide more-concrete data are important, too. Surveys of stakeholders such as learners, other educators, and parents about school library services can be a quick way to

FIGURE 13.5

S.M.A.R.T. Goals infographic.

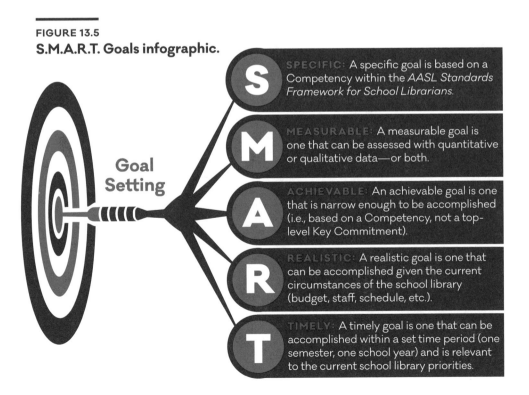

Goal Setting

S SPECIFIC: A specific goal is based on a Competency within the *AASL Standards Framework for School Librarians*.

M MEASURABLE: A measurable goal is one that can be assessed with quantitative or qualitative data—or both.

A ACHIEVABLE: An achievable goal is one that is narrow enough to be accomplished (i.e., based on a Competency, not a top-level Key Commitment).

R REALISTIC: A realistic goal is one that can be accomplished given the current circumstances of the school library (budget, staff, schedule, etc.).

T TIMELY: A timely goal is one that can be accomplished within a set time period (one semester, one school year) and is relevant to the current school library priorities.

Example of a S.M.A.R.T. Goal

SPECIFIC

Based on data analysis that includes circulation statistics, reader survey responses, and educator reports, learners read and produce products in print for the majority of class assignments and pleasure reading. Learners should demonstrate personal curiosity by reading widely and deeply in multiple formats and writing for a variety of purposes. (Learner>Explore> Think> Competency 1)

MEASURABLE

Growth in genre engagement will be measured by reader survey responses, educator feedback, learner work samples, and materials circulations that represent a wider range of genres than are currently represented.

ACHIEVABLE

By the end of the school year, more learners will explore new genres and formats for reading and writing than last year.

REALISTIC

Recent purchases for the school library include more e-books and audiobooks to enhance the current print collection. The district provided 1:1 devices for high school learners this school year, and learners have access to apps that enable them to create work products in a variety of formats.

TIMELY

During the upcoming school year.

SAMPLE GOAL

During the upcoming school year, I will encourage learners to read and write more widely and deeply in multiple formats by purchasing and promoting a wider range of genres.

determine if improvement is happening. Examination of learners' work samples and soliciting educator feedback are other examples of ways to assess progress throughout the school year.

MEASURE GROWTH

By the end of the school year (or semester), growth can be determined by looking back at the progress assessments throughout the year and by comparing beginning-of-the-year actions, attitudes, or knowledge to those at the end of the measurement time period. The school librarian can ask questions for self-reflection: Did my knowledge about this topic increase? Was I able to overcome a bias that stifled purchases for a section of the collection? Did circulation increase based on actions I took this school year to promote different formats or genres? Based on the descriptors for the four performance levels, did I show growth for my identified area?

Conclusion

In this chapter, we reviewed professional assessment approaches for school librarians. In implementation of the *AASL Standards Framework for School Librarians,* assessment is a key tool for ensuring that school librarians engage in continuous professional growth and development as well as monitor and refine their approaches to meeting learners' needs. Self-reflection is an essential starting point for self-assessment and assessment by an administrator. Assessment may be conducted using locally developed instruments or popular approaches such as those developed by Charlotte Danielson and Robert Marzano. School librarians culminate their assessment activities by creating and sharing professional goals with colleagues and administrators. Goals must be measurable with attainable evidence sources. Please see Appendix H for types of evidence.

For the beginning and novice school librarian, professional assessment is also viewed as an opportunity, indeed a responsibility, to engage in reflective practice and to seek to continuously develop and improve professional capacity and practice in alignment with the needs and goals of the learning community served. Refinement of skills and growth as an effective practitioner results through seeking opportunities for professional development and professional collaboration. Also essential is welcoming feedback from supervisors and from colleagues, including those with whom the novice collaborates.

Questions for the Reflective Practitioner

1. What are some professional competencies my evaluator/administrator should see evidence of in my teaching?

2. In what way can I improve conversations with my administrator/evaluator by focusing on evidence and support from the standards?

3. How can I develop a personal growth plan based on the *AASL Standards Framework for School Librarians?*

RECOMMENDED APPENDICES

APPENDIX C. Annotated List of AASL Position Statements

APPENDIX C1. Position Statement: Definition of an Effective School Library Program

APPENDIX C3. Position Statement: Instructional Role of the School Librarian

APPENDIX F. LLAMA's 14 Foundational Competencies

APPENDIX H. Evidence of Accomplishment

APPENDIX I. Useful Verbs

14

Evaluating School Libraries

Planning for an Effective School Library

AN EFFECTIVE SCHOOL LIBRARY IS CONTINUOUSLY ASSESSED AND evaluated based on the results of the assessments to ensure that it meets the needs of all members of the learning community. An effective school library is fully integrated into the curriculum through ongoing, sustained efforts and a strategic plan that serves the school's mission, educational goals and objectives, and school community stakeholders.

School librarians build and contribute to a collaborative school culture in which the principal, school librarian, other educators, and learners work together to ensure that the school library contributes fully to the educational process. School librarians, who are most knowledgeable about the school library, lead the school library evaluation by conducting ongoing formative assessment to measure progress toward long- and short-term goals and ensure that school librarians are involved in the evaluation process and are directly involved with decisions.

The school librarian also works in collaboration with other school librarians in the district, with the district-level school library supervisor or director, and with state, regional, and professional associations to incorporate research and best practices into the school library; benefit from ongoing professional learning for improvement of instruction and other aspects of the school library; and reflect current and emerging trends and laws, and social, economic, and cultural developments that impact the school community.

Evidence outcomes should be part of a well-developed school library plan. In addition to the reflective checklist (presented later in this chapter) that can be used to guide an advisory board on areas to include in a school library's strategic plan, identifying desired outcomes can assist in school library evaluation. Created with the assistance and input of key stakeholders such as administrators and other educators in the school, the evaluation of the school library considers each of the components of an effective school library and evaluates their impact on student achievement. This process allows a school librarian to assess areas of strength as well as areas for further development within the school library.

Like other areas within the educational landscape, the school library does not exist independently, nor does it function in isolation of student achievement. Outcomes-based evaluation strives to capture the impact the school library and school librarian have made on the learning and achievement of each child in a school. Instead of simply examining school library activities and instruction, the evaluation goes further to explore how the school library and school librarian have benefited learners or changed learning within the school during or after learners participated in program activities or interventions. Outcomes gained from school library experiences may include increased knowledge or skills, altered beliefs or expanded ideas, and newly gained perspectives and attitudes. It is necessary to take a holistic approach when evaluating a school library.

It is also necessary that building-, district-, and state-level school library personnel maximize the efficiency and effectiveness of their respective areas of responsibility by using strategic planning for continuous improvement. The planning process should begin with a careful review of school, district, and school library data. This data is then used as a guide to identify school library strengths and weaknesses.

School Library Responsibilities at the Building Level

CHARACTERISTICS OF AN EFFECTIVE SCHOOL LIBRARY

Identifying areas of competence at the building level, the school librarian uses school library evaluation to address short- and long-term needs and aspirations of learners and to provide a pathway to continuous improvement for the school librarian. The building-level evaluation tracks hallmarks of an effective school library such as:

- resources and policies that ensure equitable access to highly qualified school librarians and support personnel;
- carefully selected and organized collections of physical and digital materials and learning assets;
- flexible up-to-date barrier-free facilities, appropriate technology; and
- learning opportunities for school community members with diverse cultural, linguistic, financial, and learning differences.

School librarians conduct ongoing reviews of the school library's collection, technology, and management policies and update them to ensure that new and emerging resource formats and the needs of diverse learning populations are addressed.

School librarians also evaluate policies to ensure that they reflect the principles of intellectual freedom, provide learners with access to information, and protect users' privacy and confidentiality. More detail about characteristics of an effective school library is at the end of this chapter.

ASSESSING THE CURRENT STATE OF THE SCHOOL LIBRARY

The checklist provided later in this chapter can be used to assess the current state of the school library.

School Library Responsibilities at the District Level

At the district level the school library supervisor (or director) works with building-level and other district-level administrators to develop an effective process for providing school libraries that support the vision, mission, goals, and objectives of the school and district.

The school library supervisor may assist with the recruitment, supervision, and evaluation of school library personnel to ensure that the school library contributes to the learning process. The school library supervisor also helps to interpret library needs—and related budgetary needs—and monitors relevant state and federal laws that impact the delivery of programs and services. Additionally, the school library supervisor fosters the development of effective building-level school libraries that meet regional, state, and national standards.

The school library supervisor provides leadership and guidance to building-level school library staff in such areas as program planning, curriculum development, budgeting, in-service activities, facility use, and production of content. District-level school library supervisors ensure equity and consistency across all school libraries by coordinating requirements related to technical services, acquiring and processing resources and materials, and equipment circulation. They assume fiduciary responsibility to negotiate purchasing agreements and articulate a code of ethics that promotes adherence to copyright, intellectual property, privacy, and responsible use. District-level supervisors ensure that school library plans contain provisions for internal and external professional-development opportunities to foster school librarians' leadership, competence, and creativity.

District-level supervisors develop and implement plans for presenting and publicizing school library programs and services as well as communicate goals and priorities to the staff and public. For district and school administrators they prepare reports about the impact of building-level school libraries on instruction and the learning process. To ensure that the school library is positioned to contribute to the implementation and achievement of district-wide initiatives, supervisors participate in district-level committees for curriculum development, facility planning, budget, and management.

School Library Responsibilities at the State Level

State education agencies and/or state library programs often provide technical support, networking, and professional-development opportunities related to certification and endorsement requirements, and disseminate information regarding research, best practices, emerging trends, and grant opportunities for school librarians and programs.

The roles of state-level agencies include representing school librarians and school library stakeholders in the development of state education efforts and initiatives—especially those related to resources for teaching and learning, technology, information and digital literacy, and meeting state standards. State-level agencies also provide guidance to school administrators and school librarians in building or renovating school library facilities. A state agency may also represent school librarians' interests while serving as a liaison to the state library and/or to the state department of education. Additionally, a representative of a school library-related agency at the state level may participate in an unofficial capacity as a member of state-level school library professional associations. Representatives of state-level agencies are ambassadors of the school library community at the national level in a variety of professional organizations and efforts; in this capacity representatives of the agencies advocate for equitable learning opportunities through effective school libraries.

State-level personnel monitor and address state school board and legislative activities that impact school libraries. In addition to articulating school library needs in discussions related to purchases by state-level consortia, state-level personnel may address ongoing review of licensure requirements and preparation programs for administrators, school librarians, and other educators to ensure that education professionals develop and demonstrate an understanding of the importance of integrating the school library into curricular efforts and the learning community.

Evaluating the School Library Using the Key Commitments

The following checklist is most effective when completed by the school librarian and the school library advisory committee working together. The advisory committee may include the school library staff as well as a representative from the administration team, classroom educators, parents, and, perhaps, learners. Elements incorporated in the School Library Evaluation Checklist represent school library Alignments from the *AASL Standards Integrated Framework* evident in an effective school library. These elements include many facets of a school library: instructional responsibilities, curriculum alignment, collection development, policy development, technology integration, advocacy and promotion of the effective use of the school library and its services, facilities and learning environment, management of personnel and resources, budget development, and professional development. When evaluated together, these elements comprise an effective school library.

Achieving inclusion of all these elements is the shared responsibility of all stakeholders at the school, district, and state level.

School Library Evaluation Checklist

INQUIRE

Building-level

☐ The school librarian collaborates with educators to design and teach engaging inquiry-based learning experiences as well as assessments that incorporate multiple literacies and foster critical thinking.

☐ The school librarian uses a systematic instructional development and information search process in working with educators to improve integration of learning technology into curriculum.

☐ The school librarian participates in curriculum development and implementation through membership on instructional, curriculum, textbook, technology, professional development, and new program adoption committees.

☐ School library policies ensure that learners and educators have access to the school library and to qualified professional staff throughout the school day.

District-level

☐ The district-level school library supervisor or director designs and supervises implementation of a learning technology curriculum (in coordination with district- and building-level instructional leaders and school librarians).

☐ The district-level school library supervisor or director coordinates the planning and development of Pre-K-12 library technology integration programs that serve the learners and staff within the schools.

☐ The district-level school library supervisor or director coordinates the planning and development of K-12 school libraries that serve the learners and educators within the schools.

☐ The district-level school library supervisor or director develops an effective plan and process for providing school libraries that support the philosophy, goals, and objectives of the school district.

INCLUDE

Building-level

☐ Resources are selected according to principles of intellectual freedom, and provide learners with access to information that represents diverse points of view in a pluralistic society.

☐ The school librarian develops and maintains a teaching and learning environment that is inviting, safe, flexible, and conducive to learning.

☐ The school library ensures equitable physical access to facilities by providing barrier-free, universally designed environments. Facilities and resources are readily accessible before, during, and after school hours and during vacation periods.

☐ Each school, regardless of size or level, has at least one full-time certified school librarian.

☐ School librarians are evaluated with instruments that address their unique responsibilities and contributions according to established district practices for all professional personnel.

District-level

☐ Responsibility for leading and managing the school library in each school is shared equally by the school librarian, the principal, and a district-level school library supervisor or director, who jointly develop goals, establish priorities, and allocate the resources necessary to accomplish the mission.

☐ The school librarian, the principal, and the district-level school library supervisor or director cooperatively plan the budget.

☐ The district-level school library supervisor or director monitors state and federal laws pertaining to school library and technology-integration programs.

☐ The district-level school library supervisor or director monitors and publicizes the status of district compliance with regional, state, and national accreditation requirements, and with school library and technology standards.

COLLABORATE

Building-level

- ☐ The school librarian participates in the implementation of collaboratively planned learning experiences by providing group and individual instruction, assessing learner progress, and evaluating activities.

- ☐ The school librarian provides an environment in which collaboration, innovation, and creative problem solving thrive.

- ☐ The school librarian welcomes and encourages input to create consensus on library policies and procedures.

- ☐ The school librarian serves on decision-making teams in the school and participates in school improvement and accreditation activities.

District-level

- ☐ The district-level school library supervisor or director assists librarians in developing library goals and objectives.

- ☐ Planning at the district level involves district school library administrators, school library administrators, school library and technology-integration staff, school administrators, classroom educators, learners, and community members, as appropriate.

- ☐ The district-level school library supervisor or director advises district and school administrators of new developments in school library practice, media for learning, technology, instructional strategies, and research.

- ☐ The district-level school library supervisor or director assists principals, school librarians, and others in applying district policies that relate to school libraries.

- ☐ The district-level school library supervisor or director has a leading role in the district technology committee that has responsibility for the ongoing review and updating of a multiyear technology plan for school board and state approval.

- ☐ The district-level school library supervisor or director works with principals to recruit, supervise, and evaluate school librarians and technology-integration personnel.

- ☐ The district-level school library supervisor or director develops the district budget, including allocations for each school, in cooperation with principals and school librarians.

CURATE

Building-level

☐ A collection-development policy, approved by the school board, is in place. The policy includes criteria and procedures for selection and reconsideration, including a process for handling challenges raised about materials in the collection.

☐ In accordance with district policy, the school librarian develops and maintains a diverse collection of resources appropriate to the curriculum, the learners, and the teaching styles and instructional strategies used within the school community.

☐ Collections and equipment are circulated and accessed according to procedures that ensure confidentiality of records and promote access.

☐ Circulation policies and procedures assure that access to information is not impeded by fees, loan restrictions, or other barriers.

☐ The school library has a vibrant Web presence, which provides access to a wide variety of digital resources that have been carefully created or selected, and vetted according to the district and school collection-development policies.

District-level

☐ The district-level school library supervisor or director ensures standardization of technical services (circulation, classification, catalog, processing, standard nomenclature, naming conventions, etc.).

☐ The district-level school library supervisor or director guides school librarians in selection of materials and equipment to ensure unified ordering and taking advantage of economy of scale for periodicals, supplies, and equipment for all schools in the district.

☐ The district-level school library supervisor or director investigates and negotiates district-wide licensing of products and services.

☐ The district-level school library supervisor or director monitors collections, services, and equipment to provide data on usage, relevance, and currency.

EXPLORE

Building-level

☐ The school librarian creates an environment that is conducive to active and participatory learning, resource-based instructional practices, and collaboration with teaching staff.

☐ The school librarian uses a variety of instructional methods with different user groups and encourages personal creativity and innovation.

☐ The school librarian evaluates, promotes, and uses existing and emerging technologies to support teaching and learning.

☐ The school librarian supplements other school resources, connects the school with the global learning community, communicates with learners and with other educators, and provides 24–7 access to school library technology-integration services.

District-level

☐ The district-level school library supervisor or director fosters development of exemplary school libraries at each level and assists school libraries and school librarians in meeting regional, state, and national standards.

☐ The district-level school library supervisor or director provides for district in-service training for school librarians to foster leadership, competence, and creativity in developing instruction, services, and programs for the school library.

☐ The district-level school library supervisor or director develops—or finds and then implements—plans for presenting and publicizing school library programs and services.

☐ The district-level school library supervisor or director arranges for school librarians to evaluate new resources, services, and equipment.

ENGAGE

Building-level

☐ The school librarian promotes the ethical use of information and understands copyright, fair use, licensing of intellectual property, privacy concerns related to use of digital resources and the Internet, and ethical online behavior, and assists users with their understanding and observance of the same.

☐ The school library and school librarian demonstrate a commitment to maintaining intellectual freedom.

☐ School library personnel remain current and engage in continuing education activities to ensure instruction and activities reflect the most-recent developments in professional practices, information technologies, and educational research.

☐ The school librarian provides educators and other staff with learning opportunities related to new technologies, use, and production of a variety of media, and laws and policies regarding information.

☐ The school librarian shares with the learning community collaboratively developed and up-to-date district policies concerning such issues as materials selection, circulation, reconsideration of materials, copyright, privacy, and responsible use of technology and social media.

District-level

☐ The district-level school library supervisor or director ensures that frequent and timely communication to stakeholders is maintained through school and library websites, newsletters to parents and guardians, e-mail, social media, and other formats, such as local cable-access television, video/audio streaming, and on-demand vodcasts and podcasts.

☐ The district-level school library supervisor or director articulates a code of ethics that promotes adherence to policies and guidelines for honoring copyright and intellectual property of others, privacy, and responsible use of the Internet.

☐ The district-level school library supervisor or director provides leadership in evaluating the impact of new and existing technologies and program features, and encourages use of the most-effective technologies and strategies to support teaching and learning.

☐ The district-level school library supervisor or director prepares reports for district and school administrators on the building-level school libraries' impact on the instructional process and success.

Outcomes-Based Evaluation

At the building and district level, practitioners seek to ensure that the school library's mission, goals, and objectives are aligned with the school's and district's long-range strategic plans and are clearly understood and fully supported by the administration and educational staff, the learners, and the community. An important indicator of effectiveness is the use of evidence-based practice and action research that creates data used to inform continuous improvement.

While this chapter has focused on evaluation conducted by school librarians alone and with a number of stakeholders, even pre-service school librarians can be involved in school library evaluation activities. Throughout their preparation programs and in the completion of meaningful and relevant practicum experiences, novice school librarians are provided with opportunities to synthesize and apply knowledge, develop and refine professional skills, and demonstrate their capabilities to employ multiple means of assessment to identify learning community needs and improve the school library as articulated in the AASL Standards frameworks. In addition, field experiences of pre-service school librarians afford them the opportunity to engage in reflective dialogue with colleagues based on observation of instruction, learner work, user experience, facility and resources analysis, and assessment data, and help novices make connections to research-based effective practice.

As part of the planning process, the school library is evaluated on a regular basis to review overall goals and objectives in relation to user and instructional needs and to assess the efficiency and effectiveness of specific activities. School library and personnel evaluations follow district-wide policies and procedures, focus on performance, and are based upon appropriate collected data and evidence. The planning process results in periodic reports that emphasize and document progress toward stated goals and objectives.

Questions for the Reflective Practitioner

1. Is evidence of conformance with the *National School Library Standards* visible in my current school library? Would this evidence be visible to other stakeholders?

2. How can I use the new national standards frameworks when discussing the strengths and weaknesses of my school library?

3. How can I use the national standards frameworks to develop a plan for my school library? Who should I include in this planning process?

RECOMMENDED APPENDICES

APPENDIX C. Annotated List of AASL Position Statements

APPENDIX C1. Position Statement: Definition of an Effective School Library Program

APPENDIX C5. Position Statement: Role of the School Library Program

APPENDIX E. Interpretations of the Library Bill of Rights

APPENDIX H. Evidence of Accomplishment

APPENDIX I. Useful Verbs

PART IV

Scenarios for Professional Learning

15

Getting Started with the Standards

WHILE THESE STANDARDS HAVE EVOLVED FROM PREVIOUS AASL standards, the standards frameworks in this book *are* new. To help you envision how to apply them to planning and practice, we've developed a series of scenarios to help you get started. Many include the personas introduced in the first chapter, but we have included additional characters to help you envision the standards when put into action. The scenarios are not simultaneous or sequential, but they all do occur in the same district. In addition to helping us, the members of the AASL Standards and Guidelines Editorial Board keep stakeholders' priorities in the forefront; as we worked on the standards, these personas can help you and other educators in your school reflect on ways the new standards can guide practice and learning in your school.

Scenarios are used in active and collaborative teaching to foster the deep, problem-based learning that helps learners remember and apply new concepts. Scenarios promote higher-level learning outcomes that require application, synthesis, and evaluation (Shaw 2010).

Using scenarios in professional learning allows school librarians, learners, and other stakeholders to

- connect with prior knowledge and help build on it;
- be presented with a real-world context that could plausibly be something they encounter (i.e., be "authentic");
- envision themselves and standards users; and
- be guided by a limited amount of structure, description, and direction because self-directed learning is the intended use for these scenarios. The scenarios contain sufficient detail to make the issues clear, but with enough aspects not detailed so that learners have to make assumptions before proceeding or explore assumptions to determine which are the best to make (Norton 2004).

The scenarios in this section provide concrete examples of the standards' concepts. As mentioned previously, many of the scenarios feature personas created by the standards implementation task force to help you see how people in various roles would use and/or benefit from the standards. We have included questions at the conclusion of each scenario to enable school librarians, pre-service school librarians, and educators of school librarians to practice analytical skills and decision-making skills through application of standards' concepts in real-life situations.

RECOMMENDED APPENDICES

APPENDIX C. Annotated List of AASL Position Statements

APPENDIX E. Interpretations of the Library Bill of Rights

APPENDIX F. LLAMA's 14 Foundational Competencies

APPENDIX G. Code of Ethics of the American Library Association

APPENDIX I. Useful Verbs

District School Library Director

SCENARIO

District school library director Margot is a passion-ate, hardworking supervisor. She has been in her position for nine years. Recently, reduced budgets, more demands on educators, changing demo-graphics, and additional national, state, and local developments have challenged many neighboring districts' survival.

Margot's district has a solid history of exemplary school libraries, and its school librarians are a dedicated and passionate group of educators who represent a wide range of experiences and approaches to their practice. However, as in many school districts, school librarians come and go due to a variety of factors. As a result, Margot often has new school librarians with varying levels of experience and expertise.

The school district's mission is to prepare learners to be creators, problem solvers, strategists, and thinkers. Margot wants the district's school libraries to reflect this important commitment, so she engages her school librarians in professional learn-ing that is relevant for the entire learning community. She believes the new AASL Standards further school library programming and practices that prepare learners to be ready for college, career, and community. Margot is aware of the challenge of getting her diverse group of school librarians to adjust their practice to embrace new standards and move ahead. She wants all of the school librarians to implement the new standards in ways that engage and empower learners. She hopes to revi-talize her seasoned school librarians and help them work collaboratively to create school libraries centered on learning and teaching. She wants every school library in the district to be a place where all learners flourish and succeed.

MARGOT'S RESPONSE TO THE NEW STANDARDS

After several careful readings of the new standards and participation in an AASL webinar about them, Margot decided on her course of action. Her initial thought was to assign each school librarian one of the Shared Foundations on which to focus during the school year. After much consideration, Margot decided that perhaps the better approach was to align what she wanted the school librarians to do with the way she approaches her own work. She decided to help each of the school librarians understand why new standards will improve their practice. She designed a profes-sional learning experience that would empower the school librarians to personalize their learning experiences by sharing their perceptions of the standards' impor-tance to their practice.

Margot developed a full-day workshop in which school librarians worked collaboratively to unpack standards. She provided a professional-development structure that allowed each school librarian to speak about the given topic before others spoke again. This strategy allowed everyone to participate and no one to monopolize or opt out of the discussion. Margot provided specific discussion prompts:

1. Consider the word "inquire" and what it means to your practice as a school librarian and for your learners.
2. Repeat prompt 1 five times, each time replacing "inquire" with one of these words: "include," "collaborate," "curate," "explore," and "engage."

After the participants discussed each prompt, the school librarians at each table shared with the whole group.

After the school librarians had completed their discussions, they began looking at the new standards. Margot provided a brief overview of how the standards were organized and introduced the Domains and Shared Foundations. First the school librarians looked at the learner standards for the Shared Foundation Inquire. They used markers to highlight the most important elements of each standard. Then the school librarians looked at and discussed the correlating school librarian standard. This discussion included conversations about how each standard looked in practice. The table came to consensus on the best ideas from their table and shared them in a collaborative online document they could use in their planning for the upcoming year.

At the end of the workshop, Margot asked each school librarian to select two school librarian standards on which to focus during the school year and respond to these prompts in a short online survey:

1. Describe where your school is currently in meeting each selected standard.
2. Identify the evidence you will use to make your assessment of your school's progress toward this standard.
3. Outline the action steps you will use to meet the standard.
4. Identify the supports that you will need from the district supervisor and your principal.

QUESTIONS FOR FURTHER DISCUSSION

- What are Margot's next steps?
- How does she monitor and assess each school librarian's progress in using the standards? How will her approach be different with Noah, Helen, and Inez? (Noah's, Helen's, and Inez's scenarios are described later in the chapter.)
- How does Margot communicate with the principals and the central office administrators about the new standards and the work the district school librarians are doing to meet their own standards and help learners meet theirs?
- How does Margot ensure that school librarians are sharing with their principals the progress the school librarians are making toward their standard-related goals?
- How will Margot help provide principals with an alignment of the new standards with the district's existing evaluation system for school librarians?
- What supports will Margot need to provide for the school librarians in her district? What scaffolds should Margot develop for the new school librarians? For struggling school librarians?

Elementary School Librarian

SCENARIO

Elementary school librarian Helen is considered one of the very best. Not only does she set the bar high within her own school district, but colleagues and administrators from throughout the state and the region beat a path to her door to observe her in action and take notes on the school library she has developed. You name it: Helen is on the case. Learning commons approach? Check. Makerspace? Check. Social media presence? Check. The list goes on.

While Helen is a dynamic and successful school librarian, she also knows that she is very lucky. She works in a supportive community that values the school library. She certainly merits credit for some of that. The learners, the educators, and the parents love her. When last year's high school valedictorian mentioned Helen as an influence in his commencement address, the graduating seniors leapt to their feet applauding loudly in enthusiastic appreciation. Yes, an elementary educator remembered—and with great affection—by the high school kids!

But deserving as she is, Helen realizes that many other school librarians do not have it so good. Helen is part of a connected team of school librarians and fortunate to have an effective supervisor, Margot, who emphasizes continuous professional learning and works with each of the school librarians, and their respective principals, to ensure that the school  librarians have the resources they need to do their jobs. Helen has a very healthy budget and a full-time school library assistant; as a result, the majority of her time is focused on learners and educators. Helen is also fortunate that her principal, Jim, is very supportive. Annually, Jim emphasizes to all educators but especially the educators new to the school—even if they are experienced educators—that he expects them to work with Helen and provide guided-inquiry opportunities for their learners. He checks in with Helen frequently, and if a teacher has not made it into Helen's plan book within the first month of school, Jim makes it a point to seek out the teacher and reemphasize this expectation. Yes, life is good for Helen. That is, it *was* good until Margot showed up one morning to take stock of where the elementary school library was in regards to the new *National School Library Standards*.

Margot and some of Helen's colleagues had recently attended a regional workshop on the new standards. Helen was unable to get away because the third-grade team was in the middle of a unit of study for which she was needed, but she knew she could rely on Margot to fill her in. Margot called one morning soon after the workshop to see if she and Helen could meet right away. Margot had unsettling news.

Margot indicated to Helen that while the workshop was very informative, it was also a little unnerving. In the new iteration, not only are learner standards articulated, but what were previously called program "guidelines" are now also referred to as "school library standards," and standards for the school librarian had been added. A framework structure ties all three together, but it was clear to Margot that the district had work to do to adapt to the new format and language.

HELEN'S RESPONSE TO THE NEW STANDARDS

Initially, Helen was not too concerned. After all, they'd already used the AASL and national and state educational technology standards to build the school libraries, so the elementary school should be in great shape, and not much effort would be needed to refresh and move forward. However, as she and Margot began to tick through the document, Helen began to realize that while she'd been caught up with trends and trying to keep the school library edgy and relevant, perhaps she had lost focus on the learners and their learning, and may not have moved forward in that area.

Helen expressed this thought to Margot, noting that she saw a great deal of emphasis throughout the standards on the personalization of learning. Helen acknowledged that she was not sure they had positioned school library instruction to address personalization of learning as much as they might have. At the elementary school the work had been focused on creating and providing learning opportunities across grade bands and in the various content areas, and not so much on individual inquiry or need. Helen also said that while she and her classroom educator colleagues always worked on instructional differentiation, she wondered whether they had really done their best to personalize *everyone's* learning opportunities.

Margot agreed with Helen's assessment and thought that this realization was a place to begin. Margot had another meeting to attend, and, as she rose to leave, she asked Helen to step up to the challenge to help her colleagues reflect on where they are and where they need to grow to provide learning personalization for all—especially as it related to the Shared Foundation of Include and the learner Competency of "Demonstrating an interest in other perspectives during learning activities." Margot asked Helen to conduct an honest and reflective inventory of what is happening—or not happening—at the elementary school with regard to the learners, the school library, and Helen's own role. Standards implementation was already on the agenda for the next department meeting, and Margot intended to have Helen share her insights with her colleagues as a place for everyone to begin.

Before Margot hurried off to her appointment, Helen promised to give the assignment her best effort. However, truth be told, the component of the standards that now focused on school librarian Competencies made her uneasy. Although the district has been using a modified version of a school librarian evaluation instrument (based on the Danielson framework) previously provided by AASL, this new set of standards clearly articulated that school librarian effectiveness was an especially critical part of the learning equation.

Helen took a deep breath and wondered where to begin.

QUESTIONS FOR FURTHER DISCUSSION

- What tools or strategies might be available to Helen to assist her in the process of examining her own effectiveness, especially as it relates to the Shared Foundation of Include?
- What can Helen suggest to Margot and the district's team of school librarians as an entry point for professional development in relation to specific Competencies within the functional Domain "Think" as stated in the Include framework?

  » Think: School librarians direct learners to contribute a balanced perspective when participating in a learning community by:

  1. Engaging learners to articulate an awareness of the contributions of a range of learners.
  2. Guiding learners as they adopt a discerning stance toward points of view and opinions expressed in information resources and learning products.
  3. Differentiating learning experiences that support learners' understanding of cultural relevancy and placement within the global learning community.

- How should Helen inform Jim of her concern regarding personalization of learning, and how can she include the principal and the elementary school educators in addressing it?

Middle School Librarian

SCENARIO

Noah is an established school librarian who will be moving from elementary to middle school level starting this fall. At his elementary school he had created a strong library that included activities and instruction to build literacy and the love of reading, and taught solid curriculum-based lessons that drew on a wide range of resources. Collaborating with the classroom educators and developing strong lessons helped Noah thrive in the elementary level, and he is starting to plan how to develop his school library at the middle school level, where the structure and emphasis in the school library may be different. Even though he is part of a strong network of school librarian colleagues in his county, sometimes he still feels isolated in the building. As a result, he joined both the state-level organization of school librarians and AASL to benefit from the conferences and resources offered.

NOAH'S RESPONSE TO THE NEW STANDARDS

Noah had been reading on the AASL website and hearing at the fall state conference that new AASL Standards were being developed. How different were they going to be from the current standards that he had to use for his professional-growth goals every year? How were the new standards going to reflect the evolving technological changes that Noah likes to share with the classroom educators and use in his lessons, and also allow him to use the state content standards that are the basis for learner testing? Most importantly, how easy would the new AASL Standards be to apply and use with new content and older learners in the middle school library?

When the new standards were released by AASL, Margot, Noah's district supervisor, organized a county-wide meeting for each of the different levels, elementary and secondary. Margot wanted to be proactive and give the school librarians an opportunity to review the standards and brainstorm ideas to give structure to how the new standards could be used for professional growth and used in daily lessons. She divided the school librarians into six groups, one for each Shared Foundation: Inquire, Include, Collaborate, Curate, Explore, Engage. In the group the school librarians reviewed the Key Commitment for the Shared Foundation and the Competencies for the learner, school librarian, and school library. Then each group brainstormed how to best introduce the new standards to the classroom educators and create lesson plans based on the Competencies.

At the meeting for school librarians at the secondary level, Noah was placed in the Explore group with eight other school librarians. Although he was eager to learn about the new standards, he was nervous at first because he recognized some group members as being vocally resistant to having new standards because implementing the new standards would require changes to their school library instruction and activities. After reviewing the new standards, the group realized that the new standards used updated language and pedagogical techniques to develop a framework that embraced the essence of the previous standards while developing a forward-looking vision.

After much discussion, the group agreed the most effective way to introduce the new standards to the faculty was during a staff meeting or professional-development time, and agreed that they needed the support of the administration. Using a wiki shared with librarians county-wide, the group wrote down specific curriculum elements and necessary skills from each grade level that connected with the Competencies in the Domains of Think, Create, Share, and Grow. The school librarians would use these specific examples to connect with the classroom educators at the initial faculty meeting.

This opportunity to work with the other district middle school librarians helped Noah to build a community within his district and introduce him to the new middle school curriculum. The first step for Noah would be to meet with his new principal to explain the purpose of the new AASL Standards and how they support student learning, school librarians' professional growth, and the school library as a whole. After the beginning-of-the-semester whole faculty meeting, Noah would meet with the individual grade-level and department chairs to brainstorm and collaborate on lessons, learning, and incorporating the new AASL Standards together.

QUESTIONS FOR FURTHER DISCUSSION

- What challenges might Noah face as he introduces new school library standards to his new colleagues, both administrators and other educators?
- What AASL resources are available to help Noah present the new standards to his administrator?
- How can Noah create more opportunities (virtually and in person) to brainstorm ideas for specific grade-level lessons?
- How can Noah demonstrate to classroom educators that AASL Standards complement and support the state testing standards?
- What assessments can Noah develop to use in the school library to incorporate new AASL Standards and state content standards?

High School Librarian

SCENARIO

Inez is one of two full-time certified school librarians in a suburban high school serving just over 1,400 learners. She is a graduate of the school and has been a school librarian there for twelve years. Educators and learners enjoy working with Inez, and they are always eager to learn about new technology tools and strategies from her. In fact, Inez is something of a "tech guru," and at annual technology conferences is a frequent presenter about innovative teaching techniques and new technologies coming down the pike. Social media is her "go to" communication method, and her posts on a variety of social media platforms about school library happenings ensure that other educators, learners, parents, and the community know about all of the new, exciting programs and resources available at the school.

Inez's co-school librarian, Samantha, is in her twenty-fourth year as a school librarian. She isn't all that comfortable with new technology, and she relies on Inez to handle all "that techy stuff." But, Samantha is enthusiastic about reading promotion and has an extensive knowledge of classic and modern literature across genres. Learners and staff go to Samantha first when they want to know what to read next. If Inez is the tech guru, then Samantha is the "reading guru" at the school. Together, Samantha and Inez seem to be the ideal pair to manage the large, well-funded high school library.

Although state library standards emphasize the importance of paraprofessionals to support certified school librarians, Inez and Samantha must rely on learner workers and parent volunteers to assist with shelving books, handling circulation, doing book repair, and other duties that pull the two school librarians from working directly with learners and with other educators. The school principal, Leon, is aware of Inez and Samantha's desire for a paid school library assistant, but he struggles to secure funding and, truth be told, doesn't truly understand why the school librarians can't just do checkout and shelving themselves since that's what he remembers his high school librarian doing the majority of the time.

INEZ'S RESPONSE TO THE NEW STANDARDS

Inez recognizes that the new *AASL Standards Integrated Framework* gives her the platform on which to base improvements for the school library that she suggests to school administrators. The new standards also provide a conversation starter to help Inez talk to Samantha about competencies that should be addressed with learners and exemplified in the school librarians' own professional practice.

Inez is already an active member and presenter for state and national technology conferences, but after reading the new *National School Library Standards*, she realizes that she has much to offer her school library professional organization and its members, too. Inez decides to focus in particular on school library standards under the Shared Foundation Explore. After reading the Competencies in the Share Domain, Inez knew she had some work to do to help her school library reach its full potential. And because she has experience in tech-related professional-learning networks and in presenting at conferences, she can see herself sharing her journey with others who might need encouragement and guidance along the way.

Inez also envisions working with Samantha and a school library advisory council—which the school does not yet have—of school and community stakeholders to delve into all of the school library standards Domains and Alignments to look for areas for potential growth. For years Inez and Samantha have tried to make stakeholders aware of the full role of the school librarian and of the need for paraprofessional help in the school library. Inez hopes that asking parents, other educators, learners, and administrators to investigate the standards and take an honest look at the current school library instruction and activities will result in stakeholders' becoming aware of the importance of what the school librarians have been saying for years. Inez hopes for buy-in and full support of others who recognize the positive impact an effective school library has on the entire school community.

Inez also noticed that the second Alignment in Explore's Share Domain for school libraries is about encouraging families and the community to participate in school library planning, advocacy, and activities. Although she regularly posts school library events and photos through social media, she does so in a "one-sided" fashion by telling her community what is going to happen or sharing about what did happen. The new AASL Standards helped her to see that two-way communication is essential and that, to best meet the needs of those the school library serves, she and Samantha should seek input from all stakeholders.

QUESTIONS FOR FURTHER DISCUSSION

- What is a possible agenda for the first meeting of the new school library advisory council? What should Inez focus on the first time she brings together this group of stakeholders?
- What are some ways that Inez can seek input from learners, parents, and others on a regular basis for the purpose of improving the school library programs and services?
- How can Inez reach out to Samantha to strengthen their partnership as co-school librarians?
- How can Inez use the AASL Standards to initiate conversations with her principal about the role of a school librarian?

Pre-Service Educator and Researcher

SCENARIO

Athena is a pre-service educator in a rigorous school librarian preparation program. She enjoys teaching and is active in national and state professional organizations. Her research interests include measuring effective integration of school library standards and exploring how school librarians engage in teaching and learning in schools. She believes this work allows her to remain current with best practices in the field.

Athena works at a university with an ALA-accredited Master's in Library and Information Science program that incorporates a CAEP-accredited school librarian preparation program. Athena's learners are earning a master's degree and teaching licensure in school librarianship. Candidates in her school librarian preparation program fall into three groups:

1. Current classroom educators who want to add the school librarian endorsement to their current teaching license, in addition to earning their master's degree.

2. "Nontraditional" learners who are returning to college to earn a master's degree with school librarian licensure to embark on a second career. In addition to their school librarian preparation courses, to address the gaps in their pedagogical knowledge and experience, these career-changing learners are also required to take professional education coursework such as courses in child development, learning theory, and teaching methodologies.

3. Learners who take only one or two courses in the program for professional development or to meet teaching license recertification requirements.

The university's school librarian preparation program has a reputation for meeting the needs of pre-service school librarians in all three of the categories described above and, in doing so, cultivating innovative information professionals.

The learners already in the field of education are typically seasoned educators with five to fifteen years of experience. Many of them are highly qualified educators considered innovators in their schools. Most are actively engaged in leadership initiatives, and the learners who are currently educators are often the first educators approached to serve on a curriculum committee or be part of a leadership "think tank." These educators enjoy teaching and know that learners who are engaged love learning. However, in recent years, with their packed pacing guides and endless bouts of standardized testing, educators have had a harder time engaging learners. Searching for something a bit different and feeling as though they need a change, these educators find the work of the school librarian enticing. Athena is able to appeal to them at the university's recruitment fairs. The school librarian preparation program offers these prospective learners an opportunity to further their careers and further develop many of the skills they most love to employ as classroom educators.

Similarly, for those coming from outside education, the school library program seems like a good fit for candidates who want a new career that enables them to have a direct positive influence on the lives of learners and communities.

ATHENA'S RESPONSE TO THE NEW STANDARDS

When Athena read the new AASL Standards, she immediately asked herself, "What areas of the new AASL Standards might a new school librarian, or anyone in the profession, reference when confronted with statements that the school library may no longer be relevant to learning?"

Athena realized that, for practicing school librarians who attend her university's program for professional development and licensure renewal, her use of the new AASL Standards to guide her instruction will immediately show her learners ways to rejuvenate their practices and update their approaches to teaching and learning.

Athena also discussed the new standards with her university colleagues; all of them frequently reflect—individually and as a group—on program coursework content to ensure that it provides the core competencies of school librarianship while also addressing the required pedagogical content knowledge for program completers who must develop a thorough understanding of

- teaching for learning;
- enacting a school librarian's role in supporting reading and ethical use of information;
- employing strategies for building support among stakeholders;
- gaining influence as an educational leader; and
- managing a school library.

Contemplating the new AASL Standards provided the school library faculty at the university with new opportunities for reflection; they were unanimous in their agreement to use the AASL Standards as frameworks for reaching each group of their dynamic learners.

As a result of reflection and discussion, Athena decides that, not only does she want to show candidates how to use the AASL Standards frameworks to structure lessons for K–12 learners, but she also plans to use the standards to guide development of her own course syllabi and assignments. Athena's use of the new *National School Library Standards* will help candidates shape their teaching philosophies and the school libraries they build after they have been hired as school librarians.

Athena knows she must make the standards approachable and relevant to each learner in her program. She has carefully reviewed the new standards to examine how she might present this set of standards to those already working in education. What would educators expect to see and understand about school library standards that may complement or be slightly different from how these experienced educators already approach standards in their current teaching roles? At the same time, she is aware that many of her learners may be unfamiliar with the role of standards in education. She strives to plan ways to scaffold the introduction of the standards. She wonders whether she should begin by focusing on the Shared Foundation Collaborate—especially the school librarian's collaboration with other educators in the building.

QUESTIONS FOR FURTHER DISCUSSION

- What areas of the new AASL Standards could a pre-service school librarian use to help support and affirm the decision to become a school librarian?
- What will some of the key differences in a classroom educator's professional life be after switching to the role of school librarian? What are some of the ways in which she will interact differently with other members of her school community?
- In what way does Explore's Key Commitment "Discover and innovate in a growth mindset developed through experience and reflection" align with the innovative pedagogies experienced educators are already attempting to implement in their classrooms? How will this teaching look different in the school library setting?

School Library Assistant/ Paraprofessional

SCENARIO

Abigail, a school library assistant, is a caring and passionate staff member of Excellence Elementary School (EES). EES is one of ten elementary schools in the district, and she works hard to prepare learners for secondary school academically, socially, and emotionally. Although EES is not the best funded or highest achieving school, administrators and staff consistently demonstrate their dedication for all the learners in their charge.

As part of the EES team, Abigail works with Susannah, a school librarian with fifteen years of experience who works half time at EES and half-time at another district elementary school. Susannah is innovative, technologically savvy, and focused on integrating the school library into curriculum. However, she is in the EES school library only in the mornings and spends most of that time providing instruction to learners on a fixed schedule. Abigail works full-time and supports Susannah in myriad ways. Abigail is proud of the role her work in the school library has played in the lives of thousands of children, educators, and parents over the years.

Although Susannah works at EES only half time, EES administrators do their best to follow AASL's position statement "Appropriate Staffing for School Libraries" (AASL 2016b) by ensuring that Abigail can provide full-time clerical support and can keep the school library open full-time to support flexible use when Susannah is not teaching.

During classes held in the school library, Abigail assists Susannah by checking books out to learners. In between classes, Abigail engages in primarily technical and clerical tasks. In addition to circulation, Abigail processes new books and adds records for them into the school's library management system. Abigail also spends time shelving and preparing book displays. Additionally, she assists learners and educators with requests for materials, basic technical troubleshooting and using school library supplies and equipment.

Abigail is critical to the success of the school library and works collaboratively to accomplish Susannah's goals for the school library. For example, Abigail routinely helps to pull together statistics that will serve to support Inquire's Create Domain for school libraries so that Susannah can communicate progress toward measurable outcomes in her monthly bulletin that informs educators, administrators, and parents of the school library's activities and its connection to the curriculum.

Although Abigail's primary role is to provide clerical and technical support to the school library, she also provides support to the school's educational team. For example, the school's technology committee asked her to pull together pricing quotes that help them prioritize technology purchases.

ABIGAIL'S RESPONSE TO THE NEW STANDARDS

Abigail has heard that new standards for school libraries have been developed, and she is wondering how those standards affect someone in the school library assistant role, how she can use the standards to help Susannah keep the school library thriving, and how she can stay abreast of new concepts in the standards to benefit her school community. Abigail is hoping for more training on how these standards will affect her role and the school library.

Unfortunately, budget cuts in the district have eliminated contract days for paraprofessional training. As a result, Abigail and the other school library assistants are no longer included in professional-development events. Abigail does not have a college degree but took a few education courses at the local university about ten years ago. She is a member of her state school library association but is not really sure what opportunities that might afford her.

Susannah has said that she is happy to provide information about the new standards, but since she only works part-time at EES, little time is available for her to help Abigail. Instead, Susannah helped Abigail get connected with AASL resources including webinars, online classes, and scholarships to attend conferences. Susannah has also given Abigail permission to engage with these resources during a small portion of her workday. While Susannah is teaching in the mornings, and after Abigail has done book checking and shelving, she reads articles, watches webinars, or participates in e-mail list and blog discussions.

Once a week Abigail and Susannah sit down together to discuss what Abigail has learned and how they can apply her new knowledge to improve the school library and its value to the school community. Abigail is grateful for Susannah's support and has been enjoying learning new things. She is even considering going back to school.

QUESTIONS FOR FURTHER DISCUSSION

- What AASL resources are available to Abigail that will support her growth in her role of school library assistant?
- How do the AASL Standards relate to Abigail's role in the school library?
- How can Susannah use the new standards to focus and expand Abigail's role?

- How can Abigail and Susannah work together to implement the new school library standards?
- How does Abigail's training benefit the school library and the whole school community?
- What can Susannah do to help, not only Abigail, but the other school library assistants in her district who are no longer provided with in-district training?

Appendices

Implementation Plan Overview

A Strategic Plan for Implementation of the
*National School Library Standards for Learners,
School Librarians, and School Libraries*

INTRODUCTION

THIS APPENDIX IS AN OVERVIEW OF THE PHILOSOPHY AND PRINCIPLES THAT guide the *AASL National School Library Standards Implementation Plan.* The full implementation plan can be found on the AASL Standards website at <www.standards.aasl.org/implementation>.

The strategic implementation plan was created by the AASL Standards and Guidelines Implementation Task Force to support states, school systems, and individual schools preparing to implement the association's *National School Library Standards for Learners, School Librarians, and School Libraries.*

The implementation plan provides an implementation and advocacy roadmap for the association and its volunteers, members of the profession, and school library stakeholders engaging with the AASL Standards. The plan was intentionally designed to speak to specific audience segments. It explains AASL's standards, engages early adopters in developing exemplars of practice, and equips school librarians to understand, apply, and use the standards in their local educational settings. The task force developed this plan in parallel to the work of the AASL Standards and Guidelines Editorial Board so that AASL could support the school library community with resources immediately upon launch of the standards and follow up with a strategic plan for continued assistance and engagement. The interaction between the plan and its intended users was the implementation task force's top priority and the primary concern behind every step and action taken by the task force. This Appendix has been included as a summary explanation of our vision for how the association will support school librarians and stakeholders as they learn and adopt the new standards.

The Charge

The AASL Standards and Guidelines Implementation Task Force was charged with

- developing a plan to support states, school systems, and individual schools preparing to implement the association's learning and program standards,
- introducing the standards, and

- building awareness, understanding, and commitment to using the standards to guide school library practice.

In addition, the plan reflects the association's strategic goals and addresses professional development, marketing communication and branding, and advocacy and community engagement.

Multiple Pathways

A central principle of this implementation plan is that it honors adults as learners and includes multiple pathways for different learning needs. We (the members of the AASL Standards and Guidelines Implementation Task Force) understood that different user groups would respond to different messages and require different entry points. We solved dilemmas by returning to our understanding of the user's experience, and considered how he or she would respond to the products we had in mind. Although our approach resulted in a complex web of initiatives and products, we created a plan that is global, straightforward, and simple. The primary goals and objectives are brief. The real work is embedded in the action steps.

Personas

To identify specific adult learning needs, we created personas. A persona is depicted as a specific person but is not a real individual; rather, it is synthesized from observations of many people. Each persona represents a significant portion of people in the real world; use of personas enables the designer to focus on a manageable and memorable cast of characters. Personas aid designers to create content or products for different kinds of people as they design for a specific somebody, rather than a generic everybody (Mulder and Yaar 2007). For summary descriptions of the personas used by AASL's implementation task force and editorial board, see chapter 1. The personas are described in greater depth on the AASL Standards website at <www.standards.aasl.org/implementation>.

Adults as Learners

In considering learning needs, we have applied concepts from theoretical models to provide for a range of situations and needs. The Ways of Knowing model acknowledges that adult learners have varying perspectives, ways of knowing, and learning; see row A in table A-1 (Drago-Severson 2009). The Concerns-Based Adoption Model is a framework for understanding the stages that learners move through as they adopt innovative practices; see row B in table A-1 (Hord et al. 1987). For example, a new professional might want sequential steps for accomplishing a task. This person, an instrumental learner, typically seeks facts and wants to know "the right way" to do things. This person's needs are entirely different from the professional who is ready to learn by teaching or by experimenting with a given model. Although learning needs vary, all learners have instrumental needs in different contexts; concrete information is necessary when learning new material. We also considered the importance of providing social structures for learning and opportunities for some to grow professionally by inventing something new. Row C of table A-1 contains learning experiences appropriate for each type of knower and for each stage in the Concerns-Based Adoption Model.

Adaptable Action Plan

The goals and objectives of the proposed implementation plan are intentionally broad, universal, and brief (see Implementation Plan Goals and Objectives below). The goals establish themes for action and hint at entry points designed for different users. We know that all school librarians will need basic information and tools to get started; quick-start guides will explain the standards to all user groups. In addition to this action step, we intend to engage early adopters in developing materials to equip other practitioners to adopt the standards.

Implementation Plan Goals and Objectives

GOAL 1. Explain the structure, purpose, and value of the AASL Standards to school librarians, stakeholders, and partners beyond the school community.

Objectives 1.1 Develop consistent, sharable branding and messaging for the standards to be used across traditional and social media.

1.2 Introduce AASL Standards to key stakeholders, including state and regional school library leaders, national educational organizations, state departments of education, and school administrator organizations.

1.3 Create and sustain excitement and conversations about the AASL Standards.

GOAL 2. Engage innovators in developing tools to explain the structure, purpose, and value of the AASL Standards to school librarians, stakeholders, and partners beyond the school library community.

Objectives 2.1 Identify and engage with "movers and shakers" in the school library profession.

2.2 Encourage practitioners to develop and share implementation models and metrics for AASL Standards.

2.3 Engage with stakeholders outside the profession.

GOAL 3. Equip practitioners to understand, apply, and use the AASL Standards in their educational settings.

Objectives 3.1 Design professional-development opportunities for practitioners.

3.2 Foster building personal learning networks and crowd-sourcing of resources related to AASL Standards.

3.3 Ensure implementation support through AASL publications, websites, and online tools.

TABLE A-1

Learning experiences aligned with Ways of Knowing and with stages in the Concerns-Based Adoption Model.

	INSTRUMENTAL KNOWERS	SOCIALIZING KNOWERS	SELF-AUTHORING KNOWERS	SELF-TRANSFORMING KNOWERS
A. WAYS OF KNOWING	**Ask: What are the basics?** **Characteristics:** Looking for the correct way to do things, they want to feel supported and valued.	**Ask: What should I know?** **Characteristics:** Collaborative and reflective, they want to contribute and appreciate the contributions of others.	**Ask: What do I want and need to know and learn?** **Characteristics:** Internally motivated and comfortable with ambiguity.	**Ask: What can we learn together that we could not learn alone?** **Characteristics:** Focused on an exchange of ideas and perspectives.

ORIENTATION → PREPARATION → MECHANICAL → ROUTINE → REFINEMENT → INTEGRATION

	ORIENTATION → PREPARATION	MECHANICAL → ROUTINE	ROUTINE → REFINEMENT	REFINEMENT → INTEGRATION
B. CONCERNS-BASED ADOPTION MODEL	Learn more and make plans to begin implementation.	Begin implementation. Implementation becomes routine.	Routine implementation leads to refinement to better suit the needs of the setting and learner.	Refinement of implementation leads to thinking beyond the library/school/district setting to maximize impact.
C. LEARNING EXPERIENCES TO SUPPORT IMPLEMENTATION AND PROFESSIONAL GROWTH	• Studying concrete examples and models. • Receiving goals with step-by-step processes for achieving them.	• Watching demonstrations and having opportunities to practice. • Sharing work and ideas in safe spaces. • Collaborating with others and reflecting on one's own learning.	• Participating in opportunities to share ideas, develop goals, and give feedback to others. • Giving and getting feedback (warm and cool) on goals and implementation strategies. • Responding to reflective prompts and discussions.	• Participating in opportunities to discuss implementation in diverse communities of practitioners. • Giving and getting feedback to and from a variety of practitioners. • Taking advantage of opportunities for reflection and engaging in metacognition.

> 3.4 Prepare library and information science and continuing education faculty members to integrate the AASL Standards in university programs of study.
>
> **GOAL 4.** Evaluate progress toward implementing AASL Standards and adjust for changing conditions.
>
> ***Objectives*** 4.1 Document effectiveness of AASL Standards implementation efforts.
>
> 4.2 Review and adjust implementation strategic plan for continued relevance.

The real work takes form in the action steps, which have been planned for a three-year period (see Snapshot of Strategic Plan). The implementation task force has created materials to support the launch of the standards. Following launch, a standing committee will guide, monitor, and evaluate standards implementation. The spreadsheet format of the plan will permit this future committee to filter, track, evaluate, and revise throughout the implementation period. Because the plan is designed to evolve in response to changes in the educational landscape, the committee will also develop new actions to adjust or extend support for implementation of the standards.

Snapshot of Strategic Plan

GOAL 1.

Explain the structure, purpose, and value of the AASL Standards to school librarians, stakeholders, and partners beyond the school community.

Goal 1. Objective 2.

Introduce AASL Standards to key stakeholders, including state and regional school library leaders, national educational organizations, state departments of education, and school administrator organizations.

Goal 1. Objective 2. (Selected Action Steps)

Noah Who Needs Help	Create a "Top 5 First Steps" infographic ad/flyer about understanding and implementing the new standards document; make an interactive PDF with links to online resources and professional development.
Noah Who Needs Help	Publish brief webcast(s) (5 minutes) that focus on walking through the documents and the implementation online portal.
Leon the Lead Learner	Create an infographic ad/flyer targeted to administrators: What does an "effective school library program" with a certified school librarian using the AASL Standards look like? What value does it bring to the educational ecosystem? What value does it provide for learners?
Patty the Parent	Create an infographic for the parent showcasing the gains school libraries provide to her child, and how she can get involved, support, and advocate for the school library.

Works Cited

Drago-Severson, Ellie. 2009. *Leading Adult Learning: Supporting Adult Development in Our Schools.* Thousand Oaks, CA: Sage.

Hord, Shirley M., et al. 1987. *Taking Charge of Change.* Alexandria, VA: ASCD.

Mulder, Steve, and Ziv Yaar. 2007. *The User Is Always Right: A Practical Guide to Creating and Using Personas for the Web.* Berkeley, CA: New Riders.

AASL Standards and Guidelines Implementation Task Force

Mary Keeling, Chair
Judy Deichman
Sara Kelly Johns
Kate Lechtenberg
Ellen McNair
Jeanie Phillips
Joyce Valenza

AASL Board Liaisons

Ken Stewart, 2015–2016
Diane Chen, 2016–2017

AASL Staff

Sylvia Knight Norton, Executive Director
Stephanie Book, Staff Liaison, Manager, Communications

For more information on the AASL Standards and Guidelines Implementation Task Force's process, detailed profiles for each persona, or to view the specific actions within the *AASL National School Library Standards Implementation Plan,* visit the AASL Standards website at <www.standards.aasl.org/implementation>.

History of School Library Standards and Guidelines

1915 **The Development of the Modern High School Library.** In this *Library Journal* article, Mary E. Hall proposed a school library classroom. This document specified comfortable and functional furniture and decor as well as collection contents (Hall 1915).

1917 **Standard High School Library Organization for Accredited Secondary Schools of Different Sizes.** Symposium on a Standard Library Equipment for High Schools Contributed by Leaders in the Movement for Better High School Libraries, presented at a meeting of the North Central Association of Colleges and Secondary Schools March 21–24, 1917. C. C. Certain, chairman. This draft document later became the 1918 Standards.

1918 **Standard Library Organization and Equipment for Secondary Schools of Different Sizes.** Report of the Committee on Library Organization and Equipment, National Education Association, *Proceedings of the National Education Association*, 1918, 691–719. C. C. Certain, chairman.

1918 **Standard Library Organization and Equipment for Secondary Schools of Different Sizes.** National Education Association, Department of Secondary Education, 1918. C. C. Certain, chairman. These are the same as the 1918 proceedings, but published separately and later endorsed and published by ALA in 1920. The 1920 ALA book can be downloaded at <https://archive.org/details/libraryo00natistandardrich>.

1920 **Standard Library Organization and Equipment for Secondary Schools.** Published by the New York State Library, *Library School Bulletin 45*, University of the State of New York, 1920. [This bulletin is a reprint of the 1918 standards with notes particular to New York State certification and the University of the State of New York Regents policy.]

1925 **Elementary School Library Standards.** Report of the Joint Committee on Elementary School Library Standards, 1925. C. C. Certain, chairman [Joint Committee of the NEA Department of Elementary School Principals and ALA School Librarians' Section].

These were the first elementary school library standards, although few elementary schools had libraries. This report recommended moving books from classroom collections to a central school library (Woolls, Weeks and Coatney 2013).

1939 Evaluation Criteria. Cooperative Study of Secondary School Standards, the Middle States Association of Colleges and Secondary Schools, 1939 and 1950. State and accrediting agencies developed standards based on the Certain standards or the accrediting standards.

1945 School Libraries for Today and Tomorrow: Functions and Standards. American Library Association, Committees on Post-War Planning, Divisions of Libraries for Children and Young People and American Association of School Librarians, 1945. Mary Peacock Douglas, AASL school library standards committee chair, and Frances Henne, committee member, authored this forty-three-page booklet including quantitative and qualitative standards that guided future standards (Kester and Jones 2004).

1954 School Library Standards. U.S. Department of Health, Education, and Welfare, Office of Education, 1954. Nora E. Beust edited this review and history of standards and regulations, including a survey of the states; this document is not a new set of standards.

1960 Standards for School Library Programs. American Association of School Librarians, a Division of the American Library Association, 1960. This document was created in cooperation with nineteen educational organizations. The writing committee was chaired by Frances Henne and prepared with input from the National Council of Teachers of English and the National Education Association Department of Audiovisual Instruction (Kester and Jones 2004).

1969 Standards for School Media Programs. American Association of School Librarians and the National Education Association Department of Audiovisual Instruction, 1969. This document was drafted in cooperation with representatives from twenty-seven educational organizations and coordinated by Frances Henne. The terms "media," "media specialist," "media center," and "media program" were used for the first time (Kester and Jones 2004).

1975 Media Programs: District and School. American Association of School Librarians and Association for Educational Communications and Technology (AECT), 1975. (AECT was formerly the National Education Association's Department of Audiovisual Instruction.)

1988 Information Power: Guidelines for School Library Media Programs. American Association of School Librarians and Association for Educational Communications and Technology, 1988.

1998 **Information Power: Building Partnerships for Learning.** American Association of School Librarians and Association for Educational Communications and Technology, 1998. This document included Information Literacy Standards for Student Learning. Student learning standards were introduced in this document, and the standards do not include facility and collection specifications.

2007 **Standards for the 21st-Century Learner.** American Association of School Librarians, 2007. This stand-alone document was created in response to the AASL Strategic Plan and included student learning standards as well as school librarians' common beliefs. Again, the focus was on the students, not the collection.

2009 **Standards for the 21st-Century Learner in Action.** American Association of School Librarians, 2009. This document included benchmarks and examples to support implementation of AASL's *Standards for the 21st-Century Learner.*

2009 **Empowering Learners: Guidelines for School Library Programs.** American Association of School Librarians, 2009. This document added professional standards and program guidelines to AASL's *Standards for the 21st-Century Learner.*

2017 **National School Library Standards for Learners, School Librarians, and School Libraries.** American Association of School Librarians and American Library Association, 2018. This document includes standards for learners, school librarians, and school libraries.

APPENDIX C

Annotated List of AASL Position Statements

A POSITION STATEMENT PRESENTS A LIST OF REASONS TO SUPPORT A PAR-
ticular viewpoint. Position statements can be used to advocate for specific approaches to issues that impact learners, school librarianship, and school libraries. AASL has developed many position statements that will help you define stances, policies, and procedures for learners, educators, administrators, and the community.

In this document, we have included the full text of the position statements that were developed specifically to illustrate AASL's commitment to the Every Student Succeeds Act (ESSA). Additional position statements are described below and available on the AASL website.

APPENDIX C1. DEFINITION OF AN EFFECTIVE SCHOOL LIBRARY PROGRAM: An effective school library program has a certified school librarian at the helm, provides personalized learning environments, and offers equitable access to resources to ensure a well-rounded education for every learner.

APPENDIX C2. APPROPRIATE STAFFING FOR SCHOOL LIBRARIES: Every learner in every school should have access to an updated school library with a certified school librarian.

APPENDIX C3. INSTRUCTIONAL ROLE OF THE SCHOOL LIBRARIAN: School librarians are instructors as well as collaborators with fellow educators in the pursuit of learning in school libraries.

APPENDIX C4. PREPARATION OF SCHOOL LIBRARIANS: In addition to meeting state certification requirements, school librarians should hold a master's degree or equivalent from a program that combines academic and professional preparation in library and information science, education, and technology.

APPENDIX C5. ROLE OF THE SCHOOL LIBRARY PROGRAM: An effective school library program plays a crucial role in preparing learners for informed living in an information-rich society.

Additional AASL Position Statements

Notes about each position statement follow; the full text of position statements is available on the AASL website at <**http://www.ala.org/aasl/positionstatements**> (accessed February 11, 2017).

COMMON CORE COLLEGE- AND CAREER-READINESS STANDARDS. As learners strive to meet the rigor of the Common Core State Standards, certified school librarians will play an essential part in ensuring that 21st-century information-literacy skills, dispositions, responsibilities, and assessments are integrated throughout all curriculum areas. AASL has led the way in addressing information literacy through the *Standards for the 21st-Century Learner*; and the *Standards for the 21st-Century Learner in Action* provided a coherent framework of development from pre-kindergarten through twelfth grade. With the integration of these standards with the Common Core State Standards, learners have the opportunity to be well prepared as lifelong learners facing the challenges of college and careers. (adopted 03/01/2010)

CONFIDENTIALITY OF LIBRARY RECORDS. Records held in libraries that connect specific individuals with specific resources, programs, or services are confidential and not to be used for purposes other than routine record keeping: i.e., to maintain access to resources, to assure that resources are available to users who need them, to arrange facilities, to provide resources for the comfort and safety of patrons, or to accomplish the purposes of the program or service. The library community recognizes that children and youth have the same rights to privacy as adults. (revised 02/06/2012)

DIGITAL CONTENT AND E-BOOKS IN SCHOOL LIBRARY COLLECTIONS. Digital content, e-books, e-readers, and other digital devices are essential components of school library collections. These collections will remain in a period of transition for some time while school librarians balance the selection of devices and formats, including print, e-book, and digital materials. Schools and districts will need to provide funding and support for this powerful means of accessing information and for the requisite experimentation in the face of ever-changing options. School librarians and administrators need a cooperative spirit of tolerance as school librarians explore emerging digital devices and new ways of purchasing and lending materials. (adopted 06/28/13)

DIVERSITY IN THE ORGANIZATION. Diversity is an integral facet of the American landscape, and it permeates all professions, including school librarianship. Diversity in its many dimensions—ethnicity, nationality, race, culture, religion, gender, sexual orientation, socioeconomic background, mental and physical abilities, learning styles, values, and viewpoints—enriches the school. In this setting diversity provides rich opportunities for school librarians to collaborate with educators and administrators to create meaningful learning experiences that foster cultural competence, sensitivity, appreciation, and respect for differences in the school library and classrooms. Persuasive benefits of fostering an inclusive environment are learner success and empowerment. (adopted 01/08/2011)

FLEXIBLE SCHEDULING. Classes must be flexibly scheduled to visit the school library on an as-needed basis to facilitate just-in-time research, training, and use of technology with the guidance of the educator, who is the subject specialist, and the school librarian, who is the information-search process specialist. The lesson plans resulting from this collaboration recognize that the length of the learning experience is dependent on learning needs rather than a fixed school library period. Regularly scheduling classes in the school library to provide educator release time or preparation time prohibits this best practice. Learners and educators must be able to come to the school library throughout the day to use information sources, read for pleasure, and collaborate with other learners and educators. (adopted 09/2011, revised 06/2014)

LABELING BOOKS WITH READING LEVELS. Labeling and shelving books with reading levels or grade levels displayed on the spine allow learners to see the reading levels of peers. As a result, the confidentiality of learners' reading levels is threatened. Only a learner, the child's parents or guardian, the educator, and the school librarian as appropriate should have knowledge of a learner's reading capability. Nonstandard shelving practices make it difficult for school library staff and patrons to locate specific titles. More importantly, if books in the school library are arranged by reading level, learners may have no understanding of how materials are arranged in most school and public libraries, and learners' ability to select books in other libraries will be adversely affected. (adopted 07/18/2011)

QUANTITATIVE STANDARDS. School librarians should engage in continuous evaluation of the effectiveness of the school library program to meet patrons' needs to access ideas and information through the resources of the school library. Such an evaluation should be locally based, responsive to community needs, and flexible to allow for new formats, new modes of access, and changing demographics. National attempts to provide quantitative measures would lose this local context and flexibility. Rather than relying on quantitative standards that promote compliance with an inflexible and minimal threshold list, school librarians need to demonstrate the dispositions of deep commitment and inquiry required by continuous program assessment and advocacy with stakeholders. (adopted 06/28/13)

ROLE OF THE SCHOOL LIBRARIAN IN READING DEVELOPMENT. When learners read "real books" and write to communicate for an authentic purpose, learning becomes relevant, interesting, and motivational, and learners are prepared for lifelong learning. Acquisition, organization, and dissemination of resources to support the reading program through the school library are cost-effective for the entire school district. (revised 9/1/2010)

ROLE OF THE SCHOOL LIBRARIAN IN SENIOR/CAPSTONE PROJECTS. AASL's *Standards for the 21st-Century Learner* has identified skills and dispositions learners need to successfully complete a senior or capstone project. School librarians possess the knowledge of instructional strategies, resources, and technology to work with learners in developing these skills and dispositions. Additionally, school librarians possess unique leadership skills and expertise that enable them to play an important role in design, coordination, and implementation of senior/capstone projects. (adopted 06/2014)

SCHOOL LIBRARIAN'S ROLE IN READING. With a deep knowledge of the wide variety of authentic reading materials available in the school library and elsewhere, the school librarian has a key role in supporting instruction in comprehension strategies for reading print and online materials. In collaboration with classroom educators and reading specialists, school librarians co-design, co-implement, and co-evaluate interdisciplinary lessons and units of instruction that result in increased learning. (revised 09/01/2010)

THE SCHOOL LIBRARY SUPERVISOR. The leadership of a qualified school library supervisor is an essential component in the delivery of quality school library programs throughout a district or other jurisdiction. In collaboration with qualified school librarians and competent school library support personnel, the school library supervisor works to ensure that best practices support learners and that equitable access to resources is available to all learners in the schools. (adopted 06/94; revised 05/12)

SUPPORT FOR NATIONAL BOARD OF PROFESSIONAL TEACHING STANDARDS CERTIFICATION. National Board assessment focuses on what accomplished school librarians should know and do in the context of their daily work. AASL members are encouraged to pursue National Board certification as a way of demonstrating their accomplished practice and as a means of professional development. (revised 09/01/2010)

VALUE OF INDEPENDENT READING IN THE SCHOOL LIBRARY PROGRAM. To become lifelong readers, learners must have access to current, high-quality, interesting, and extensive collections of books and other print materials in their school libraries, classrooms, and public libraries. To develop a love of reading, learners also need: contact with adults who read regularly and widely and who serve as positive reading role models; certified school librarians and educators who demonstrate their enthusiasm for reading by reading aloud and booktalking; time during the school day dedicated to reading for pleasure, information, and exploration; opportunities specifically designed to engage young people in reading; schools that create an environment where independent reading is valued, promoted, and encouraged; and opportunities that involve caregivers, parents and other family members in reading. (adopted June 1994; revised July 1999, September 2010)

APPENDIX C1

Definition of an Effective School Library Program

AASL Position Statement

Position

THE AMERICAN ASSOCIATION OF SCHOOL LIBRARIANS (AASL) SUPPORTS THE position that an effective school library program has a certified school librarian at the helm, provides personalized learning environments, and offers equitable access to resources to ensure a well-rounded education for every learner.

As a fundamental component of college, career, and community readiness, the effective school library program:

1. is adequately staffed, including a state-certified school librarian who
   a. is an instructional leader and teacher,
   b. supports the development of digital learning, participatory learning, inquiry learning, technology literacies, and information literacy, and
   c. supports, supplements, and elevates the literacy experience through guidance and motivational reading initiatives;
2. has up-to-date digital and print materials and technology, including curation of openly licensed educational resources; and
3. provides regular professional development and collaboration between classroom educators and school librarians.

Effective school libraries are dynamic learning environments that bridge the gap between access and opportunity for all K–12 learners. Under the leadership of the school librarian, the school library provides learners access to resources and technology, connecting classroom learning to real-world events. By providing access to an array of well-managed resources, school libraries enable academic knowledge to be linked to deeper, personalized learning. The expanded learning environment of the school library ensures the unique interests and needs of individual learners are met. In this way, effective school library programs prepare learners for college, career, and community.

Under the leadership of a certified school librarian, the effective school library program delivers a well-rounded educational program (AASL 2009a). This program focuses on accessing and evaluating information, providing digital learning training and experiences, and developing a culture of reading. The program uses a variety of engaging and relevant resources. Robust school libraries have high-quality, openly licensed digital and print resources, technology tools, and broadband access. This environment is essential to providing equitable learning opportunities for all learners. More than 60 studies in two dozen states show that the "levels of library funding, staffing levels, collection size and range, and the instructional role of the librarian all have a direct impact on student achievement" (Gretes 2013).

In an effective school library program, the school librarian serves as an instructional leader, program administrator, teacher, instructional partner, and information specialist (AASL 2009). Working with classroom educators, the school librarian develops information literacy and digital literacy instruction for all students. Serving as an instructional leader, the school librarian contributes to curricular decisions and facilitates professional learning. Additionally, as the school library program administrator, the school librarian oversees and manages the program and works with school and community partners. These partnerships result in expanded and improved resources and services for all learners.

An effective school library program plays a crucial role in bridging digital and socioeconomic divides. School library programs staffed with state-certified professionals provide an approachable, equitable, personalized learning environment necessary for every learner's well-rounded education.

Background

The Every Student Succeeds Act (ESSA) includes language for "effective school library programs" in the provisions of Title I, Part A; Title II, Part A; Title II, Part B, Subpart 2; Title II, Part B, Subpart 2, Section 2226; and Title IV, Part A. The definition of an effective school library program provides guidance to administrators, school boards, and school librarians in implementing ESSA.

DEFINITIONS

- *Collaboration:* Working with a member of the teaching team to plan, implement, and evaluate a specialized instructional plan.
- *Community Readiness:* The ability to be a productive, active, engaged member of a democratic society.
- *School Librarian Instructional Role:* See Appendix C3: Instructional Role of the School Librarian Position Statement.

REFERENCES

American Association of School Librarians. 2012. *2012 School Libraries Count! National Longitudinal Survey of School Library Programs.* <www.ala.org/aasl/sites/ala.org.aasl/files/content/researchandstatistics/slcsurvey/2012/AASL-SLC-2012-WEB.pdf> (accessed May 20, 2016).

American Association of School Librarians. 2009. *Empowering Learners: Guidelines for School Library Programs.* Chicago, IL. <www.ala.org/aasl/standards/guidelines> (accessed July 7, 2016).

Gretes, Frances. 2013. *School Library Impact Studies: A Review of Findings and Guide to Sources.* Harry & Jeanette Weinberg Foundation. <www.baltimorelibrary project.org/wp-content/uploads/downloads/2013/09/Library-Impact-Studies .pdf> (accessed May 25, 2016).

DISCLAIMER

The position taken by the American Association of School Librarians (AASL) represents the organization and cannot be applied to individual members or groups affiliated with the association without their direct confirmation.

Approved June 25, 2016

APPENDIX C2

Appropriate Staffing for School Libraries

AASL Position Statement

Position

THE AMERICAN ASSOCIATION OF SCHOOL LIBRARIANS (AASL) SUPPORTS THE position that every learner in every school, including independent schools and public charter schools, should have access to an updated school library with a certified school librarian. The success of a school library program, no matter how well designed, ultimately depends on the quality and number of personnel responsible for managing the instructional program and the school library's physical and virtual resources. A certified school librarian, supported by technical and clerical staff, is crucial to an effective school library program. Every learner, educator, and administrator in every school building at every grade level should have access to a fully staffed school library throughout the school day.

The following minimum school library staffing requirements define an effective school library program structured to transform teaching and learning throughout the school community:

1. The school library program is serviced by one or more certified school librarians working full-time in the school library.
2. The specific number of additional school librarians is determined by the school's instructional programs, services, facilities, size, and number of learners and educators.
3. In addition to library-degreed professionals, highly trained technical and clerical support staff are necessary for all school library programs at every grade level. Each school should employ at least one full-time technical assistant or clerk for each school librarian. Some programs, facilities, and levels of service will require more than one support staff member for each professional.
4. The school district is served by a district school library supervisor who provides leadership and support for the building-level school library programs by providing resources, professional development, and leadership in developing and implementing the district's school library program. The district school library supervisor is a member of the administrative team and helps determine the criteria and policies for the district's curriculum and instructional programs. The

221

district library supervisor communicates the mission, strategic plan, goals, and needs of the school and district school library programs to the superintendent, board of education, other district-level personnel, and the community.

Background

The staffing of school libraries will be guided by the language for effective school library programs in the Every Student Succeeds Act (ESSA). A certified school librarian is essential to an effective school library program, yet only two-thirds of school libraries are staffed with certified school librarians (Davis 2009).

DEFINITIONS

- *Effective School Library Program.* See Appendix C1: Definition of an Effective School Library Program.

REFERENCES

Davis, Denise M. 2009. "The Condition of U.S. Libraries: School Library Trends, 1999-2009." American Library Association. <http://www.ala.org/research/sites/ala.org.research/files/content/librarystats/librarymediacenter/Condition_of_Libraries_1999.20.pdf> (accessed July 7, 2016).

RECOMMENDED READING LIST

American Association of School Librarians. 2012. *2012 School Libraries Count! National Longitudinal Survey of School Library Programs.* <www.ala.org/aasl/sites/ala.org.aasl/files/content/researchandstatistics/slcsurvey/2012/AASL-SLC-2012-WEB.pdf> (accessed May 20, 2016).

American Association of School Librarians. 2009. *Empowering Learners: Guidelines for School Library Programs.* Chicago, IL. <http://www.ala.org/aasl/standards/guidelines> (accessed July 7, 2016).

Library Research Service. n.d. "School Libraries Impact Studies." <https://www.lrs.org/data-tools/schoollibraries/impact-studies>.

Scholastic Library Publishing. 2016. *School Libraries Work! A Compendium of Research Supporting the Effectiveness of School Libraries.* <www.scholastic.com/slw2016>.

DISCLAIMER

The position taken by the American Association of School Librarians (AASL) represents the organization and cannot be applied to individual members or groups affiliated with the association without their direct confirmation.

Approved June 25, 2016

Instructional Role of the School Librarian

AASL Position Statement

Position

THE AMERICAN ASSOCIATION OF SCHOOL LIBRARIANS (AASL) SUPPORTS THE position that school librarians are instructors as well as collaborators with fellow educators in the pursuit of learning in school libraries, classrooms, learning commons, makerspaces, labs, and virtual learning spaces. School librarian instruction results in students who read and utilize print and digital resources for curricular and personalized learning needs. School librarians teach students how to be inquiring learners who evaluate and use both print and digital information efficiently, effectively, and ethically, with the goal of developing lifelong learning and literacy skills (AASL 2007). School librarians lead the way in digital learning and literacies by teaching and providing professional development in their school communities and districts.

The role of the school librarian is to guide learners and fellow educators through the intersection of formal and informal learning. The instruction the school librarian offers is integral to a well-rounded education. As educators and instructional partners school librarians are critical to teaching and learning in the school community. The school librarian plays a prominent role in instructing learners, faculty, and administrators in a range of literacies, including information, digital, print, visual, and textual literacies. As leaders in literacy and technology, school librarians are perfectly positioned to instruct every learner in the school community through both traditional and blended learning.

Background

In the ever-changing information and education landscape, the instructional role of school librarians is vitally important for educators and learners. As print and digital literacies, inquiry, and reading motivation have become crucial elements of teaching and learning, school librarians as educators and information specialists play a key instructional role in successful schools.

DEFINITIONS

- *Digital Learning:* Learning materials and resources displayed on a digital device and shared electronically with other users. Digital learning content can be both open and/or commercial content (U.S. Dept. of Education 2016).
- *Digital Literacy:* The ability to use information and communication technologies to find, evaluate, create, and communicate information, requiring both cognitive and technical skills (ALA 2013).
- *Information Literacy:* A set of abilities requiring individuals to recognize when information is needed and have the ability to locate, evaluate, and use effectively the needed information (ACRL 2000).

REFERENCES

American Association of School Librarians. 2007. "Standards for the 21st-Century Learner." <www.ala.org/aasl/standards/learning> (accessed April 28, 2016).

American Library Association. January 2013. "Digital Literacy, Libraries, and Public Policy: Report of the Office for Information Technology Policy's Digital Literacy Task Force." <http://www.districtdispatch.org/wp-content/uploads/2013/01/2012_OITP_digilitreport_1_22_13.pdf> (accessed August 15, 2016).

Association of College and Research Libraries. 2000. "Information Literacy Competency Standards for Higher Education." <www.ala.org/acrl/standards/informationliteracycompetency> (accessed May 25, 2016).

U.S. Department of Education. "Definitions." <http://www.ed.gov/race-top/district-competition/definitions> (accessed May 13, 2016).

RECOMMENDED READING LIST

American Association of School Librarians. 2010. ALA/AASL Standards for Initial Preparation of School Librarians. <www.ala.org/aasl/sites/ala.org.aasl/files/content/aasleducation/schoollibrary/2010_standards_with_rubrics_and_statements_1-31-11.pdf>.

American Association of School Librarians. "School Librarians and the Every Student Succeeds Act (ESSA)." <essa.aasl.org/>.

American Library Association. June 18, 2013. "ALA Task Force Releases Digital Literacy Recommendations." <www.ala.org/news/press-releases/2013/06/ala-task-force-releases-digital-literacy-recommendations> (accessed May 13, 2016).

Association of College and Research Libraries. 2000. "Information Literacy Competency Standards for Higher Education." <www.ala.org/acrl/standards/informationliteracycompetency> (accessed May 25, 2016).

Johnston, Melissa. 2012. "School Librarians as Technology Integration Leaders: Enablers and Barriers to Leadership Enactment." *School Library Research* 15. <www.ala.org/aasl/sites/ala.org.aasl/files/content/aaslpubsandjournals/slr/vol15/SLR_School_Librarians_as_Technology_Integration_Leaders_V15.pdf>.

U.S. Department of Education. "Every Student Succeeds Act." <www.ed.gov/essa> (accessed April 28, 2016).

Wine, Lois. 2016. "School Librarians as Technology Leaders: An Evolution in Practice." *Journal of Education for Library & Information Science* 57 (2): 207–20.

DISCLAIMER

Approved June 25, 2016

Preparation of School Librarians

AASL Position Statement

Position

THE AMERICAN ASSOCIATION OF SCHOOL LIBRARIANS (AASL) SUPPORTS THE position that, in addition to meeting state certification requirements, school librarians hold a master's degree or equivalent from a program that combines academic and professional preparation in library and information science, education, and technology. The graduate degree is earned at a college or university whose program is recognized by appropriate bodies such as the American Library Association (ALA), the American Association of School Librarians/Council for the Accreditation of Educator Preparation (CAEP), or state education agencies. The academic program of study includes directed field experience coordinated by a college/university faculty member and takes place in an effective school library program under the direct supervision of a certified, full-time school librarian.

Background

In order to address the critical need for a reading-rich environment in the ever-changing information landscape, the preparation of school librarians is vitally important. As technology has become a crucial element of teaching and learning, school librarians as educators and information specialists play a key role in the success of schools.

Definitions

- *Information Technologies:* Modern information, computer, and communication technology products, services, or tools, including the Internet, computer devices, and other hardware, software applications, data systems, and other electronic content (including multimedia content) and data storage.
- *School Librarian Instructional Role:* See Appendix C3: Instructional Role of the School Librarian Position Statement.

Recommended Reading List

American Association of School Librarians. 2010. ALA/AASL Standards for Initial Preparation of School Librarians. <www.ala.org/aasl/sites/ala.org.aasl/files/content/aasleducation/schoollibrary/2010_standards_with_rubrics_and_statements_1-31-11.pdf> (accessed May 20, 2016).

American Library Association. 2015. "Standards for Accreditation of Master's Programs in Library and Information Studies." <www.ala.org/accredited programs/sites/ala.org.accreditedprograms/files/content/standards/Standards_2015_adopted_02-02-15.pdf> (accessed February 11, 2017).

Council for the Accreditation of Educator Preparation. 2015. "CAEP Accreditation Standards." <www.caepnet.org/~/media/Files/caep/standards/final-board-amended-20150612.pdf> (accessed February 11, 2017).

DISCLAIMER

The position taken by the American Association of School Librarians (AASL) represents the organization and cannot be applied to individual members or groups affiliated with the association without their direct confirmation.

Approved June 25, 2016

Role of the School Library Program
AASL Position Statement

Position

THE AMERICAN ASSOCIATION OF SCHOOL LIBRARIANS (AASL) SUPPORTS THE position that an effective school library program (please see Appendix C1. Definition of an Effective School Library Program) plays a crucial role in preparing learners for informed living in an information-rich society. The school library program provides learning opportunities that enable learners to become efficient, effective, and creative users of information. Further, the school library program encourages learners to examine the authority of authors and the bias of sponsors; to assess the importance of currency of information to the topic at hand; to determine the scope and relevance of information to meet their needs; and to create and share new ideas, resources, products, and information. This instruction occurs best in the context of the school curriculum where learners are guided by a standard of excellence set by their classroom educators in collaboration with the school librarian.

The school library program is not confined by the school library walls, but rather, with the use of technology and online resources, connects to the community and branches throughout the entire school. The school library program provides the mechanism for learners to access the resources they need 24/7, whether in the school library, in the classroom, or in the learner's home.

Beyond its curricular role, the effective school library program gives each individual member of the learning community a venue for exploring questions that arise out of personalized learning, individual curiosity, and personal interest. As part of the school library program, the school librarian provides leadership and instruction to both learners and staff on how to use information technologies constructively, ethically, and safely. The school librarian offers expertise in accessing and evaluating information and collections of quality physical and virtual resources. In addition, the school librarian possesses dispositions that encourage broad and deep exploration of ideas and responsible use of information technologies. These attributes add value to the school community.

School library programs also provide opportunities for learners to read for enjoyment. School librarians' skills in the selection and evaluation of resources are critical in providing learners, staff, and families with open, non-restricted access to a high-quality collection of reading materials that reflect personal interests and academic needs in multiple formats.

School librarians take a leadership role in organizing and promoting literacy projects and events that encourage learners to become lifelong learners and readers.

The school library program is based on long-range goals developed through strategic planning that reflect the mission of the school. The school librarian participates fully in all aspects of the school's instructional program, including federally mandated programs and reform efforts. The school library program provides flexible and equitable access to collections, technology, and a state-certified school librarian for all learners and staff, physically as well as virtually. The collection includes materials that meet the needs of all learners, represents various points of view on current and historical issues, and offers a wide variety of interest areas. Policies, procedures, and guidelines are developed to maintain the effective school library program. The school library staff and budget are sufficient to support the school's instructional program and meet the needs of the school library program's goals.

For learners, the school library represents one of America's most cherished freedoms: the freedom to speak and hear what others have to say. Learners have the right to choose what they will read, view, or hear and are expected to develop the ability to think clearly, critically, and creatively about their choices, rather than allowing others to do this for them.

Background

Citizens of this information world must have the skills and dispositions to access information efficiently and to critically assess the sources they rely upon for decision making, problem solving, and generation of new knowledge. The effective school library program plays a critical role in schools in instructing learners on how to access information efficiently and critically assess resources.

DEFINITIONS

- *Effective School Library Program:* See Appendix C1. Definition of an Effective School Library Program Position Statement.
- *Learning Community:* A group of people (can include learners) who share common academic goals and attitudes who meet regularly to share expertise and work collaboratively to improve instruction and the academic performance of learners (Stronge, Richard and Catano 2008, 7).
- *Information Technologies:* Modern information, computer, and communication technology products, services, or tools, including the Internet, computer devices and other hardware, software applications, data systems, personal electronic devices, and other electronic content (including multimedia content) and data storage.
- *Virtual Resources:* Resources that are not physical in nature, such as computer hardware platforms, operating systems, storage devices, computer network resources, electronic databases, and e-books.

REFERENCES
Stronge, James H., Holly B. Richard, and Nancy Catano. 2008. *Qualities of Effective Principals.* Alexandria: ASCD.

RECOMMENDED READING LIST

Harvey, II, Carl A. 2010. "The Teacher's Take, Part 2: The Instructional Role of the School Librarian." *School Library Monthly* 26 (5): 45–47.

Heindel, Maegan Coffin., et al. 2014. "Demonstrating the Essential Role of the School Librarian." *Knowledge Quest* 42 (3): 74.

Young, Robyn. 2012. "Digital Learning: The Role of the School Librarian." *School Library Monthly* 29 (1):33.

DISCLAIMER

Approved June 25, 2016

APPENDIX D

Library Bill of Rights

THE AMERICAN LIBRARY ASSOCIATION AFFIRMS THAT ALL LIBRARIES ARE forums for information and ideas, and that the following basic policies should guide their services.

    I. Books and other library resources should be provided for the interest, information, and enlightenment of all people of the community the library serves. Materials should not be excluded because of the origin, background, or views of those contributing to their creation.

    II. Libraries should provide materials and information presenting all points of view on current and historical issues. Materials should not be proscribed or removed because of partisan or doctrinal disapproval.

    III. Libraries should challenge censorship in the fulfillment of their responsibility to provide information and enlightenment.

    IV. Libraries should cooperate with all persons and groups concerned with resisting abridgment of free expression and free access to ideas.

    V. A person's right to use a library should not be denied or abridged because of origin, age, background, or views.

    VI. Libraries which make exhibit spaces and meeting rooms available to the public they serve should make such facilities available on an equitable basis, regardless of the beliefs or affiliations of individuals or groups requesting their use.

Adopted June 19, 1939, by the ALA Council; amended October 14, 1944; June 18, 1948; February 2, 1961; June 27, 1967; January 23, 1980; inclusion of "age" reaffirmed January 23, 1996.

Although the Articles of the Library Bill of Rights are unambiguous statements of basic principles that should govern the service of all libraries, questions do arise concerning application of these principles to specific library practices. See the documents designated by the

Intellectual Freedom Committee as *Interpretations of the Library Bill of Rights* <www .ala.org/advocacy/intfreedom/librarybill/interpretations> (Accessed December10, 2016).

A history of the Library Bill of Rights is found in *A History of ALA Policy on Intellectual Freedom: A Supplement to the Intellectual Freedom Manual,* Ninth Edition. (available for purchase from ALA Editions) <www.alastore.ala.org/detail.aspx?ID=11364>.

Interpretations of the Library Bill of Rights

ALTHOUGH THE ARTICLES OF THE LIBRARY BILL OF RIGHTS ARE UNAMBIGU-
ous statements of basic principles that should govern the service of all libraries, questions do arise concerning application of these principles to specific library practices and situations.

These interpretations can be used to advocate for specific approaches to issues that impact school librarianship and school libraries. ALA has developed many interpretations that will help school librarians define stances, policies, and procedures for learners, educators, administrators, and the community.

The documents described below have been designated by the Intellectual Freedom Committee as Interpretations of the Library Bill of Rights and provide background information detailing the philosophy and history of each topic. For convenience and easy reference, the documents are presented in alphabetical order. These documents are policies of the American Library Association, having been adopted by the ALA Council.

Interpretations featured in this document:

APPENDIX E1. *Access for Children and Young Adults to Nonprint Materials:* Library collections of nonprint materials raise a number of intellectual freedom issues, especially regarding minors. Article V of the Library Bill of Rights states, "A person's right to use a library should not be denied or abridged because of origin, age, background, or views." (Adopted June 28, 1989, by the ALA Council; amended June 30, 2004.)

APPENDIX E2. *Access to Resources and Services in the School Library Program:* The school library program plays a unique role in promoting intellectual freedom. It serves as a point of voluntary access to information and ideas and as a learning laboratory for learners as they acquire critical-thinking and problem-solving skills needed in a pluralistic, global society. Although the educational level and program of the school necessarily shapes the resources and services of a school library program, the principles of the Library Bill of Rights apply equally to all libraries, including school libraries. (Adopted July 2, 1986, by the ALA Council; amended January 10, 1990; July 12, 2000; January 19, 2005; July 2, 2008; and July 1, 2014.)

APPENDIX E3. *Advocating for Intellectual Freedom:* Educating the American public, including library staff, on the value of intellectual freedom is fundamental to the mission of libraries of all types. Intellectual freedom is a universal human right that involves both physical and intellectual access to information and ideas. Libraries provide physical access through facilities, resources, and services, and foster awareness of intellectual freedom rights within the context of educational programs and instruction in essential information-literacy skills. (Adopted July 15, 2009, by the ALA Council; amended July 1, 2014.)

APPENDIX E4. *Challenged Resources:* The American Library Association declares as a matter of firm principle that it is the responsibility of every library to have a clearly defined materials selection policy in written form that reflects the Library Bill of Rights, and that is approved by the appropriate governing authority. (Adopted June 25, 1971; amended July 1, 1981; January 10, 1990; January 28, 2009, and July 1, 2014, by the ALA Council.)

APPENDIX E5. *Diversity in Collection Development:* Intellectual freedom, the essence of equitable library services, provides for free access to all expressions of ideas through which any and all sides of a question, cause, or movement may be explored. Toleration is meaningless without tolerance for what some may consider detestable. Librarians cannot justly permit their own preferences to limit their degree of tolerance in collection development because freedom is indivisible. (Adopted July 14, 1982, by the ALA Council; amended January 10, 1990; July 2, 2008; and July 1, 2014.)

APPENDIX E6. *Internet Filtering:* In the span of a single generation the Internet has revolutionized the basic functions and operations of libraries and schools, and expanded exponentially both the opportunities and challenges these institutions face in serving their users. During this time, many schools and libraries in the United States have installed content filters on their Internet access. This filtering is done for a variety of reasons, including the requirement to comply with the Children's Internet Protection Act (CIPA) to be eligible to receive federal funding through the Library Services and Technology Act and Title III of the Elementary and Secondary Education Act, or discounts through the Universal Service discount program (E-rate). Filtering is also implemented to comply with state filtering requirements that may also be tied to state funding. The rationale for filtering is that filtered access is better than no access. (Adopted June 30, 2015, by the ALA Council.)

APPENDIX E7. *Privacy:* Privacy is essential to the exercise of free speech, free thought, and free association. (Adopted June 19, 2002, by the ALA Council; amended on July 1, 2014.)

Please consult the ALA website for the most current versions and most complete list of Interpretations of the Library Bill of Rights <**www.ala.org/advocacy/intfreedom/ librarybill/interpretations**> (accessed February 1, 2017).

Access to Digital Information, Services, and Networks

Freedom of expression is an inalienable human right and the foundation for self-government. Freedom of expression encompasses the freedom of speech and the corollary right to receive information. Libraries and librarians protect and promote these rights by selecting, producing, providing access to, identifying, retrieving, organizing, providing instruction in the use of, and preserving recorded expression regardless of the format or technology. (Adopted January 24, 1996; amended January 19, 2005; and July 15, 2009, by the ALA Council.)

Access to Library Resources and Services for Minors

Library policies and procedures that effectively deny minors equal and equitable access to all library resources available to other users violate the Library Bill of Rights. The American Library Association opposes all attempts to restrict access to library services, materials, and facilities based on the age of library users. (Adopted June 30, 1972, by the ALA Council; amended July 1, 1981; July 3, 1991; June 30, 2004; July 2, 2008 under previous name "Free Access to Libraries for Minors"; and July 1, 2014.)

Access to Library Resources and Services Regardless of Sex, Gender Identity, Gender Expression, or Sexual Orientation

The American Library Association stringently and unequivocally maintains that libraries and librarians have an obligation to resist efforts that systematically exclude materials dealing with any subject matter, including sex, gender identity, or sexual orientation. Librarians have a professional obligation to ensure that all library users have free and equal access to the entire range of library services, materials, and programs.

Economic Barriers to Information Access

A democracy presupposes an informed citizenry. The First Amendment to the U.S. Constitution mandates the right of all persons to free expression, and the corollary right to receive the constitutionally protected expression of others. The publicly supported library provides free, equal, and equitable access to information for all people of the community the library serves. While the roles, goals, and objectives of publicly supported libraries may differ, they share this common mission. (Adopted June 30, 1993, by the ALA Council.)

Evaluating Library Collections

The continuous review of library materials is necessary as a means of maintaining an active library collection of current interest to users. In the process, materials may be added, and physically deteriorated or obsolete materials may be replaced or removed in accordance with the collection maintenance policy of the library and the needs of the community it serves. Continued evaluation is closely related to the goals and responsibilities of all libraries and is a valuable tool in collection development. This procedure is not to be used as a convenient means to remove materials presumed to be controversial or disapproved of by segments of the community. (Adopted February 2, 1973, by the ALA Council; amended July 1, 1981; June 2, 2008.)

Exhibit Spaces and Bulletin Boards

Libraries often provide exhibit spaces and bulletin boards. The uses made of these spaces should conform to the Library Bill of Rights. Article I includes the statement, "Materials should not be excluded because of the origin, background, or views of those contributing to their creation." Article II states in part, "Materials should not be proscribed or removed because of partisan or doctrinal disapproval." Article VI maintains that exhibit space should be made available "on an equitable basis, regardless of the beliefs or affiliations of individuals or groups requesting their use." (Adopted July 2, 1991, by the ALA Council; amended June 30, 2004, and July 1, 2014.)

Expurgation of Library Materials

Expurgating library materials is a violation of the Library Bill of Rights. Expurgation as defined by this interpretation includes any deletion, excision, alteration, editing, or obliteration of any part of books or other library resources by the library, its agent, or its parent institution (if any). (Adopted February 2, 1973, by the ALA Council; amended July 1, 1981; January 10, 1990; July 2, 2008; and July 1, 2014.)

Importance of Education to Intellectual Freedom

Through education, programming, and instruction in information skills, libraries empower individuals to explore ideas, access and evaluate information, draw meaning from information presented in a variety of formats, develop valid conclusions, and express new ideas. Such education facilitates intellectual access to information and offers a path to intellectual freedom.

Intellectual Freedom Principles for Academic Libraries

A strong intellectual freedom perspective is critical to the development of academic library collections and services that dispassionately meet the education and research needs of a college or university community. The purpose of this statement is to outline how and where intellectual freedom principles fit into an academic library setting, thereby raising consciousness of the intellectual freedom context within which academic librarians work. (Approved by ACRL Board of Directors: June 29, 1999 and adopted July 12, 2000, by the ALA Council; amended on July 1, 2014.)

Labeling Systems

The American Library Association affirms the rights of individuals to form their own opinions about resources they choose to read, view, listen to, or otherwise access. Libraries do not advocate the ideas found in their collections or in resources accessible through the library. The presence of books and other resources in a library does not indicate endorsement of their contents by the library or librarian. Likewise, providing access to digital information does not indicate endorsement or approval of that information by the library or librarian. Labeling systems are not consistent with these principles of intellectual freedom. (Adopted on June 30, 2015, by ALA Council.)

Library-Initiated Programs as a Resource

Library-initiated programs support the mission of the library by providing users with additional opportunities for acquiring information, furthering their educations, and enjoying recreation. (Adopted January 27, 1982, by the ALA Council; amended June 26, 1990; July 12, 2000.)

Meeting Rooms

As part of their services, many libraries provide meeting rooms for individuals and groups. Article VI of the Library Bill of Rights states in part that such facilities should be made available to the public served by the given library "on an equitable basis, regardless of the beliefs or affiliations of individuals or groups requesting their use." (Adopted July 2, 1991, by the ALA Council.)

Minors and Internet Activity

The digital environment offers opportunities both for accessing information created by others and for creating and sharing new information. The rights of minors in schools and libraries to retrieve, interact with, and create information posted on the Internet are extensions of their First Amendment rights. (Adopted July 15, 2009, by the ALA Council; amended on July 1, 2014.)

Prisoners' Right to Read

The American Library Association asserts a compelling public interest in the preservation of intellectual freedom for individuals of any age held in jails, prisons, detention facilities, juvenile facilities, immigration facilities, prison work camps, and segregated units within any facility. (Adopted June 29, 2010, by the ALA Council.)

Rating Systems

Libraries, no matter their size, contain an enormous wealth of viewpoints and are responsible for making those viewpoints available to all. However, libraries do not advocate or endorse the content found in their collections or in resources made accessible through the library. Rating systems appearing in library public access catalogs or resource discovery tools conflict with these principles of intellectual freedom. (Adopted on June 30, 2015, by ALA Council.)

Religion in American Libraries

The First Amendment guarantees the right of individuals to believe and practice their religion or practice no religion at all, and prohibits government from establishing or endorsing a religion or religions. Librarians have a professional responsibility to be inclusive rather than exclusive in collection development. Libraries serve all members of their communities and within their budgetary constraints should address all information concerns of all members—including their religious information needs. Collections should reflect those needs by providing access to diverse religious thought without becoming a proponent of any of them. (Adopted June, 2016, by the ALA Council.)

Restricted Access to Library Materials

Libraries are a traditional forum for the open exchange of information. Attempts to restrict access to library materials violate the basic tenets of the Library Bill of Rights. (Adopted February 2, 1973, by the ALA Council; amended July 1, 1981; July 3, 1991; July 12, 2000; June 30, 2004; January 28, 2009; and July 1, 2014.)

Services to People with Disabilities

ALA recognizes that persons with disabilities are a large and often neglected part of society. In addition to many personal challenges, some persons with disabilities face economic inequity, illiteracy, cultural isolation, and discrimination in education, employment, and the broad range of societal activities. The library plays a catalytic role in their lives by facilitating their full participation in society. (Adopted January 28, 2009, by the ALA Council.)

Universal Right to Free Expression

Freedom of expression is an inalienable human right and the foundation for self-government. Freedom of expression encompasses the freedoms of speech, press, religion, assembly, and association, and the corollary right to receive information. (Adopted January 16, 1991, by the ALA Council; amended on July 1, 2014.)

User-Generated Content in Library Discovery Systems

If a publicly funded library by policy or practice chooses to invite everyone to contribute user-generated content to the library's discovery system, the library then may not limit or exclude a particular user's content based upon the content's subject or viewpoint. Publicly funded libraries may define the time, place, or manner in which the user contributes the content to the library's discovery system. Such restrictions must be reasonable and cannot be based upon the beliefs or affiliations of the user or the views expressed in the user-generated content. (Adopted January 12, 2016, by the ALA Council.)

A history of the Library Bill of Rights is found in *A History of ALA Policy on Intellectual Freedom: A Supplement to the Intellectual Freedom Manual,* Ninth Edition. (available for purchase from ALA Editions) <**www.alastore.ala.org/detail.aspx?ID=11364**>.

Access for Children and Young Adults to Nonprint Materials

An Interpretation of the Library Bill of Rights

LIBRARY COLLECTIONS OF NONPRINT MATERIALS RAISE A NUMBER OF INTEL-lectual freedom issues, especially regarding minors. Article V of the Library Bill of Rights states, "A person's right to use a library should not be denied or abridged because of origin, age, background, or views" (ALA 1980).

The American Library Association's principles protect minors' access to sound, images, data, games, software, and other content in all formats such as tapes, CDs, DVDs, music CDs, computer games, software, databases, and other emerging technologies. ALA's Free Access to Libraries for Minors: An Interpretation of the Library Bill of Rights states:

> . . . The "right to use a library" includes free access to, and unrestricted use of, all the services, materials, and facilities the library has to offer. Every restriction on access to, and use of, library resources, based solely on the chronological age, educational level, literacy skills, or legal emancipation of users violates Article V.
>
> . . . [P]arents—and only parents—have the right and responsibility to restrict access of their children—and only their children—to library resources. Parents who do not want their children to have access to certain library services, materials, or facilities should so advise their children. Librarians and library governing bodies cannot assume the role of parents or the functions of parental authority in the private relationship between parent and child. (ALA 2004)

Lack of access to information can be harmful to minors. Librarians and library governing bodies have a public and professional obligation to ensure that all members of the community they serve have free, equal, and equitable access to the entire range of library resources regardless of content, approach, format, or amount of detail. This principle of library service applies equally to all users, minors as well as adults. Librarians and library governing bodies must uphold this principle in order to provide adequate and effective service to minors.

Policies that set minimum age limits for access to any nonprint materials or information technology, with or without parental permission, abridge library use for minors. Age limits based on the cost of the materials are also unacceptable. Librarians, when dealing with minors, should apply the same standards to circulation of nonprint materials as are applied to books and other print materials except when directly and specifically prohibited by law.

Recognizing that librarians cannot act in loco parentis, ALA acknowledges and supports the exercise by parents of their responsibility to guide their own children's reading and viewing. Libraries should provide published reviews and/or reference works that contain information about the content, subject matter, and recommended audiences for nonprint materials. These resources will assist parents in guiding their children without implicating the library in censorship.

In some cases, commercial content ratings, such as the Motion Picture Association of America (MPAA) movie ratings, might appear on the packaging or promotional materials provided by producers or distributors. However, marking out or removing this information from materials or packaging constitutes expurgation or censorship.

MPAA movie ratings, Entertainment Software Rating Board (ESRB) game ratings, and other rating services are private advisory codes and have no legal standing (ALA 1990). For the library to add ratings to nonprint materials if they are not already there is unacceptable. It is also unacceptable to post a list of such ratings with a collection or to use them in circulation policies or other procedures. These uses constitute labeling, "an attempt to prejudice attitudes" (ALA 2005), and are forms of censorship. The application of locally generated ratings schemes intended to provide content warnings to library users is also inconsistent with the Library Bill of Rights.

The interests of young people, like those of adults, are not limited by subject, theme, or level of sophistication. Librarians have a responsibility to ensure young people's access to materials and services that reflect diversity of content and format sufficient to meet their needs.

REFERENCES

American Library Association. 1980. "Library Bill of Rights." <www.ala.org/advocacy/intfreedom/librarybill> (accessed March 14, 2017).

———. 1990. "Expurgation of Library Materials: An Interpretation of the Library Bill of Rights." <www.ala.org/Template.cfm?Section=interpretations&Template=/ContentManagement/ContentDisplay.cfm&ContentID=8540> (accessed March 14, 2017).

———. 2004. "Free Access to Libraries for Minors: An Interpretation of the Library Bill of Rights." <www.ala.org/Template.cfm?Section=interpretations&Template=/ContentManagement/ContentDisplay.cfm&ContentID=8639> (accessed March 14, 2017).

———. 2005. "Labels and Rating Systems: An Interpretation of the Library Bill of Rights." <www.ala.org/Template.cfm?Section=interpretations&Template=/ContentManagement/ContentDisplay.cfm&ContentID=8657> (accessed March 14, 2017).

Adopted June 28, 1989, by the ALA Council; amended June 30, 2004.

Access to Resources and Services in the School Library Program

An Interpretation of the Library Bill of Rights

THE SCHOOL LIBRARY PLAYS A UNIQUE ROLE IN PROMOTING, PROTECTING, and educating about intellectual freedom. It serves as a point of voluntary access to information and ideas and as a learning laboratory for learners as they acquire critical thinking and problem-solving skills needed in a pluralistic society. Although the educational level and program of the school necessarily shape the resources and services of a school library, the principles of the American Library Association's Library Bill of Rights apply equally to all libraries, including school libraries. Under these principles, all learners have equitable access to school library facilities, resources, and instructional programs.

School librarians assume a leadership role in promoting the principles of intellectual freedom within the school by providing resources and services that create and sustain an atmosphere of free inquiry. School librarians work closely with educators to integrate instructional activities in classroom units designed to equip learners to locate, evaluate, and use a broad range of ideas effectively. Intellectual freedom is fostered by educating learners in the use of critical thinking skills to empower them to pursue free inquiry responsibly and independently. Through resources, programming, and educational processes, learners and educators experience the free and robust debate characteristic of a democratic society.

School librarians cooperate with other individuals in building collections of resources that meet the needs as well as the developmental and maturity levels of learners. These collections provide resources that support the mission of the school district and are consistent with its philosophy, goals, and objectives. Resources in school library collections are an integral component of the curriculum and represent diverse points of view on both current and historical issues. These resources include materials that support the intellectual growth, personal development, individual interests, and recreational needs of learners.

While English is, by history and tradition, the customary language of the United States, the languages in use in any given community may vary. Schools serving communities in which other languages are used make efforts to accommodate the needs of learners for whom English is a second language. To support these efforts, and to ensure equitable access to resources and services, the school library provides resources that reflect the linguistic pluralism of the community.

Members of the school community involved in the collection development process employ educational criteria to select resources unfettered by their personal, political, social, or religious views. Learners and educators served by the school library have access to resources and services free of constraints resulting from personal, partisan, or doctrinal disapproval. School librarians resist efforts by individuals or groups to define what is appropriate for all learners or educators to read, view, hear, or access regardless of technology, formats or method of delivery.

Major barriers between learners and resources include but are not limited: to imposing age, grade-level, or reading-level restrictions on the use of resources; limiting the use of interlibrary loan and access to electronic information; charging fees for information in specific formats; requiring permission from parents or educators; establishing restricted shelves or closed collections; and labeling. Policies, procedures, and rules related to the use of resources and services support free and open access to information.

It is the responsibility of the governing board to adopt policies that guarantee learners access to a broad range of ideas. These include policies on collection development and procedures for the review of resources about which concerns have been raised. Such policies, developed by persons in the school community, provide for a timely and fair hearing and assure that procedures are applied equitably to all expressions of concern. It is the responsibility of school librarians to implement district policies and procedures in the school to ensure equitable access to resources and services for all learners.

Adopted July 2, 1986, by the ALA Council; amended January 10, 1990; July 12, 2000; January 19, 2005; July 2, 2008; and July 1, 2014.

Advocating for Intellectual Freedom

An Interpretation of the Library Bill of Rights

EDUCATING THE AMERICAN PUBLIC, INCLUDING LIBRARY STAFF, ON THE value of intellectual freedom is fundamental to the mission of libraries of all types. Intellectual freedom is a universal human right that involves both physical and intellectual access to information and ideas. Libraries provide physical access through facilities, resources, and services and foster awareness of intellectual freedom rights within the context of educational programs and instruction in essential information skills.

The universal freedom to express information and ideas is stated in the Universal Declaration of Human Rights, Article 19:

> Everyone has the right to freedom of opinion and expression; this right includes freedom to hold opinions without interference and to seek, receive, and impart information and ideas through any media and regardless of frontiers.

The importance of education to the development of intellectual freedom is expressed in the Universal Declaration of Human Rights, Article 26:

1. Everyone has the right to education. Education shall be free, at least in the elementary and fundamental stages.
2. Education shall be directed to the full development of the human personality and to the strengthening of respect for human rights and fundamental freedoms. It shall promote understanding, tolerance and friendship among all nations, racial, or religious groups, and shall further the activities of the United Nations for the maintenance of peace.

In addition, Article I of the American Library Association's Library Bill of Rights "affirms that all libraries are forums for information and ideas." Physical access to information is listed as the first principle:

> Books and other library resources should be provided for the interest, information, and enlightenment of all people of the community the library serves. Materials should not be excluded because of the origin, background, or views of those contributing to their creation.

Article II of the Library Bill of Rights emphasizes the importance of fostering intellectual access to information by providing materials that allow users to evaluate content and context and find information representing multiple points of view:

> Libraries should provide materials and information presenting all points of view on current and historical issues. Materials should not be proscribed or removed because of partisan or doctrinal disapproval.

Libraries of all types foster education by promoting the free expression and interchange of ideas, leading to empowered lifelong learners. Libraries use resources, programming, and services to strengthen intellectual and physical access to information and thus build a foundation of intellectual freedom: developing collections (both real and virtual) with multiple perspectives and individual needs of users in mind; providing programming and instructional services framed around equitable access to information and ideas; and teaching information skills and intellectual freedom rights integrated appropriately throughout the spectrum of library programming.

Through educational programming and instruction in information skills, libraries empower individuals to explore ideas, access and evaluate information, draw meaning from information presented in a variety of formats, develop valid conclusions, and express new ideas. Such education facilitates intellectual access to information and offers a path to a robust appreciation of intellectual freedom rights.

Adopted July 15, 2009, by the ALA Council; amended July 1, 2014.

APPENDIX E4

Challenged Resources
An Interpretation of the Library Bill of Rights

"LIBRARIES: AN AMERICAN VALUE" STATES, "WE PROTECT THE RIGHTS OF individuals to express their opinions about library resources and services." The American Library Association declares as a matter of firm principle that it is the responsibility of every library to have a clearly defined written policy for collection development that includes a procedure for review of challenged resources. Collection development applies to print and media resources or formats in the physical collection. It also applies to digital resources such as databases, e-books and other downloadable and streaming media.

Content filtering is not equivalent to collection development. Content filtering is exclusive, not inclusive, and cannot effectively curate content or mediate access to resources available on the Internet. This should be addressed separately in the library's acceptable use policy. These policies reflect the American Library Association's Library Bill of Rights and are approved by the appropriate governing authority.

Challenged resources should remain in the collection and accessible during the review process. The Library Bill of Rights states in Article I that "Materials should not be excluded because of the origin, background, or views of those contributing to their creation," and in Article II, that "Materials should not be proscribed or removed because of partisan or doctrinal disapproval." Freedom of expression is protected by the Constitution of the United States, but constitutionally protected expression is often separated from unprotected expression only by a dim and uncertain line. The Supreme Court has held that the Constitution requires a procedure designed to examine critically all challenged expression before it can be suppressed.[1] This procedure should be open, transparent, and conform to all applicable open meeting and public records laws. Resources that meet the criteria for selection and inclusion within the collection should not be removed.

Therefore, any attempt, be it legal or extra-legal,[2] to regulate or suppress resources in libraries must be closely scrutinized to the end that protected expression is not abridged.

NOTES

1. Bantam Books, Inc. v. Sullivan, 372 U.S. 58 (1963).
2. "Extra-legal" refers to actions that are not regulated or sanctioned by law. These can include attempts to remove or suppress materials by library staff

and library board members that circumvent the library's collection development policy, or actions taken by elected officials or library board members outside the established legal process for making legislative or board decisions. "Legal process" includes challenges to library materials initiated and conducted pursuant to the library's collection development policy, actions taken by legislative bodies or library boards during official sessions or meetings, or litigation undertaken in courts of law with jurisdiction over the library and the library's governing body.

Adopted June 25, 1971; amended July 1, 1981; January 10, 1990; January 28, 2009, and July 1, 2014, by the ALA Council.

Diversity in Collection Development
An Interpretation of the Library Bill of Rights

COLLECTION DEVELOPMENT SHOULD REFLECT THE PHILOSOPHY inherent in Article II of the American Library Association's Library Bill of Rights: "Libraries should provide materials and information presenting all points of view on current and historical issues. Materials should not be proscribed or removed because of partisan or doctrinal disapproval."

Library collections must represent the diversity of people and ideas in our society. There are many complex facets to any issue, and many contexts in which issues may be expressed, discussed, or interpreted. Librarians have an obligation to select and support access to content on all subjects that meet, as closely as possible, the needs, interests, and abilities of all persons in the community the library serves.

Librarians have a professional responsibility to be inclusive in collection development and in the provision of interlibrary loan. Access to all content legally obtainable should be assured to the user, and policies should not unjustly exclude content even if it is offensive to the librarian or the user. This includes content that reflect a diversity of issues, whether they be, for example, political, economic, religious, social, ethnic, or sexual. A balanced collection reflects a diversity of content, not an equality of numbers.

Collection development responsibilities include selecting content in different formats produced by independent, small and local producers as well as information resources from major producers and distributors. Content should represent the languages commonly used in the library's service community and should include formats that meet the needs of users with disabilities. Collection development and the selection of content should be done according to professional standards and established selection and review procedures. Failure to select resources merely because they may be potentially controversial is censorship, as is withdrawing resources for the same reason.

Over time, individuals, groups, and entities have sought to limit the diversity of library collections. They cite a variety of reasons that include prejudicial language and ideas, political content, economic theory, social philosophies, religious beliefs, sexual content and expression, and other potentially controversial topics. Librarians have a professional responsibility to be fair, just, and equitable and to give all library users equal protection in guarding against violation of the library patron's right to read, view, or listen to content protected by the First Amendment, no matter what the viewpoint of the author, creator, or selector. Librarians have an obligation to protect library collections from removal of content based on personal bias or prejudice.

Intellectual freedom, the essence of equitable library services, provides for free access to all expressions of ideas through which any and all sides of a question, cause, or movement may be explored. Librarians must not permit their personal beliefs to influence collection development decisions.

Adopted July 14, 1982, by the ALA Council; amended January 10, 1990; July 2, 2008; and July 1, 2014.

See also Diversity Standards: Cultural Competency for Academic Libraries (2012) <www .ala.org/acrl/standards/diversity> (accessed February 11, 2017).

APPENDIX E6

Internet Filtering
An Interpretation of the Library Bill of Rights

IN THE SPAN OF A SINGLE GENERATION, THE INTERNET HAS REVOLUTIONIZED the basic functions and operations of libraries and schools and expanded exponentially both the opportunities and challenges these institutions face in serving their users. During this time, many schools and libraries in the United States have installed content filters on their Internet access. They have done so for a variety of reasons, not least of which is the requirement to comply with the Children's Internet Protection Act (CIPA) in order to be eligible to receive federal funding or discounts through the Library Services and Technology Act, Title III of the Elementary and Secondary Education Act, and the Universal Service discount program (E-rate), or to comply with state filtering requirements that may also be tied to state funding. Their rationale for filtering is that it is better to have filtered access than no access.

CIPA specifically requires public libraries and schools seeking e-rate discounts for Internet connections to install technology protection measures, i.e., content filters, to block two categories of visual images that are unprotected by the First Amendment: obscene images and images of child pornography. These are categories of images the Supreme Court has consistently ruled outside the constitutional protection of the First Amendment. CIPA also requires those libraries and schools to block a third category of images for minors under the age of 17 that courts deem "harmful for minors" that are constitutionally protected for adults but not for minors. CIPA does not require libraries and schools to block any other constitutionally protected categories of images, or any constitutionally protected categories of speech.

Research demonstrates that filters consistently both over- and underblock the content they claim to filter. Filters often block adults and minors from access to a wide range of constitutionally protected speech. Content filters are unreliable because computer code and algorithms are still unable to adequately interpret, assess, and categorize the complexities of human communication whether expressed in text or image. In the case of websites containing sexually explicit images, the success rate of filters is frequently no greater than chance. In addition, the use of content filters cedes vital library and school resource and service decisions to external parties (private companies and contractors) who then exercise unknown and unaccountable influence over basic functions of the library or school and users' access to library or school resources and services (Batch 2014). In addition to this research, the experience of librarians and educators working within the constraints of CIPA suggests that filters are unreliable and routinely circumvented by technologically adept users.

Most content filters are designed and marketed for a much larger market than libraries and schools, and offer options for filtering wide categories of protected speech such as objectionable language, violence, and unpopular or controversial opinion, as well as entire categories of Internet-based services such as e-mail and social media. In addition, many content filters operate on an "opt out" model where the filter defaults "on" unless the user is given the option to shut it off. Categories frequently are set to default to the most stringent settings and may only be adjusted by administrative intervention.

Unblocking for adults on request was a key factor in the Supreme Court decision to uphold CIPA in public libraries (US v. ALA 2003). This has proved to be equivocal in actual practice in some libraries, because of the unwillingness or inability of libraries to unblock when requested, especially when system administrators may be outside of library administrative control. While some filtering systems allow librarians at the local or end user level to modify the filter settings, others restrict that authorization to the highest administrative levels, creating lengthy delays in the processing of user requests to unblock erroneously filtered content.

This same situation also occurs in schools. Such delays represent de facto blocking for both library users and K-12 learners, because most users rarely have the flexibility or time to wait hours or even days for resources to become available. This dilemma is exacerbated by the secrecy surrounding category definitions and settings maintained by the filtering industry, frequently under the guise of trade secrets. There are also issues of user privacy when users must identify themselves and their interests when asking for specific websites to be unblocked. Certainly, both adults and learners researching highly personal or controversial topics will be reluctant to subject themselves to administrative review in order to have access to information that should be freely available to them.

In schools, the CIPA requirements have frequently been misinterpreted with the result of overly restrictive filtering that blocks many constitutionally protected images and texts. Educators are unable to use the wealth of Internet resources for instruction, and minor learners are blocked from content relevant to their school assignments and personal interests. Interactive websites and social media sites are frequently restricted, and are thus unavailable to educators for developing assignments that teach learners to live and work in the global digital environment. In many cases learners are prevented from creating and sharing their documents, videos, graphics, music and other original content with classmates or the wider world; thus, valuable learning opportunities are lost. These situations occur in schools when school librarians, educators and educational considerations are excluded from the development and implementation of appropriate, least-restrictive filtering policies and procedures. Minor learners and the school librarians and educators who are responsible for their learning experience, should not be blocked from accessing websites or web-based services that provide constitutionally protected content that meets educational needs or personal interests even though some may find that content objectionable or offensive. Minors and the adult educators who instruct them should be able to request the unblocking of websites that do not fall under the categories of images required to be filtered under the Children's Internet Protection Act.

CIPA-mandated content filtering has had three significant impacts in our schools and libraries. First, it has widened the divide between those who can afford to pay for personal access and those who must depend on publicly funded (and filtered) access. Second, when content filtering is deployed to limit access to what some may consider objectionable or offensive, often minority viewpoints religions, or controversial topics are included in the categories of what is considered objectionable or offensive. Filters thus become the tool of bias and discrimination and marginalize users by denying or abridging their access to these materials. Finally, when over-blocking occurs in public libraries and schools, library users, educators, and learners who lack other means of access to the Internet are limited to the content allowed by unpredictable and unreliable filters.

The negative effects of content filters on Internet access in public libraries and schools are demonstrable and documented. Consequently, consistent with previous resolutions, the American Library Association cannot recommend filtering (ALA 1997, 2001). However, the ALA recognizes that local libraries and schools are governed by local decision makers and local considerations and often must rely on federal or state funding for computers and Internet access. Because adults and, to a lesser degree minors, have First Amendment rights, libraries and schools that choose to use content filters should implement policies and procedures that mitigate the negative effects of filtering to the greatest extent possible. The process should encourage and allow users to ask for filtered websites and content to be unblocked, with minimal delay and due respect for user privacy.

REFERENCES

United States v. American Library Association, Inc. 2003. 539 U.S. 194.

American Library Association. 1997. "Resolution on the Use of Filtering Software in Libraries" <www.ala.org/advocacy/intfreedom/statementspols/ifresolutions/resolutionuse> (accessed March 14, 2017).

———. 2001. "Resolution on Opposition to Federally Mandated Internet Filtering." <www.ala.org/advocacy/intfreedom/statementspols/ifresolutions/resolutionopposition> (accessed March 14, 2017).

Kristen R. Batch. 2014. *Fencing Out Knowledge: Impacts of the Children's Internet Protection Act 10 Years Later.* <http://connect.ala.org/files/cipa_report.pdf> (accessed March 14, 2017).

Adopted June 30, 2015, by the ALA Council.

APPENDIX E7

Privacy

An Interpretation of the Library Bill of Rights

INTRODUCTION

PRIVACY IS ESSENTIAL TO THE EXERCISE OF FREE SPEECH, FREE thought, and free association. The courts have established a First Amendment right to receive information in a publicly funded library.[1] Further, the courts have upheld the right to privacy based on the Bill of Rights of the U.S. Constitution.[2] Many states provide guarantees of privacy in their constitutions and statute law.[3] Numerous decisions in case law have defined and extended rights to privacy.[4]

In a library (physical or virtual), the right to privacy is the right to open inquiry without having the subject of one's interest examined or scrutinized by others. Confidentiality exists when a library is in possession of personally identifiable information about users and keeps that information private on their behalf.[5] Confidentiality extends to "information sought or received and resources consulted, borrowed, acquired or transmitted" (see Appendix G ALA Code of Ethics featured in this volume), including, but not limited to: database search records, reference questions and interviews, circulation records, interlibrary loan records, information about materials downloaded or placed on "hold" or "reserve," and other personally identifiable information about uses of library materials, programs, facilities, or services.

Protecting user privacy and confidentiality has long been an integral part of the mission of libraries. The ALA has affirmed a right to privacy since 1939.[6] Existing ALA policies affirm that confidentiality is crucial to freedom of inquiry.[7] Rights to privacy and confidentiality also are implicit in the Library Bill of Rights' guarantee of free access to library resources for all users.[8]

Rights of Library Users

The *Library Bill of Rights* affirms the ethical imperative to provide unrestricted access to information and to guard against impediments to open inquiry. Article IV states: "Libraries should cooperate with all persons and groups concerned with resisting abridgement of free expression and free access to ideas." When users recognize or fear that their privacy or confidentiality is compromised, true freedom of inquiry no longer exists.

In all areas of librarianship, best practice leaves the user in control of as many choices as possible. These include decisions about the selection of, access to, and use of information. Lack of privacy and confidentiality has a chilling effect on users' choices. All users have a right to be free from any unreasonable intrusion into or surveillance of their lawful library use.

Users have the right to be informed what policies and procedures govern the amount and retention of personally identifiable information, why that information is necessary for the library, and what the user can do to maintain his or her privacy. Library users expect and in many places have a legal right to have their information protected and kept private and confidential by anyone with direct or indirect access to that information. In addition, Article V of the *Library Bill of Rights* states: "A person's right to use a library should not be denied or abridged because of origin, age, background, or views." This article precludes the use of profiling as a basis for any breach of privacy rights. Users have the right to use a library without any abridgement of privacy that may result from equating the subject of their inquiry with behavior.[9]

Responsibilities in Libraries

The library profession has a long-standing commitment to an ethic of facilitating, not monitoring, access to information. This commitment is implemented locally through the adoption of and adherence to library privacy policies that are consistent with applicable federal, state, and local law.

Everyone (paid or unpaid) who provides governance, administration, or service in libraries has a responsibility to maintain an environment respectful and protective of the privacy of all users. Users have the responsibility to respect each others' privacy.

For administrative purposes, librarians may establish appropriate time, place, and manner restrictions on the use of library resources.[10] In keeping with this principle, the collection of personally identifiable information should only be a matter of routine or policy when necessary for the fulfillment of the mission of the library. Regardless of the technology used, everyone who collects or accesses personally identifiable information in any format has a legal and ethical obligation to protect confidentiality.

Libraries should not share personally identifiable user information with third parties or with vendors that provide resources and library services unless the library has obtained the permission of the user or has entered into a legal agreement with the vendor. Such agreements should stipulate that the library retains control of the information, that the information is confidential, and that it may not be used or shared except with the permission of the library.

Law enforcement agencies and officers may occasionally believe that library records contain information that would be helpful to the investigation of criminal activity. The American judicial system provides a mechanism for seeking release of such confidential records: a court order issued following a showing of good cause based on specific facts by a court of competent jurisdiction. Libraries should make such records available only in response to properly executed orders.

Conclusion

The American Library Association affirms that rights of privacy are necessary for intellectual freedom and are fundamental to the ethics and practice of librarianship.

NOTES

1. Court opinions establishing a right to receive information in a public library include *Board of Education. v. Pico*, 457 U.S. 853 (1982); *Kreimer v. Bureau of Police for the Town of Morristown*, 958 F.2d 1242 (3d Cir. 1992); and *Reno v. American Civil Liberties Union*, 117 S.Ct. 2329, 138 L.Ed.2d 874 (1997).

2. See in particular the Fourth Amendment's guarantee of "[t]he right of the people to be secure in their persons, houses, papers, and effects, against unreasonable searches and seizures," the Fifth Amendment's guarantee against self-incrimination, and the Ninth Amendment's guarantee that "[t]he enumeration in the Constitution, of certain rights, shall not be construed to deny or disparage others retained by the people." This right is explicit in Article Twelve of the United Nations' Universal Declaration of Human Rights <www.un.org/Overview/rights .html>: "No one shall be subjected to arbitrary interference with his privacy, family, home or correspondence, nor to attacks upon his honour and reputation. Everyone has the right to the protection of the law against such interference or attacks." See: This right has further been explicitly codified as Article Seventeen of the International Covenant on Civil and Political Rights <www.ohchr.org/EN/ ProfessionalInterest/Pages/CCPR.aspx>, a legally binding international human rights agreement ratified by the United States on June 8, 1992.

3. Ten state constitutions guarantee a right of privacy or bar unreasonable intrusions into citizens' privacy. Forty-eight states protect the confidentiality of library users' records by law, and the attorneys general in the remaining two states have issued opinions recognizing the privacy of users' library records. See: <www.ala .org/advocacy/privacyconfidentiality/privacy/stateprivacy>.

4. Cases recognizing a right to privacy include: *NAACP v. Alabama*, 357 U.S. 449 (1958); *Griswold v. Connecticut* 381 U.S. 479 (1965); *Katz v. United States*, 389 U.S. 347 (1967); and *Stanley v. Georgia*, 394 U.S. 557 (1969). Congress recognized the right to privacy in the Privacy Act of 1974 and Amendments (5 USC Sec. 552a), which addresses the potential for government's violation of privacy through its collection of personal information. The Privacy Act's "Congressional Findings and Statement of Purpose" states in part: "the right to privacy is a personal and fundamental right protected by the Constitution of the United States." See: <caselaw.lp.findlaw.com/scripts/ts_search.pl?title=5&sec=552a>.

5. The phrase "personally identifiable information" was established in ALA policy in 1991. Personally identifiable information can include many types of library records, including: information that the library requires an individual to provide in order to be eligible to use library services or borrow materials, information

that identifies an individual as having requested or obtained specific materials or materials on a particular subject, and information that is provided by an individual to assist a library staff member to answer a specific question or provide information on a particular subject. Personally identifiable information does not include information that does not identify any individual and that is retained only for the purpose of studying or evaluating the use of a library and its materials and services. Personally identifiable information does include any data that can link choices of taste, interest, or research with a specific individual.

6. Article Eleven of the *Code of Ethics for Librarians* <www.ala.org/ala/issues advocacy/proethics/codeofethics/coehistory/1939code.pdf> (1939) asserted that "It is the librarian's obligation to treat as confidential any private information obtained through contact with library patrons." Article Three of the 2008 Code (see Appendix G in this book) states: "We protect each library user's right to privacy and confidentiality with respect to information sought or received and resources consulted, borrowed, acquired, or transmitted."

7. See the newest version of these ALA Policies <www.ala.org/advocacy/>: "Access for Children and Young Adults to Nonprint Materials"; "Access to Library Resources and Services for Minors"; "Freedom to Read"; "Libraries: An American Value"; "Library Principles for a Networked World"; "Policy Concerning Confidentiality of Personally Identifiable Information about Library Users"; "Policy on Confidentiality of Library Records"; "Suggested Procedures for Implementing Policy on the Confidentiality of Library Records." Use the ALA website <ala.org> search box to quickly locate these documents.

8. Adopted June 18, 1948; amended February 2, 1961, and January 23, 1980; inclusion of "age" reaffirmed January 23, 1996, by the ALA Council.

9. Existing ALA Policy <http://www.ala.org/advocacy/intfreedom/statementspols/otherpolicies/policyconcerning> asserts, in part, that: "The government's interest in library use reflects a dangerous and fallacious equation of what a person reads with what that person believes or how that person is likely to behave. Such a presumption can and does threaten the freedom of access to information."

10. See: "Guidelines for the Development and Implementation of Policies, Regulations and Procedures Affecting Access to Library Materials, Services and Facilities." <http://www.ala.org/advocacy/intfreedom/statementspols/otherpolicies/guidelinesdevelopmentimplementation>.

Adopted June 19, 2002, by the ALA Council; amended on July 1, 2014.

LLAMA's 14 Foundational Competencies

Library Leadership & Management Association, a division of the American Library Association

1. COMMUNICATION SKILLS

A leader effectively employs a wide range of well-developed verbal, nonverbal and written communication methods to interact with employees and stakeholders, conveying information clearly and efficiently and using active listening for consistent, mutual understanding.

> Barrett, D. J. 2006. "Strong Communication Skills a Must for Today's Leaders." *Handbook of Business Strategy* 7 (1): 385–90.

2. CHANGE MANAGEMENT

A leader provides an environment open to innovation and collaboration by ensuring continuous two-way communication, flexibility, and willingness to learn from mistakes made, and by providing the training necessary to make the change happen.

> Kanter, R. M. 1999. "The Enduring Skills of Change Leaders." *Leader to Leader* (13): 16–17.

3. TEAM BUILDING (PERSONNEL)

A leader unifies a group of individuals behind a commonly-shared vision by using strong communication skills to encourage dedication to mutual accountability, investment in the team's goal and purpose, and support for success of the team and its members.

> Kouzes, J., and B. Posner. 2002. *The Leadership Challenge,* 2nd ed. San Francisco: Wiley, 155.
> KU Work Group for Community Health and Development. 2015. "Chapter 13, Section 4: Building Teams: Broadening the Base for Leadership." Lawrence, KS: University of Kansas. <http://ctb.ku.edu/en/table-of-contents/leadership/leadership-ideas/team-building/main>.

4. COLLABORATION AND PARTNERSHIPS

A leader works, and encourages others to work, in cooperation with others within the library as well as with other organizations in order to achieve a common goal. Leaders look for ways to strengthen the role of the library in the community by seeking out opportunities to work with others in a mutually beneficial way, engaging stakeholders, and building relationships.

Mattessich, P. W., M. Murray-Close, and B. R. Monsey. 2001. *Collaboration: What Makes It Work*, 2nd ed. Saint Paul, MN: Wilder Foundation.

Smallwood, C., ed. 2010. *Librarians as Community Partners: An Outreach Handbook.* Chicago: American Library Association.

5. EMOTIONAL INTELLIGENCE

A leader is effective in understanding and improving the way he or she perceives and manages his or her own and other people's emotions, applying concepts such as self-awareness, self-regulation, motivation, empathy, and social skills to inform interpersonal interactions.

Goleman, D. 1995. *Emotional Intelligence*. New York: Bantam.

Salovey, P., J. Mayer, and D. Caruso. 2004. "Emotional Intelligence: Theory, Findings, and Implications." *Psychological Inquiry* 197–215.

6. PROBLEM SOLVING

A leader solves problems – taking proactive measures to avoid conflicts and address issues when they arise, and guiding employees to find appropriate information that allows them to generate and evaluate a diverse set of alternative solutions – to prevent issues from escalating and to encourage employees' abilities to do the same.

Griswold, A. 2013. "*4 Problem-Solving Tactics of Great Leaders.*" *Business Insider (November 8). <www.businessinsider.comproblem-solving-tactics-of-great-leaders -2013-11>.*

*Reiter-Palmon, R., and J. J. Illies. 2004. "Leadership and Creativity: Un*derstanding Leadership from a Creative Problem-Solving Perspective." *Leadership Quarterly* 15 (1): 55–77. <http://digitalcommons.unomaha.edu/psychfacpub/31>.

7. EVIDENCE-BASED DECISION MAKING

A leader makes use of research derived from trials, literature reviews, or other activities that provide objective information on issues of concern in order to help determine whether a particular policy or program will work at their organization and to demonstrate its effectiveness.

Cartwright, N., and J. Hardie. 2012. *Evidence-Based Policy: A Practical Guide to Doing It Better*. Oxford: Oxford University Press.

Evidence Based Library and Information Practice. <https://ejournals.library.ualberta .ca/index.php/EBLIP/index>.

8. CONFLICT RESOLUTION (PERSONNEL)

A leader supports differences of opinion, and helps individuals resolve conflict in a constructive manner when it threatens to become counterproductive to the organization's mission and strategic goals, encouraging communication, collaboration, and compromise.

Cloke, K., and J. Goldsmith. 2011. *Resolving Conflicts at Work: Ten Strategies for Everyone on the Job.* San Francisco: Jossey-Bass.

Montgomery, J. G., E. I. Cook, P. J. Wagner, and G. T. Hubbard. 2005. *Conflict Management for Libraries: Strategies for a Positive, Productive Workplace.* Chicago: American Library Association.

9. BUDGET CREATION AND PRESENTATION

A leader creates a budget that considers the needs of the department or organization, incorporates the input of team members, and reflects the institutional mission and priorities, and then communicates the value of library services to stakeholders, presenting qualitative and quantitative data to making a case for their proposed budget.

Doost, Roger K. 2007. "Budgets and Budgeting." In *Encyclopedia of Business and Finance*, 2nd ed. Vol. 1, edited by B. S. Kaliski, 58–60. Detroit: Macmillan Reference USA.

10. FORWARD THINKING

A leader maintains an understanding of important trends and developments in the library landscape, and uses that understanding to position their library to take advantage of opportunities as they arise, moving the library forward from a position of strength.

Kouzes, J., and B. Posner. 2010. "Focusing on the Future Sets Leaders Apart." In *The truth about leadership*, 45–60. San Francisco: Jossey-Bass.

11. CRITICAL THINKING

A leader applies critical thinking, which implies a high level of understanding, the ability to break a problem down into its constituent parts, and the skills to effectively analyze and assess the issues, to their library's challenges to identify and implement solutions.

Halpern, D. 2013. *Thought and Knowledge: An Introduction to Critical Thinking*, 5th ed. New York: Psychology Press.

12. ETHICS

A leader uses ethics in the process of deciding what should be done, reflecting on the reasons for a proposed course of action that takes into account the organization's decision-making process, its system of production and maintenance, and its culture and values, with the goal of bringing forth the resources so that people can make better decisions.

Brown, M. 2000. *Working Ethics: Strategies for Decision Making and Organizational Responsibility.* Berkeley, CA: Basic Resources.

13. PROJECT MANAGEMENT

A leader takes deliberate steps to execute, monitor, analyze and report on the progress of a work group charged with the creation of a unique product, service or result in order to deliver the on-time/on-budget results, learning and integration that the project and its stakeholders require.

> Kerzner, H. 2003. *Project Management: A Systems Approach to Planning, Scheduling, and Controlling*, 8th ed. New York: Wiley.
>
> Project Management Institute. 2013. *A Guide to the Project Management Body of Knowledge* (PMBOK® guide), 5th ed. Newtown Square, PA: Project Management Institute.

14. MARKETING AND ADVOCACY

A leader collaboratively creates key activities and goals of the organization and aggressively seeks out opportunities to communicate the goals with both internal and external constituencies.

> Heyman, D. R. 2011. Nonprofit Management 101: A Complete and Practical Guide for Leaders and Professionals. San Francisco: Jossey-Bass.
>
> Rosenbach, W. E., R. Taylor, and M. A. Youndt. 2012. *Contemporary Issues in Leadership*, 7th ed. Boulder, CO: Westview.
>
> Sarjeant-Jenkins, R. 2012. "Why Market? Reflections of an Academic Library Administrator." *Library Leadership & Management* 26 (1): 1–8. <https://journals.tdl.org/llm/index.php/llm/article/view/5903>.

Read background information about the development of the LLAMA Foundational Leadership Competencies in LLAMA's white paper at <**www.ala.org/llama/leadership -and-management-competencies#LLAMA's 14 FoundationalCompetencies**>.

Code of Ethics of the American Library Association

AS MEMBERS OF THE AMERICAN LIBRARY ASSOCIATION, WE RECOGNIZE THE importance of codifying and making known to the profession and to the general public the ethical principles that guide the work of librarians, other professionals providing information services, library trustees and library staffs.

Ethical dilemmas occur when values are in conflict. The American Library Association Code of Ethics states the values to which we are committed, and embodies the ethical responsibilities of the profession in this changing information environment.

We significantly influence or control the selection, organization, preservation, and dissemination of information. In a political system grounded in an informed citizenry, we are members of a profession explicitly committed to intellectual freedom and the freedom of access to information. We have a special obligation to ensure the free flow of information and ideas to present and future generations.

The principles of this Code are expressed in broad statements to guide ethical decision making. These statements provide a framework; they cannot and do not dictate conduct to cover particular situations.

I. We provide the highest level of service to all library users through appropriate and usefully organized resources; equitable service policies; equitable access; and accurate, unbiased, and courteous responses to all requests.

II. We uphold the principles of intellectual freedom and resist all efforts to censor library resources.

III. We protect each library user's right to privacy and confidentiality with respect to information sought or received and resources consulted, borrowed, acquired or transmitted.

IV. We respect intellectual property rights and advocate balance between the interests of information users and rights holders.

V. We treat co-workers and other colleagues with respect, fairness, and good faith, and advocate conditions of employment that safeguard the rights and welfare of all employees of our institutions.

VI. We do not advance private interests at the expense of library users, colleagues, or our employing institutions.

VII. We distinguish between our personal convictions and professional duties and do not allow our personal beliefs to interfere with fair representation of the aims of our institutions or the provision of access to their information resources.

VIII. We strive for excellence in the profession by maintaining and enhancing our own knowledge and skills, by encouraging the professional development of co-workers, and by fostering the aspirations of potential members of the profession.

Adopted at the 1939 Midwinter Meeting by the ALA Council; amended June 30, 1981; June 28, 1995; and January 22, 2008.

Evidence of Accomplishment

ONE OF THE JOYS OF BEING A SCHOOL LIBRARIAN IS NEVER HAVING TWO days that are the same! In the midst of meeting hectic schedules and enacting many roles, school librarians can easily lose track of the many ways in which they impact the school community. The list below contains activities, interactions, and tasks school librarians often perform that generate evidence of accomplishments in support of teaching and learning in the school library and beyond. Use this list to determine progress toward professional goals, gather evaluation materials for administrators, or engage parents and educators. This list is just a starting point—be sure to record and save additional artifacts produced as part of your work. This evidence will help you show others the difference your practice makes to learners and the school community.

A

advocacy
____ circulating petitions
____ legislative testimony
____ writing press releases

agenda
____ in-service
____ school library staff meeting
____ school library staff training

assessment
____ alternative
____ authentic venues
____ citations, works cited pages, and annotated bibliographies
____ communication log
____ data-driven decision making
____ double-entry journal
____ exit slips
____ formative
____ "I learned" statements
____ muddiest point
____ note-taking sample
____ one-minute paper
____ online information-literacy test
____ online rubric generator
____ performance-based
____ portfolios
____ pre- and post-tests
____ real-world
____ recorded observation
____ reflection log
____ rubrics
____ school library program
____ school library's role in state
____ smartphones and other smart devices
____ student response system (SRS)

and "clickers"
____ student work samples
____ summative
____ tablet computers
____ test retakes

authorship
____ article in *Knowledge Quest* (AASL)
____ article in local newspaper
____ article in professional trade journal
____ article in *School Library Research* journal (AASL)
____ article in school newspaper
____ article in state school library association journal
____ e-reader content
____ newsletter for parents
____ professional textbook, commercial publisher
____ publish professional textbook with national association (AASL)

award
____ professional, AASL Awards
____ professional, other

B

blog
____ librarian's
____ student-authored

book
____ award voting
____ club and literature circle
____ talk and book hook

budget
____ fund-raising
____ keeping financial records

C

cataloging
____ preprocessed

cataloging and social networking
____ online service

certification
____ National Board Certified Teacher (NBCT)
____ state school librarian

chart
____ scope and sequence

circulation
____ family literacy material
____ online public access catalog (OPAC) statistics
____ school library automation system installation/conversion/update
____ "sick kid" packet
____ summer reading

club
____ book
____ computer
____ cybersecurity
____ manga
____ poetry
____ other

code
____ computer

committee
____ career and college readiness
____ curriculum
____ Friends of the School Library
____ instructional and curriculum
____ intervention or RTI activities
____ parent-teacher organization (PTO)
____ reading literacy and promotion
____ school improvement
____ school library planning committee
____ strategic planning
____ technology

community
____ alumni outreach
____ parent outreach
____ parent-teacher
____ school library outreach

evaluation process   E
- ____ school librarian
- ____ school library program

event
- ____ Banned Books Week (ALA)
- ____ Banned Websites Awareness Day (AASL)
- ____ book fair
- ____ brown-bag lunch
- ____ Drop Everything And Read (D.E.A.R).
- ____ El día de los niños/El día de los libros
- ____ family literacy "read over"
- ____ general
- ____ hack-a-thon
- ____ National Library Legislative Day (ALA)
- ____ National Library Week (ALA)
- ____ poetry slam
- ____ Read across America (Dr. Seuss's birthday)
- ____ read-alouds
- ____ Right-to-Read Week (RTR)
- ____ School Library Month
- ____ Teen Read Week (TRW)
- ____ Teen Tech Week (TTW)

evidence
- ____ personal learning network (PLN) participation
- ____ student photos and clips
- ____ thank you notes

facilities   F
- ____ computer lab and classroom
- ____ design
- ____ information desk
- ____ learning commons design
- ____ makerspace
- ____ mobile furniture
- ____ mobile shelving

- ____ planning
- ____ reading nooks
- ____ school library centralization
- ____ self-checkout
- ____ signage
- ____ simultaneous usage of space
- ____ video production

feedback
- ____ from administrators
- ____ from board of education
- ____ from focus group
- ____ from needs assessment
- ____ from online microblogging service response
- ____ from online survey service
- ____ from periodic
- ____ from social networking profile service "friend count"
- ____ from student
- ____ from student panel
- ____ from suggestion box
- ____ from survey

grant   G
- ____ applications submitted
- ____ federal
- ____ Frances Henne (YALSA/VOYA)
- ____ local
- ____ professional, AASL Grants
- ____ Reading Is Fundamental (RIF)
- ____ received
- ____ state

guide
- ____ database searching
- ____ How To and Getting Started
- ____ online pathfinder
- ____ online subject

impact studies
- ____ student learning

intervention
- ____ response to (RTI)

job description J
____ adult volunteer
____ Friends of the School Library
____ paraprofessional
____ school library planning committee
____ student volunteer

leadership L
____ instructional
____ professional association
____ school building and district

learning management system
____ class taught by school librarian (ex., how to use Moodle)

lesson
____ blog
____ Boolean logic and operators
____ collaborative
____ digital citizenship
____ digital literacy
____ distance learning
____ field trip
____ global disposition
____ information literacy
____ interactive whiteboard
____ media literacy
____ print and online resources evaluation criteria
____ reflective process
____ student orientation
____ subject tagging
____ technological
____ textual literacy
____ transition to college (T2C)
____ virtual literacy
____ Web 2.0 tools
____ wiki

letter
____ student to author
____ thank you to school library

licensure
____ teaching

link to
____ college online public access catalog (OPAC)
____ free online state-created career and college resources
____ homework help at public library
____ public library's online public access catalog (OPAC)
____ websites

list
____ audiobook, preloaded audio and video player, portable media player (mp3)
____ book award winners
____ common school library vocabulary
____ e-reader, tablet computer
____ interactive e-book
____ local expert and speakers bureau
____ new acquisitions
____ online public access catalog section, "popular reads of your learners"
____ reading
____ webliographies, webquests

log
____ collaboration
____ communication
____ e-mail

manual M
____ school library policy and procedure

materials selection
____ learner input
____ policy

media storage and collaborative service
____ voice, text, music, podcasts, photographs, and videos)

membership
____ American Association of School Librarians (AASL)

____ American Library Association (ALA)
____ library consortium
____ parent-teacher organization (PTO)
____ professional association
____ regional library system
____ state library association

mentoring
____ new educator
____ pre-service school librarian
____ student assistants

modeling
____ information literacy
____ persistence through self-directed tinkering and making
____ safe, responsible, ethical and legal information behaviors
____ use of a variety of communication tools and resources
____ use of personal and professional learning networks

open house   O
____ school building
____ school library

partnership   P
____ academic library
____ curriculum leadership
____ historical society
____ Information Technology (IT) department
____ legislative
____ local business
____ public library
____ researcher-practitioner (RPP)

performance evaluation form
____ school librarian: goal setting
____ school librarian: rubric

performance evaluation process
____ school library staff

phone
____ introductory calls to parents
____ polls

podcast
____ school library

policy
____ academic integrity
____ confidentiality
____ copyright
____ cybersafety and acceptable use (AUP)
____ donation
____ ethics
____ intellectual freedom
____ inventory
____ materials selection
____ privacy
____ reconsideration
____ school library collection development
____ weeding and deselection

presentation
____ board of education
____ learners in school library
____ national school library conference
____ stakeholder organizations
____ state school library conference

products
____ learner-created

professional development
____ association journal, *Knowledge Quest* (AASL)
____ Fall Institute (AASL)
____ National Conference (AASL)
____ professional trade journals
____ school librarian recertification
____ state conference
____ webinar
____ workshop, institute

program guidelines
____ *AASL Standards Framework for School Libraries*
____ *Empowering Learners* (AASL)

program planning
____ action research process
____ goals and objectives
____ learner assessment
____ mission and vision statements
____ school library planning committee
____ school library program evaluation

promotional material
____ ALA "READ" posters of learners, educators, and staff
____ contest and game
____ reading

promotional tool
____ public service announcement (PSA)
____ school building announcement
____ social networking and microblogging

public library
____ interlibrary loans
____ instructional collaboration
____ resource sharing

publicity
____ services and resources to learners, staff, and the community

purchasing
____ cooperative contracts

R

reflective process
____ school librarian's

resource sharing
____ via union catalog
____ with college library
____ with public library

rewards
____ bookmark, prize, coupon

S

schedule
____ fixed
____ flexible
____ reservation system

school district initiative
____ bring your own device (BYOD)
____ college and career readiness
____ face-to-face and/or virtual participation
____ student-created
____ sustained silent reading (SSR)

school library collection
____ alignment and analysis
____ analysis
____ artifacts of student learning
____ diverse, balanced, and multi-cultural
____ English language learners (ESL)
____ foreign languages
____ free or fee-based electronic databases
____ large-print materials
____ mapping and analysis tool
____ open educational resources (OERs)
____ range of ability and levels

school library collection tool
____ online curation tool

school library display
____ student-created
____ community member-created
____ educator-created

school library marketing plan

school library posters
____ infographic
____ informational
____ literature-based

school library program evaluation
____ collaborative

school library report
____ annual

school library strategic plan
____ with mission and vision statements

school library training
____ advisory committee
____ Friends of the School Library volunteers

school library training *(cont'd)*
____ paraprofessional
____ parent volunteer
____ planning committee
____ student volunteers

social networking profile service
____ school librarian's page

software
____ school library automation

staff development
____ emerging technologies
____ one-on-one
____ one-shots
____ tutorial
____ webinar

standards
____ Common Core State Standards (CCSS)
____ *National School Library Standards for Learners, School Librarians, and School Libraries*
____ Partnership for 21st Century Skills (P21 Framework)
____ state academic content

statistics
____ audiobook, preloaded audio and/or video player, portable media player (mp3)
____ circulation
____ data collection
____ e-book downloads
____ e-reader, tablet computers
____ free online plagiarism and citation checker
____ interlibrary loan
____ learning commons usage
____ online book reviews
____ program assessment

student product
____ blog
____ book review

____ cartoon and art
____ contest entry
____ gallery walk
____ graphic organizer
____ inquiry-research-based project
____ interview
____ invention
____ microblogging response
____ model or game
____ note-taking sample
____ oral presentation
____ recipe
____ robot
____ rubric or checklist
____ slide show or slide show presentation
____ social networking profile page
____ speech or debate
____ spreadsheet
____ statistics
____ tag or word cloud
____ timeline
____ video or video clip creation
____ website
____ wiki
____ writing contest

supplies
____ student stations

T

teaching
____ adult education
____ blended course
____ college adjunct
____ community college
____ evidence-based practice
____ online college course
____ PSEO course

teaching strategy
____ activating prior knowledge
____ active learning
____ Bloom's Taxonomy

____ brain teasers
____ brainstorming
____ chunking
____ fish bowl
____ free writing
____ graphic organizer
____ guided inquiry
____ guided practice
____ independent practice
____ independent study
____ inquiry-based learning
____ inquiry method
____ intervention (RTI)
____ K-W-L
____ learning styles
____ manipulatives
____ mind maps
____ modeling
____ multiple intelligences
____ one-on-one
____ online educational video sharing service
____ optical illusions
____ peer evaluation
____ peer-led groups
____ predicting
____ problem solving
____ reading aloud
____ reading log
____ read-write-think
____ scaffolding
____ self-evaluation
____ show don't tell
____ simulations
____ small group
____ streaming video
____ student-centered
____ team building
____ think-pair-share
____ webquest
____ word wall
____ other

teaching tool
____ Best Apps for Teaching and Learning (AASL)
____ Best Websites for Teaching and Learning (AASL)
____ collaboration generator
____ free online brainstorming service
____ free online diagram generator
____ free online electronic calendar
____ free online gaming service service
____ free online interactive graphic organizer
____ free online mind-mapping tool
____ free online office suite and data-storage service
____ free online plagiarism and citation-checker service
____ free online social networking service
____ free online spreadsheet storage service
____ free online video-editing service
____ free online website authoring and storage service
____ free web-based computer-to-computer telephone calling service
____ interactive whiteboard
____ online notice board generator
____ online timeline generator
____ primary and secondary documents
____ projector
____ research calculator
____ word processing summarizing feature

technology
____ assistive and adaptive
____ copier
____ e-readers
____ laptop and/or netbook
____ photo- and/or video-editing
____ scanner
____ sound system
____ tablet computers
____ television

testimonial

_____ community member

_____ educators

_____ learners and former learners

_____ parents

_____ principal

tutorial

_____ online educational video-
sharing service

_____ OPAC

_____ school library equipment

_____ software applications

_____ transition to college

V

visit

_____ author, storyteller, magician,
musician, or puppeteer

_____ class accompanied by
educator

_____ college librarian

_____ community guest

_____ expert

_____ public librarian

_____ scientist

volunteer

_____ adult

_____ pre-service school librarian

_____ student

W

website

_____ school librarian's

_____ school librarian's companion course

wiki

_____ school librarian's

workshop

_____ community: college application
process, college finances, and
careers

_____ community: cyber safety

_____ community: homework

_____ community: literacy

_____ community: parents

_____ community: social media

Adapted from: Owen, Patricia. 2012. _A 21st-Century Approach to School Librarian Evaluation._ Chicago: American Library Association.

Useful Verbs

THE LANGUAGE OF THE *AASL STANDARDS INTEGRATED FRAMEWORK* IS empathetic, inclusive, and active; the standards include many of the verbs below. These verbs will help you customize the Competencies in the AASL Standards to your local curriculum, professional activities, or school library elements. This list is intended to be a starting point; feel free to add your own verbs. Some verbs fit in more than one Domain, but are listed in only one Domain.

A learner or a school librarian...

DOMAIN	VERB
Think	Accepts, Accesses, Addresses, Adopts, Analyzes, Assesses, Believes, Chooses, Compares, Conceives, Contrasts, Defines, Discerns, Dissects, Establishes, Evaluates, Finds, Identifies, Inquires, Knows, Matches, Monitors, Navigates, Observes, Plans, Prepares, Probes, Questions, Recalls, Recognizes, Remembers, Seeks, Selects, Thinks
Create	Adapts, Adjusts, Builds (on), Classifies, Combines, Composes, Creates, Cultivates, Designs, Develops, Differentiates, Dissects, Enhances, Estimates, Extends, Formulates, Incorporates, Infers, Innovates, Integrates, Invents, Makes, Modifies, Organizes, Originates, Proposes, Scaffolds, Solves, Structures, Supports, Tests, Tinkers
Share	Acts as a resource, Advocates, Balances, Champions, Clarifies, Collaborates, Communicates, Delivers, Demonstrates, Depicts, Discusses, Empowers, Encourages, Engages, Illustrates, Includes, Influences, Instructs, Listens, Makes, Mentors, Models, Partners, Promotes, Proposes, Relates, Rephrases, Shares, Shows, Showcases, Summarizes, Translates, Tells

(continued on page 272)

Grow	Accommodates, Administers, Appreciates, Challenges, Chooses, Constructs, Directs, Commits, Engages, Enhances, Ensures, Extends, Facilitates, Flourishes, Fosters, Grows, Guides, Innovates, Instructs, Leads, Manages, Masters, Mentors, Models, Personalizes, Reflects , Respects, Responds, Stimulates, Takes responsibility, Teaches, Thrives, Understands, Uses, Values

GLOSSARY OF TERMS

Aesthetic Growth: Process in which individuals develop the ability to think about and respond to artistic/aesthetic stimuli (Housen 1983).

Agency: When learning involves the activity and the initiative of the learner, more than the inputs that are transmitted to the learner from the educator, from the curriculum, and the resources; it is learners' power to act. When learners move from being passive recipients to being much more active in the learning process, actively involved in the decisions about the learning, then they have greater agency (CORE Education 2014)

Assessment: Process of "collecting, analyzing, and reporting data" (Coatney 2003, 157) about learner accomplishments and understandings throughout a learning experience. Forms of assessment include tests, observations, self-assessments, conferences, logs, graphic organizers, surveys, checklists, rubrics, and interviews (Wiggins and McTighe 2005; Harada and Yoshina 2010).

Authentic Assessment requires learners to originate a response to a task or question, using knowledge in real-world ways, with genuine purposes, audiences, and situational variables; may include demonstrations, exhibits, portfolios, oral presentations, or essays (Donham 2008, 267; Wiggins and McTighe 2005, 337). Authentic assessment helps to measure how effectively learners apply knowledge to the real world (Collins and O'Brien 2003).

Diagnostic Assessment is the use of formal or informal measurement tools to assess an individual's area of strengths and needs for purposes of identifying appropriate learning modifications or adaptations. Two examples of diagnostic assessment tools include running records (informal) and Weschler Intelligence Scale for Children (formal) (AASL 2009c, 118).

Formative Assessment is ongoing and provides information about what learners are learning and how that learning is taking place. It gives learners feedback on their progress and provides educators with feedback on the effectiveness of their instruction (Donham 2008, 266; Harada and Yoshina 2010, 1).

Prior Learning Assessment (PLA) is the determination of learners' knowledge, skills, and abilities gained outside of the immediate learning event. This knowledge may have been gained in variety of settings and through formal and informal means, including independent study, civic activities, volunteer service, or extracurricular activities (Marzano 2007).

Summative Assessment occurs at the end of the learning process and is intended to evaluate learner performance. It also provides feedback that can be used to redesign learning experiences (Donham 2008, 266; Harada and Yoshina 2010, 1, 33).

Authentic Assessment, *see* **Assessment**

Benchmark: Statement that provides a description of learner knowledge expected at specific grades, ages, or developmental levels. Benchmarks are often used in conjunction with standards and provide concrete indicators of learner understanding (EDSource n.d.).

Collaboration: Working with a member of the teaching team to plan, implement, and evaluate a specialized instructional plan (AASL 2016b; Montiel-Overall 2006).

Collaborative Learning: Learning that involves groups of learners working together to solve a problem, complete a task, or create a product (Smith and MacGregor 1992).

Community Readiness: The ability to be a productive, active, engaged member of a democratic society (AASL 2016b).

Competency: A general statement that describes the desired knowledge, skills, and behaviors of a learner completing an educational experience. Competencies commonly define the applied skills and knowledge that enable learners to successfully perform in professional, educational, and other life contexts. Competencies are defined in terms of a "package" of observable behaviors, and therefore can be assessed or measured. (Gosselin 2016).

Convergent Thinking: Thinking that brings together information focused on solving a problem, especially one that has a single correct solution (AASL 2009c, 118).

Critical Stance: Attitude or disposition toward learning in which learners are positioned to develop an understanding of a topic or issue through objectivity, inquiry, hypothesis, analysis and evaluation, comparing and contrasting, and consideration of implications (AASL 2009c, 118).

Critical Thinking: "Reasonable thinking that is focused on deciding what to believe or do" (Ennis 1987, 10). Critical thinking includes the ability to "set goals, to adjust strategies, to carry out tasks, to distinguish fact from opinion, to establish the authority of sources, to assess the accuracy and relevancy of information, and to detect bias and underlying assumptions" (Thomas 2004, 119).

Curation: Curation is the act of continually identifying, selecting, and sharing the best and most relevant content and resources on a specific subject to match the needs of a specific audience (Handley 2012).

Diagnostic Assessment, *see* **Assessment**

Differentiated Instruction: Teaching theory based on the belief that instructional approaches should vary and be adapted for individual and diverse learners in classrooms. The intent of differentiating instruction is "to maximize each learner's growth and individual success by meeting each learner where he or she is, and assisting in the learning process" (Hall 2002).

Digital Learning: Any learning facilitated by technology that gives learners some element of control over time, place, path, and/or pace (Digital Learning Now 2010).

Digital Literacy: The ability to use information and communication technologies to find, evaluate, create, and communicate information, requiring both cognitive and technical skills (ALA 2013).

Digital Resources: Learning materials and resources that can be displayed on a digital device and shared in a digital format with other users. Digital learning content includes both open and or commercial content (U.S. Dept. of Education 2012).

Direct Instruction: General term for the explicit teaching of a skill set. The most commonly identified steps of direct instruction include introduction/review, presenting new material, guided practice, independent practice, weekly/monthly review, and feedback/corrections (Collins and O'Brien 2003, 107).

Dispositions: Ongoing belief and attitudes that guide thinking and intellectual behavior. Often referred to as habits of mind or tendencies to respond to situations in a certain way (Katz 1988).

Divergent Thinking: Creative production or elaboration of ideas; associated with elements of creative problem solving (AASL 2009c, 118).

Domain: Learning categories, often referred to as KSA: <u>Knowledge</u> (cognitive), <u>Skills</u> (psychomotor), and <u>Attitudes</u> (affective) (Clark 2015). AASL's adaptation of these categories is: Think (cognitive), Create (psychomotor), Share (affective), with the addition of Grow (developmental) (AASL 2008).

Educators: All education professionals working in schools, including principals, teachers, staff involved in curriculum development, staff development, or operating school library, media, and computer centers, pupil support services staff, other administrators, and paraprofessionals (U.S. Dept. of Education 2012).

Effective School Library: An effective school library has a certified school librarian at the helm, provides personalized learning environments, and offers equitable access to resources to ensure a well-rounded education for every learner (AASL 2016c).

Emotional Resilience: Ability to "spring back emotionally after suffering through difficult and stressful times" (Mills and Dombeck 2005, 1). Emotional resilience requires setting realistic and attainable expectations and goals, good problem-solving skills, persistence and determination, learning from past mistakes, and an optimistic attitude (Mills and Dombeck 2005, 1).

Evaluation: A process of reviewing and analyzing data for the purpose of making informed decisions about the effectiveness of a program, project, or person (Evaluation of Learning n.d.).

Flexible Learning Environment (FLE): A learning environment that supports personalization within and outside of the classroom. Comfort, choice, and learner ownership of space are key to developing effective flexible learning environments. Reconfigurable seating options and technologies support learning (Colorado Springs School District 2014).

Formative Assessment, *see* **Assessment**

Global Perspective: Individual's awareness and understanding of the changing world with regard to global issues, culture, and connections, and the individual's roles and responsibilities as a member of the global community (Collins, Czarra, and Smith 1996, 7).

Grit: A distinct combination of passion, resilience, determination, and focus that allows a learner to maintain the discipline and optimism to persevere toward goals even in the face of discomfort, rejection, and a lack of visible progress for extended periods of time (Duckworth and Gross 2014, 319).

Growth: Refers to academic progress made over a period of time, as measured from the beginning to the end of the defined period. Achievement growth can be tracked and determined for individual learners, schools, states, or countries, and a wide variety of variables and methodologies may be used to determine whether growth is being achieved (Abbott 2013a).

Growth Mindset: In a growth mindset, people believe that their most basic abilities can be developed through dedication and hard work. This view creates a love of learning and a resilience that is essential for great accomplishment (ASCD Wisconsin 2015; Dweck 2007, iii).

Guided Inquiry: "An innovative team approach to teaching and learning where teachers and school librarians, with other experts and specialists, join together to design and implement inquiry learning. It engages children in constructing personal knowledge while using a wide range of sources of information and creatively sharing their learning with their fellow learners in an inquiry community (Kuhlthau, Maniotes, and Caspari 2007, 1).

Guided Practice: Instructional strategy that enables learners to "practice a new skill or strategy while the educator provides close monitoring, immediate feedback, and assistance as needed" (Collins and O'Brien 2003, 160).

Higher-Level Thinking/Questioning: Ability to think and question in a manner that requires consideration and application of complex concepts, problem-solving skills, and reflection (AASL 2009c, 119). Bloom's Taxonomy identifies a hierarchy of six levels of thinking, with the top three (analysis, synthesis, and evaluation) classified as higher-order thinking skills (Bloom et al. 1956).

Independent Practice: Instructional strategy that enables learners to "practice newly learned content, skills, or strategies on their own with no direct educator assistance" (Collins and O'Brien 2003, 175).

Information Literacy: Information literacy is knowing when and why information is needed, where to find it, and how to evaluate, use, and communicate it in an ethical manner (Chartered Institute of Library and Information Professionals 2004).

Information Technologies: Modern information, computer, and communication technology products, services, or tools, including the Internet, computer devices and other hardware, software applications, data systems, personal digital devices, and other digital and multimedia content and data storage (AASL 2016c).

Inquiry: Stance toward learning in which the learner is engaged in asking questions and finding answers, not simply accumulating facts presented by someone else that have no relation to previous learning or new understanding. Inquiry follows a continuum of learning experiences, from simply discovering a new idea or an answer to a question to following a complete inquiry process (Kuhlthau, Maniotes, and Caspari 2007, 1; New York City School Library System. 2010).

Instructional Role: A role of the school librarian that includes guiding learners and fellow educators through the intersection of formal and informal learning. The instruction the school librarian offers is integral to a well-rounded education. As educators and instructional partners school librarians are critical to teaching and learning in the school community. The school librarian plays a prominent role in instructing learners, faculty, and administrators in a range of literacies, including information, digital, print, visual, and textual literacies. As leaders in literacy and technology, school librarians are perfectly positioned to instruct every learner in the school community through both traditional and blended learning (AASL 2016c).

Key Commitment: The second level of the AASL Standards, which describes an essential understanding related to a Shared Foundation. Key Commitments operationally define Shared Foundations.

Leader: An individual who displays high levels of persistence, overcomes significant obstacles, attracts dedicated people, influences groups of people toward the achievement of goals, and plays key roles in guiding their organizations through crucial episodes (Collins and Porras 1997).

Learning Community: Learners, educators, and other stakeholders who share common academic goals and attitudes and who meet regularly to share expertise and work collaboratively to improve instruction and the academic performance of learners (Stronge, Richard, and Catano 2008, 7).

Learning Environment: The diverse physical locations, contexts, and cultures in which people learn. Since learners may learn in a wide variety of settings, such as outside-of-school locations and outdoor environments, the term is often used as a more-accurate or preferred alternative to "classroom," which has more limited and traditional connotations—a room with rows of desks and a chalkboard, for example (Abbott 2013b).

Learning Personalization: The process of using a diverse variety of educational programs, learning experiences, instructional approaches, and academic-support strategies that are intended to address the distinct learning needs, interests, aspirations, or cultural backgrounds of individual learners. Learning personalization may take the form of using online and/or in-person learning experiences tailored specifically to learners (Abbott 2015).

Literacy: The ability to identify, understand, interpret, create, communicate, and compute, using materials associated with varying contexts. Literacy involves a continuum of learning in enabling individuals to achieve their goals, to develop their knowledge and potential, and to participate fully in their community and wider society (UNESCO 2006).

Lower-Level Thinking/Questioning: Use of basic skills (such as recall, rote memorization, and simple comprehension) to think and question. Bloom's Taxonomy identifies a hierarchy of six levels of thinking; the lowest three are knowledge, comprehension, application (Bloom et al. 1956).

Mastery: A thorough understanding of a concept or skill such that the learner has the ability to teach others because "[t]eaching back demonstrates the learner's ability to grasp the problem, choose a process, develop a solution, and articulate the reasoning behind their choices, or it reveals where there are gaps in their understanding" (Teach 4 Mastery 2017). Mastery is not just knowing a fact, but it is using that fact in increasingly complex situations (Block 1971; Bloom 1968).

Media Literacy: Ability to "access, analyze, evaluate and create messages in a variety of forms—from print to video to the Internet. Media literacy builds an understanding of the role of media in society as well as essential skills of inquiry and self-expression necessary for citizens of a democracy" (Center for Media Literacy n.d.).

Metacognition: Metacognition is the process of "thinking about thinking." For example, good readers use metacognition before reading when they clarify their purpose for reading and preview the text (WETA 2015).

Modeling: Instructional strategy in which the educator demonstrates to the learner the behaviors, skills, or competencies that learners are to learn, with the expectation that the learners will copy the model (Coffey 2007). Modeling often involves thinking aloud or talking about how to work through a task (Schiller and Smyth 2010, 237).

Multiple Intelligences: Cognitive theory developed by Howard Gardner that proposes that intelligence is not a unitary or fixed trait, but a collection of different abilities with neurological foundations (Collins and O'Brien 2003, 230). Gardner proposed nine intelligences: linguistic, musical, logical-mathematical, visual-spatial, bodily-kinesthetic, intrapersonal, interpersonal, naturalist, and existential (Gardner 1999, 8–18).

Outcome: A very specific statement that describes in some measurable way exactly what a learner will be able to do. More than one measurable outcome may be defined for a given competency (Gosselin 2016).

Persona: A particular person within a customer segment. Personas are not meant to be exhaustive; they are meant to represent particular user types one might encounter and/or target for outreach, services, or advocacy (Mulder and Yaar 2007, 19).

Prior Learning Assessment, *see* **Assessment**

Qualified School Librarian: In addition to meeting state certification requirements, qualified school librarians hold a master's degree or equivalent from a program that combines academic and professional preparation in library and information science, education, and technology. The graduate degree is earned at a college or university whose program is recognized by appropriate bodies such as the American Library Association (ALA), the American Association of School Librarians/Council for the Accreditation of Educator Preparation (CAEP), or state education agencies. The academic program of study includes directed field experience coordinated by a college/university faculty member and takes place in an effective school library under the direct supervision of a certified, full-time school librarian (AASL 2016b)

Responsibilities: Common behaviors used by independent learners in researching, investigating, and problem solving (AASL 2009c, 119).

Scaffolding: Instructional strategy "in which a more skilled teaching partner adjusts the assistance he or she provides to fit the child's current level of performance. More support is offered when the task is new; less is provided as the child's competence increases, fostering the child's autonomy and independent mastery" (Callison 2006, 523). The gradual withdrawal of support is accomplished through instruction, questioning, modeling, feedback, etc. (Collins and O'Brien 2003, 312).

Self-Assessment: Assessment technique in which learners compare their performance, behaviors, or thoughts to assessment standards, and then use their observations to improve learning. Self-assessment requires learners to engage in reflection of their own learning and to focus not just on the task or the product, but also on the process. Self-assessment tools include journaling, rating scales, checklists, questionnaires, and rubrics (Donham 2008, 1).

Shared Foundation: The highest level of the AASL Standards that describes a core educational concept for learners, school librarians, and programs. The AASL Standards are based on six Shared Foundations: Inquire, Include, Collaborate, Curate, Explore, and Engage.

Social Networking: Ability to "connect, collaborate and form virtual communities via the computer and/or Internet. Social networking web sites are those that provide this opportunity to interact via interactive web applications. Sites that allow visitors to send emails, post comments, build web content and/or take part in live chats are all considered to be social networking sites. These kinds of sites have come to be collectively referred to as 'Web 2.0' and are considered the next generation of the Internet because they allow users to interact and participate in a way that we couldn't before" (Young Adult Library Services Association 2011).

Standards: Statements of what learners should know and be able to demonstrate. Various standards have been developed by national organizations, state departments of education, individual districts, and schools (Learn NC n.d.). *National School Library Standards for Learners, School Librarians, and School Libraries* is AASL's standards document.

Summative Assessment, *see* **Assessment**

Technology Literacy: Ability to responsibly use appropriate technology to communicate, solve problems, and access, manage, integrate, evaluate, and create information to improve learning in all subject areas and to acquire lifelong knowledge and skills in the twenty-first century (State Educational Technology Directors Association 2007, 1).

Textual Literacy: Ability to read, write, analyze, and evaluate textual works of literature and nonfiction as well as personal and professional documents (AASL 2009c, 119).

Visual Literacy: Ability to "understand and use images, including the ability to think, learn, and express oneself in terms of images" (Braden and Hortin 1982, 41).

Writing Process: Pedagogical term referring to a set of steps an individual takes while writing. They include: prewriting, writing, revising, editing, and publishing (AASL 2009c, 119).

WORKS CITED

Abbott, Stephen E., ed. 2013a. "Achievement Growth." *Glossary of Education Reform for Journalists, Parents, and Community Members.* <edglossary.org/achievement -growth> (accessed December 11, 2016).

——. 2013b. "Learning Environment." *Glossary of Education Reform for Journalists, Parents, and Community Members.* <edglossary.org/learning-environment> (accessed December 11, 2016).

——. 2015. "Personalized Learning." *Glossary of Education Reform for Journalists, Parents, and Community Members.* <http://edglossary.org/personalized -learning> (accessed January 21, 2017).

——. 2016. "Student Engagement." *Glossary of Education Reform for Journalists, Parents, and Community Members.* <http://edglossary.org/student-engagement> (accessed March 25, 2017).

American Association of School Librarians. 1960. *Standards for School Library Programs.* Chicago: ALA.

——. 2007. *Standards for the 21st-Century Learner.* <www.ala.org/aasl/pdf/ 21standards> (accessed December 11, 2016).

——. 2008. "Learning 4 Life: A National Plan for Implementation of *Standards for the 21st-Century Learner* and *Empowering Learners: Guidelines for School Libraries.*" <www.ala.org/aasl/pdf/l4l> (accessed March 12, 2017).

———. 2009a. "AASL's L4L Sample School Librarian Performance and Evaluation System." <www.ala.org/aasl/pdf/L4Leval> (accessed April 1, 2017).

———. 2009b. *Empowering Learners: Guidelines for School Library Programs.* Chicago: ALA.

———. 2009c. *Standards for the 21st-Century Learner in Action.* Chicago: ALA.

———. 2010. "ALA/AASL Standards for Initial Preparation of School Librarians." <www.ala.org/aasl/pdf/prep> (accessed March 25, 2017).

———. 2015. "AASL Executive Summary: AASL Repurposing and Managing the Brands Task Force." Unpublished report, 2015.

———. 2016a. "AASL Member and Stakeholder Consultation Process on the Learning Standards and Program Guidelines: Executive Summary." <www.ala.org/aasl/standards/researchsummary> (accessed November 15, 2016).

———. 2016b. "Appropriate Staffing for School Libraries." <www.ala.org/aasl/essa/staffing> (accessed November 15, 2016).

———. 2016c. "Definition of an Effective School Library Program." <www.ala.org/aasl/essa/effective> (accessed December 11, 2016).

———. 2016d. "Instructional Role of the School Librarian." <www.ala.org/aasl/essa/instructor> (accessed December 11, 2016).

———. 2016e."Preparation of School Librarians." <www.ala.org/aasl/essa/preparation> (accessed December 11, 2016).

———. 2016f. "Role of the School Library Program." <www.ala.org/aasl/essa/program> (accessed December 10, 2016).

———. n.d.1. "ALA and AASL: Assuring Quality in School Librarianship Education Programs." <http://www.ala.org/aasl/about/caep > (accessed July 28, 2017).

———. n.d.2. "Impact of the Loss of a State Library Consultant/Coordinator." <www.ala.org/aasl/pdf/impact> (accessed December 16, 2016).

American Association of School Librarians and Association for Educational Communications and Technology. 1975. *Media Programs: District and School.* Chicago: ALA.

———. 1988. *Information Power: Guidelines for School Library Media Programs.* Chicago: ALA.

———. 1998. *Information Power: Building Partnerships for Learning.* Chicago: ALA.

American Association of School Librarians and National Education Association Department of Audiovisual Instruction. 1960. *Standards for School Library Programs.* Chicago: ALA.

American Library Association. 2013. "Digital Literacy, Libraries, and Public Policy: Report of the Office for Information Technology Policy's Digital Literacy Task Force." <www.districtdispatch.org/wp-content/uploads/2013/01/2012_OITP _digilitreport_1_22_13.pdf> (accessed December 11, 2016).

American Library Association Committee on Post-War Planning, Post-War Planning Committee of the Division of Libraries for Children and Young People, and Planning Committee of the American Association of School Librarians. 1945. *School Libraries for Today and Tomorrow: Functions and Standards.* Chicago: ALA.

Anderson, Lorin W., and David R. Krathwohl, eds. 2001. *A Taxonomy for Learning, Teaching, and Assessing: A Revision of Bloom's Taxonomy of Educational Objectives*. New York: Addison Wesley Longman.

ASCD Wisconsin. 2015. "Growth vs Fixed Mindset." *What We Know Now* (July 10). <www.wascd.org/What-We-Know-Now/growth-vs-fixed-mindset.html> (accessed December 11, 2016).

Block, James H. 1971. *Mastery Learning: Theory and Practice*. New York: Holt, Rinehart and Winston.

Bloom, Benjamin S. 1968. "Learning for Mastery." *UCLA CSEIP Evaluation Comment* 1 (2): 1–12. <programs.honolulu.hawaii.edu/intranet/sites/programs.honolulu .hawaii.edu.intranet/files/upstf-student-success-bloom-1968.pdf> (accessed December 11, 2016).

Bloom, Benjamin S., et al. 1956. *Taxonomy of Educational Objectives Handbook 1: Cognitive Domain*. New York: McKay.

Braden, Roberts A., and John A. Hortin. 1982. "Identifying the Theoretical Foundations of Visual Literacy." *Journal of Visual/Verbal Languaging* 2 (2): 37–42.

Braxton, Barbara. 2003. "Setting S.M.A.R.T. Goals for the School Library." *Teacher Librarian* 30 (4): 45.

Bryk, Anthony S. 2015. "2014 AERA Distinguished Lecture: Accelerating How We Learn to Improve." *Educational Researcher* 44 (9): 467–77.

Bryk, Anthony S., et al. 2015. *Learning to Improve: How America's Schools Can Get Better at Getting Better*. Cambridge, MA: Harvard Education Press.

Calkins, Andrew, and Kristen Vogt. 2013. "Next Generation Learning: The Pathway to Possibility." <library.educause.edu/~/media/files/library/2013/4/ngw1301 -pdf.pdf> (accessed December 11, 2016).

Callison, Daniel. 2006. "Scaffolding." In *The Blue Book on Information Age Inquiry, Instruction and Literacy*, edited by Daniel Callison and Leslie Preddy, 523–26. Westport, CT: Libraries Unlimited.

Carbaugh, Beverly, Robert Marzano and Michael Toth. 2017. "2017 Update: The Marzano Focused Teacher Evaluation Model." Learning Sciences International. <http://www.marzanocenter.com/files/Focus%20Eval%20Model_Marzano Cust_20170321.pdf> (accessed May 1, 2017).

Center for Media Literacy. n.d. "Media Literacy: A Definition and More." <www .medialit.org/media-literacy-definition-and-more> (accessed December 11, 2016).

Chartered Institute of Library and Information Professionals. 2004. "Information Literacy—Definition." <www.cilip.org.uk/cilip/advocacy-campaigns-awards/ advocacy-campaigns/information-literacy/information-literacy> (accessed March 14, 2017).

Clark, Donald. 2015. "Bloom's Taxonomy of Learning Domains." <www.nwlink .com/~donclark/hrd/bloom.html> (accessed December 11, 2016).

Coatney, Sharon. 2003. "Assessment for Learning," in *Curriculum Connections through the Library*, edited by Barbara K. Stripling and Sandra Hughes-Hassell, 157–68. Westport, CT: Libraries Unlimited.

Coffey, Heather. 2007. "Modeling." <www.learnnc.org/lp/pages/4697> (accessed December 11, 2016).

Collins, H. Thomas, Frederick R. Czarra, and Andrew F. Smith. 1996. "Guidelines for Global and International Studies Education: Challenges, Culture, Connections." *Issues in Global Education* (135,136): 3–19. <files.eric.ed.gov/fulltext/ED415131 .pdf> (accessed December 11, 2016).

Collins, James C., and Jeremy I. Porras. 1997. *Built to Last: Successful Habits of Visionary Companies*. New York: Harper Business.

Collins, John W., III, and Nancy Patricia O'Brien, eds. 2003. *The Greenwood Dictionary of Education*. Westport, CT: Greenwood.

Colorado Springs School District 11. 2014. "Creating Flexible Learning Environments." <www.d11.org/NextGen/Pages/Environments.aspx> (accessed November 15, 2016).

CORE Education. 2014. "Trend 1: Learner Agency." <core-ed.org/legacy/thought -leadership/ten-trends/ten-trends-2014/learning-agency> (accessed December 11, 2016).

Danielson, Charlotte. 2007. *Enhancing Professional Practice: A Framework for Teaching*. Alexandria, VA: ASCD.

Danielson Group. 2013. "The Framework." <www.danielsongroup.org/framework> (accessed January 5, 2017).

Digital Learning Now. 2010. "Glossary." <www.digitallearningnow.com/education -in-the-digital-age/glossary> (accessed December 11, 2016).

Donham, Jean. 2008. *Enhancing Teaching and Learning: A Leadership Guide for School Library Media Specialists,* 2nd ed. New York: Neal-Schuman.

Duckworth, Angela L., and James J. Gross. 2014. "Self-Control and Grit: Related but Separable Determinants of Success." *Current Directions in Psychological Science* 23 (5): 319–25.

Dweck, Carol S. 2007. *Mindset: The New Psychology of Success.* New York: Ballantine.

EDSource. n.d. "Glossary of Education Terms." <edsource.org/publications/ education-glossary> (accessed December 11, 2016).

Elkins, Aaron J. 2014. "What's Expected, What's Required, and What's Measured: A Comparative Qualitative Content Analysis of the National Professional Standards for School Librarians, and Their Job Descriptions and Performance Evaluations in Florida." doctoral dissertation. Tallahassee: Florida State University.

Ennis, Robert H. 1987. "A Taxonomy of Critical Thinking Dispositions and Abilities." In *Teaching Thinking Skills: Theory and Practice,* edited by Joan Boykoff Baron and Robert J. Sternberg, 9–26. New York: Freeman.

"Evaluation of Learning." n.d. <etc.usf.edu/broward/mod3/module3.html> (accessed December 11, 2016).

Freire, Paolo. 1993. *Pedagogy of the Oppressed,* rev. ed. London: Penguin.

Gardner, Howard. 1999. *Intelligence Reframed: Multiple Intelligences for the 21st Century.* New York: Basic Books.

Gosselin, David. 2016. "Competencies and Learning Outcomes." <serc.carleton.edu/ integrate/programs/workforceneeds/competencies_and_LO.html> (accessed December 11, 2016).

Hall, Mary E. "The Development of the Modern High School Library." *Library Journal 40* (September 1915): 627.

Hall, T. 2002. "Sec-B Readings: Differentiated Instruction." <www.principals.in/ uploads/pdf/Instructional_Strategie/DI_Marching.pdf> (accessed December 9, 2016).

Handley, Ann. 2012. "Content Curation Definitions & Context for Content Marketing." *TopRank Online Marketing Blog.* <www.toprankblog.com/2010/06/content -marketing-curation-context> (accessed January 5, 2017).

Harada, Violet H., and Joan M. Yoshina. 2010. *Assessing Learning: Librarians and Teachers as Partners*, 2nd ed. Santa Barbara, CA: Libraries Unlimited.

Hermanns, William. 1983. *Einstein and the Poet: In Search of the Cosmic Man.* Brookline Village, MA: Branden.

Holmes, Oliver Wendell, Sr. 1858. *The Autocrat of the Breakfast Table.* <www .gutenberg.org/files/751/751-h/751-h.htm> (accessed March 14, 2017).

Housen, Abigail. 1983. "The Eye of the Beholder: Measuring Aesthetic Development." EdD diss., Harvard University Graduate School of Education.

Huba Mary E., and Jann E. Freed. 2000. *Learner-Centered Assessment on College Campuses: Shifting the Focus from Teaching to Learning.* Boston: Allyn and Bacon.

Johns, Sara Kelly. 2008. "AASL Standards for the Twenty-First-Century Learner: A Map for Student Learning." *Knowledge Quest* 36 (3): 4-7.

Katz, Lilian G. 1988. "What Should Young Children Be Doing?" *American Educator 12* (2): 28–33, 44–45.

Kawasaki, Guy. 2015. "Create or Curate?" <www.youtube.com/watch?v=372mSxob QDQ> (accessed March 14, 2017).

Kester, Diane D. and Jones, Plummer Alston. 2004. "Frances Henne and the Development of School Library Standards." *Library Trends* (Spring): 35-40.

Knoblock, John. 1994. *Xunzi: A Translation and Study of the Complete Works.* Stanford, CA: Stanford University Press.

Kuhlthau, Carol C., Leslie K. Maniotes, and Ann K Caspari. 2007. *Guided Inquiry: Learning in the 21st Century.* Westport, CT: Libraries Unlimited.

Learn NC. n.d. "Standards" <www.learnnc.org/reference/standards> (accessed December 11, 2016).

Marzano, Robert J. 2007. *Art and Science of Teaching.* Alexandria, VA: ASCD.

———. 2013. *The Marzano Teacher Evaluation Model.* Bloomington, IN: Marzano Research.

Mills, Harry, and Mark Dombeck. 2005. "Resilience: Underlying Attitudes and Skills." <www.mentalhelp.net/articles/resilience-underlying-attitudes-and-skills> (accessed December 12, 2016).

Montiel-Overall, Patricia 2006. "Teacher and Teacher-Librarian Collaboration: Moving toward Integration." *Teacher Librarian* 34 (2): 28–33.

Mulder, Steve, and Ziv Yaar. 2007. *The User Is Always Right: A Practical Guide to Creating and Using Personas for the Web.* Berkeley, CA: New Riders.

National Education Association Committee on Elementary School Library Standards and American Library Association. 1925. *Elementary School Library Standards.* Chicago: ALA.

National Education Association Committee on Library Organization and Equipment, and North Central Association of Colleges and Secondary Schools, approved by the American Library Association Committee on Education. 1920. *Standard Library Organization and Equipment for Secondary Schools of Different Sizes.* Chicago: ALA.

New York City School Library System. 2010. "Information Fluency Continuum: Benchmark Skills for Grades K–12 Assessment." <schools.nyc.gov/NR/rdonlyres/ 27A1E84E-65EB-4A54-80DF-51E28D34BF4F/0/InformationFluencyContinuum .pdf> (accessed December 11, 2016).

Norton, Lin. 2004. "Psychology Applied Learning Scenarios (PALS): A Practical Intro- duction to Problem-Based Learning Using Vignettes for Psychology Lecturers." <www.heacademy.ac.uk/resources/detail/resource_database/casestudies/ cs_088> (accessed December 16, 2016).

Osterwalder, Alexander, and Yves Pigneur. 2010. *Business Model Generation.* Hoboken, NJ: Wiley.

Osterwalder, Alexander, et al. 2014. *Value Proposition Design.* Hoboken, NJ: Wiley.

Robinson, Ken. 2010. "Changing Education Paradigms." <www.youtube.com/watch ?v=zDZFcDGpL4U> (accessed March 14, 2017).

Rosenberg, Marc. 2012. "Beyond Competence: It's the Journey to Mastery That Counts." *Learning Solutions Magazine* (May 21). <www.learningsolutionsmag .com/articles/930/beyond-competence-its-the-journey-to-mastery-that -counts> (accessed December 12, 2016).

Rudy, Willis (2003). *Building America's Schools and Colleges: The Federal Contribu- tion.* Cranbury, NJ: Cornwall Books.

Schiller, Jon, and Emilie Smyth. 2010. *Education in the 21st Century: How Advanced Teaching Contents Are Improving Learning Skills.* Bedford, MA: Schiller Software.

Shaw, Carolyn M. 2010. "Designing and Using Simulations and Role-Play Exercises." In *The International Studies Encyclopedia,* edited by Robert Denemark, 65676– 77. Chichester, West Sussex: Wiley-Blackwell.

Shulman, Lee S. 1998. "Theory, Practice, and the Education of Professionals." *Elementary School Journal* 98 (5): 511–26.

Sinclair, Dan. 2016. "So What is Mastery?" <teach4mastery.com/what-is-mastery> (accessed March 12, 2017).

Smith, Barbara Leigh, and Jean T. MacGregor. 1992. "What Is Collaborative Learn- ing?" In *Collaborative Learning: A Sourcebook for Higher Education,* edited by Anne S. Goodsell et al., 9–23. University Park, PA: National Center on Post- secondary Teaching, Learning, and Assessment.

State Educational Technology Directors Association. 2007. "2007 Technology Liter- acy Assessment and Educational Technology Standards Report." <www.setda .org/wp-content/uploads/2015/03/TEchnologyLiteracy2007Final.pdf> (accessed March 14, 2017).

Stronge, James H., Holly B. Richard, and Nancy Catano. 2008. *Qualities of Effective Principals.* Alexandria, VA: ASCD.

Teach 4 Mastery. 2017. "What is Mastery?" <teach4mastery.com/what-is-mastery> (accessed March 12, 2017).

Thomas, Nancy Pickering. 2004. *Information Literacy and Information Skills Instruction: Applying Research to Practice in the School Library*, 2nd ed. Westport, CT: Libraries Unlimited.

United States Department of Education. [2012.] "Definitions." <www.ed.gov/race-top/district-competition/definitions> (accessed December 10, 2016).

UNESCO. 2006. "Understandings of Literacy." *Education for All: A Global Monitoring Report.* <www.unesco.org/education/GMR2006/full/chapt6_eng.pdf> (accessed December 11, 2016).

WETA. 2015. "Glossary." <www.ldonline.org/glossary> (accessed December 11, 2016).

Wiggins, Grant P., and Jay McTighe. 2005. *Understanding by Design*, 2nd ed. Alexandria, VA: ASCD.

Williams, Connie. 2015. "The Changing Role of the School Library." <knowledge quest.aasl.org/changing-role-school-library> (accessed December 12, 2016).

Woolls, Blanche, Ann Weeks, and Sharon Coatney. 2013. *The School Library Media Manager,* 5th edition. Santa Barbara: Libraries Unlimited.

Young Adult Library Services Association. 2011. "Teens and Social Networking in School and Public Libraries: A Toolkit for Librarians and Library Workers." <www.ala.org/yalsa/sites/ala.org.yalsa/files/content/professionaltools/sn _toolkit11.pdf> (accessed March 14, 2017).

SUGGESTED FURTHER READING

THIS SECTION INCLUDES RESOURCES—FROM AASL, ALA, AND ADDITIONAL sources—that give insight into the standards' foundations in research and practice. This list is not intended to be exhaustive; these readings represent current literature that provides insight on the topics addressed in the standards.

Part I: Introduction and Overview

AASL AND ALA RESOURCES

Weisburg, Hilda K. 2017. *Leading for School Librarians: There Is No Other Option.* Chicago: ALA Neal-Schuman.

ADDITIONAL READINGS

Coatney, Sharon, and Violet H. Harada, eds. 2017. *The Many Faces of School Library Leadership*, 2nd ed. Santa Barbara, CA: Libraries Unlimited.

Freire, Paulo. 1993. *Pedagogy of the Oppressed*, rev. ed. New York: Continuum Books.

Harvey, Carl A., II. 2016. *The 21st-Century Elementary School Library Program: Managing for Results*, 2nd ed. Santa Barbara, CA: Libraries Unlimited.

Hochman, Jessica. 2016. "School Library Nostalgias." *Curriculum Inquiry* 46 (2): 132–47.

Howard, Jody K. 2017. *The School Librarian as Curriculum Leader.* Santa Barbara, CA: Libraries Unlimited.

Kompar, Fran. 2015. "Re-Imagining the School Library." *Teacher Librarian* 42 (4): 20–24.

Markless, Sharon, ed. 2016. *The Innovative School Librarian,* 2nd ed. London: Facet.

National Commission on Teaching and America's Future. 2016. What Matters Now: A New Compact for Teaching and Learning. <nctaf.org/wp-content/uploads/2016/08/NCTAF_What-Matters-Now_A-Call-to-Action.pdf> (accessed December 16, 2016).

Pace, Lillian, and Maria Worthen. 2014. *Laying the Foundation for Competency Education: A Policy Guide for the Next Generation Educator Workforce.* <www.knowledgeworks.org/sites/default/files/laying-foundation-competency-education-policy-guide.pdf> (accessed December 10, 2016).

Patrick, Susan, and Chris Sturgis. 2015. *Maximizing Competency Education and Blended Learning: Insights from Experts.* <www.competencyworks.org/wp-content/uploads/2015/03/CompetencyWorks-Maximizing-Competency-Education-and-Blended-Learning.pdf> (accessed December 10, 2016).

Perkins, David N. 2014. *Future Wise: Educating Our Children for a Changing World.* San Francisco: Jossey-Bass.

Sykes, Judith Anne. 2016. *The Whole School Library Learning Commons: An Educator's Guide.* Santa Barbara, CA: Libraries Unlimited.

Part II: Standards Frameworks

SHARED FOUNDATION: INQUIRE

AASL and ALA Publications

AASL, Achieve, David Loertscher, and Kathryn Roots Lewis. 2013. *Implementing the Common Core State Standards: The Role of the School Librarian.* <www.ala.org/aasl/sites/ala.org.aasl/files/content/externalrelations/CCSSLibrariansBrief_FINAL.pdf> (accessed December 10, 2016).

Callison, Danny, and Katie Baker. 2014. "Elements of Information Inquiry, Evolutions of Models, and Measured Reflection." *Knowledge Quest* 43 (2): 18–24.

Coleman, Mary Catherine. 2016. "Design Thinking and the School Library." *Knowledge Quest* 44 (5): 62–68.

Craddock, IdaMae. 2013. "Community Assessment in Teaching the Research Process." *Knowledge Quest* 42 (1): 58–63.

Dando, Priscille. 2016. "Traditional Literacy and Critical Thinking." *Knowledge Quest* 44 (5): 8–12.

Fuller, Cherry, et al. 2014. "Community Collaboration for Inquiry Success." *Knowledge Quest* 43 (2): 56–59.

Jacobson, Trudi E., and Emer O'Keeffe. 2014. "Seeking—and Finding—Authentic Inquiry Models for Our Evolving Information Landscape." *Knowledge Quest* 43 (2): 26–33.

Kelley-Mudie, Sara, and Jeanie Phillips. 2016. "To Build a Better Question." *Knowledge Quest* 44 (5): 14–19.

Maniotes, Leslie K., and Carol C. Kuhlthau. 2014. "Making the Shift: From Traditional Research Assignments to Guiding Inquiry Learning." *Knowledge Quest* 43 (2): 8–17.

Marriott, Catherine E. 2014. "Just Wondering: The Beginning of Inquiry." *Knowledge Quest* 43 (2): 74–76.

Naluai, Nālani. 2014. "Approaching the Inquiry Process from a Cultural Perspective." *Knowledge Quest* 43 (2): 38–41.

Ratzer, Mary Boyd. 2014. "Opportunity Knocks: Inquiry, the New National Social Studies and Science Standards, and You." *Knowledge Quest* 43 (2): 64–70.

Stubeck, Carole J. 2015. "Enabling Inquiry Learning in Fixed-Schedule Libraries." *Knowledge Quest* 43 (3): 28–34.

Wilhelm, Jeffrey D. 2014. "Learning to Love the Questions." *Knowledge Quest* 42 (5): 36–41.

Willingham, Daniel. 2014. "Making Students More Curious." *Knowledge Quest* 42 (5): 32–35.

Additional Sources

Callison, Daniel. 2015. *The Evolution of Inquiry: Controlled, Guided, Modeled, and Free.* Santa Barbara, CA: Libraries Unlimited.

Fitzgerald, Lee. 2018. *Guided Inquiry Meets Global Curriculum Reform.* Santa Barbara, CA: Libraries Unlimited.

Levitov, Deborah. 2016. "School Libraries, Librarians, and Inquiry Learning." *Teacher Librarian* 43 (3): 28–35.

MacDonell, Colleen. 2006. *Project-Based Inquiry Units for Young Children: First Steps to Research for Grades Pre-K–2.* Worthington, OH: Linworth.

Maniotes, Leslie K., ed. 2016. *Guided Inquiry Design® in Action: High School.* Santa Barbara, CA: Libraries Unlimited.

Maniotes, Leslie K., LaDawna Harrington, and Patrice Lambusta. 2015. *Guided Inquiry Design® in Action: Middle School.* Santa Barbara, CA: Libraries Unlimited.

Norfolk, Sherry, and Jane Stenson, eds. 2017. *Engaging Community through Storytelling: Library and Community Programming.* Santa Barbara, CA: Libraries Unlimited.

Todd, Ross J. 2013. "The Power of (in) the (Im)possible." *Teacher Librarian* 41 (2): 8–15.

SHARED FOUNDATION: INCLUDE

AASL and ALA Publications

Adams, Helen R. 2015. "Have Intellectual Freedom and Privacy Questions? Help Is on the Way!" *Knowledge Quest* 43 (4): 72–75.

Azano, Amy Price. 2014. "Rural, the Other Neglected 'R': Making Space for Place in School Libraries." *Knowledge Quest* 43 (1): 60–65.

Ballard, Susan. 2015. "Coming This Fall to a School Library near You: The Challenged, the Banned, & the Filtered." *Knowledge Quest* 43 (5): 32–37.

Batch, Kristen R. 2015. "Filtering Beyond CIPA: Consequences of and Alternatives to Overfiltering in Schools." *Knowledge Quest* 44 (1): 60–66.

Cesari, Lindsay. 2014. "Arranging a Library to Support Adolescent Development." *Knowledge Quest* 42 (4): 44–48.

Chmara, Theresa. 2015. "Do Minors Have First Amendment Rights in Schools?" *Knowledge Quest* 44 (1): 8–13.

Hunsinger, Valarie. 2015. "School Librarians as Equity Warriors." *Knowledge Quest* 44 (1): E10–E14.

Kim, Sung Un. 2015. "Enablers and Inhibitors to English Language Learners' Research Process in a High School Setting." *School Library Research* 18. <www.ala.org/aasl/sites/ala.org.aasl/files/content/aaslpubsandjournals/slr/vol18/SLR_EnablersandInhibitors_V18.pdf> (accessed October 11, 2016).

Magi, Trina. 2015. "Newly Revised Intellectual Freedom Manual Makes It Easier to Find the Help You Need." *Knowledge Quest* 44 (1): 32–35.

Markey, Patricia T., and Michel L. Miller. 2015. "Introducing an Information-Seeking Skill in a School Library to Students with Autism Spectrum Disorder: Using Video Modeling and Least-to-Most Prompts." *School Library Research* 18. <www.ala.org/aasl/sites/ala.org.aasl/files/content/aaslpubsandjournals/slr/vol18/SLR_IntroducingInfoSeekingSkill_V18.pdf> (accessed October 11, 2016).

Rickman, Wendy. 2015. "Collection Development Behaviors in School Librarians: LGBTQQ Books and Resources." *Knowledge Quest* 43 (5): 22–27.

Seroff, Jole. 2015. "Developing a Curriculum in Intellectual Freedom: What Our Students Need to Know." *Knowledge Quest* 44 (1): 20–24.

Stripling, Barbara K. 2015. "Creating a Culture of Intellectual Freedom through Leadership and Advocacy." *Knowledge Quest* 44 (1): 14–19.

Turner, Heather. 2014. "Library XGen: Student-Centered Spaces." *Knowledge Quest* 42 (4): 28–31.

Additional Sources

Burrows, Patricia, and Bernie Morrissey. 2015. "Fostering Cultural Awareness through Literature." *Library Media Connection* 33 (6): 36–38.

Chita-Tegmark, Meia, et al. 2012. "Using the Universal Design for Learning Framework to Support Culturally Diverse Learners." *Journal of Education* 192 (1): 17–22.

Cooke, Nicole A. 2017. *Information Services to Diverse Populations: Developing Culturally Competent Library Professionals.* Santa Barbara, CA: Libraries Unlimited.

Dadlani, Punit, and Ross J. Todd. 2015. "Information Technology and School Libraries: A Social Justice Perspective." *Library Trends* 64 (2): 329–59.

Horning, Kathleen T. 2014. "Still an All-White World?" *School Library Journal* 60 (5): 18.

Horton, Lisa. 2016. "Meeting the Needs of Lesbian, Gay, Bisexual, Transsexual, Queer, or Questioning Students through the School Library Collection." *Teacher Librarian* 44 (1): 20–22.

Hughes-Hassell, Sandra, Pauletta Brown Bracy, and Casey H. Rawson, ed. 2016. *Libraries, Literacy, and African American Youth*. Santa Barbara, CA: Libraries Unlimited.

Naidoo, Jamie Campbell. 2017. *A World of Rainbow Families: Children's Books and Media with Lesbian, Gay, Bisexual, Transgender, and Queer Themes from Around the Globe*. Santa Barbara, CA: Libraries Unlimited.

SHARED FOUNDATION: COLLABORATE

AASL and ALA Publications

Ballew, Linda M. 2014. "The Value of School Librarian Support in the Digital World." *Knowledge Quest* 42 (3): 64–68.

Boyer, Brenda L. 2015. "Collaborative Instructional Design for College Readiness." *Knowledge Quest* 44 (2): 60–65.

Dotson, Kaye B., and Christine Clark. 2015. "Together We Can." *Knowledge Quest* 44 (2): 8–15.

Green, Lucy Santos, and Stephanie Jones. 2014. "Instructional Partners in Digital Library Learning Spaces." *Knowledge Quest* 42 (4): E11–E17.

Grigsby, Susan K. S., Jennifer Helfrich, and Christa Harrelson Deissler. 2015. "A Seat at the Table." *Knowledge Quest* 44 (2): 16–23.

Harada, Violet. 2016. "A Practice-Centered Approach to Professional Development: Teacher-Librarian Collaboration in Capstone Projects." *School Library Research* 19. <www.ala.org/aasl/slr/volume19/harada> (accessed October 11, 2016).

Harper, Meghan, and Liz Deskins. 2015. "Using Action Research to Assess and Advocate for Innovative School Library Design." *Knowledge Quest* 44 (2): 24–33.

Lankau, Louise. 2015. "Connection + Collaboration = Successful Integration of Technology in a Large High School." *Knowledge Quest* 44 (2): 66–73.

Lighthart, Matthew, and Creedence Spreder. 2014. "Partners in Lifelong Learning: How Creeds Elementary School and the Pungo-Blackwater Public Library Combine Forces for the Benefit of Their Community." *Knowledge Quest* 42 (4): 32–37.

Moreillon, Judi. 2016. "Building Your Personal Learning Network (PLN): 21st-Century School Librarians Seek Self-Regulated Professional Development Online." *Knowledge Quest* 44 (3): 64–69.

Moreillon, Judi, Sue Kimmel, and Karen Gavigan. 2014. "Educating Pre-Service School Librarians for the Instructional Partner Role: An Exploration into University Curricula." *School Library Research* 17. <ala.org/aasl/sites/ala.org .aasl/files/content/aaslpubsandjournals/slr/vol17/SLR_EducatingPreservice _V17.pdf> (accessed October 11, 2016).

Rawson, Casey, Janice Anderson, and Sandra Hughes-Hassell. 2015. "Preparing Pre-Service School Librarians for Science-Focused Collaboration with Pre-Service Elementary Teachers: The Design and Impact of a Cross-Class Assignment." *School Library Research* 18. <www.ala.org/aasl/sites/ala.org.aasl/files/content/aaslpubsandjournals/slr/vol18/SLR_PreparingPreserviceSchoolLib_V18.pdf> (accessed October 11, 2016).

Schroeder, Eileen E., and Stacy Fisher. 2015. "Communicating the Emerging Roles of Librarians to Teachers through a Collaborative K–12 and Higher Education Partnership." *Knowledge Quest* 44 (2): 34–42.

Shepherd, Craig E., et al. 2015. "Fostering Technology-Rich Service-Learning Experiences between School Librarians and Teacher Education Programs." *Knowledge Quest* 44 (2): 44–52.

Additional Sources

Cooper, O. P., and Marty Bray. 2011. "School Library Media Specialist-Teacher Collaboration: Characteristics, Challenges, Opportunities." *TechTrends* 55 (4): 48–55.

Johnson, Doug. 2014. "Head for the Edge: Collaboration at a Higher Level." *Library Media Connection* 32 (5): 98.

Wallace, Virginia L., and Whitney Norwood Husid. 2016. *Collaborating for Inquiry-Based Learning: School Librarians and Teachers Partner for Student Achievement,* 2nd ed. Santa Barbara, CA: Libraries Unlimited.

SHARED FOUNDATION: CURATE

AASL and ALA Publications

Adamich, Tom. 2013. "Dewey Redux: Virtual Dewey Resources Deliver Trusted, Familiar 21st-Century Information." *Knowledge Quest* 42 (2): 70–72.

Batch, Kristen R., Trina Magi, and Michelle Luhtala. 2015. "Filtering Beyond CIPA: Consequences of and Alternatives to Overfiltering in Schools." *Knowledge Quest* 44 (1): 60–66.

Buchter, Holli. 2013. "Dewey vs Genre Throwdown." *Knowledge Quest* 42 (2): 48–55.

Buerkett, Rebecca. 2014. "Where to Start? Creating Virtual Library Spaces." *Knowledge Quest* 42 (4): E23–E27.

Degroat, Wendy. 2014. "Make Space for Poetry." *Knowledge Quest* 42 (4): E28–E32.

Doyle, Miranda. 2015. "Rethinking the 'Restricted' Shelf." *Knowledge Quest* 44 (1): 72–73.

Gordon, Carol A. 2013. "Dewey Do Dewey Don't: A Sign of the Times." *Knowledge Quest* 42 (2): E1–E8.

Grabenstein, Chris. 2013. "How Dewey Find What We're Really Looking For?" *Knowledge Quest* 42 (2): 78–80.

Harris, Christopher. 2013. "Library Classification 2020." *Knowledge Quest* 42 (2): 14–19.

Hembree, Julie. 2013. "Ready Set Soar! Rearranging Your Fiction Collection by Genre." *Knowledge Quest* 42 (2): 62–65.

Jameson, Juanita. 2013. "A Genre Conversation Begins." *Knowledge Quest* 42 (2): 10–13.

Kaplan, Tali Balas, et al. 2013. "One Size Does Not Fit All: Creating a Developmentally Appropriate Classification for Your Children's Collections." *Knowledge Quest* 42 (2): 30–37.

Kelley-Mudie, Sara. 2014. "Books and Mortar & Beyond." *Knowledge Quest* 42 (4): 54–57.

Kimmel, Sue C. 2014. *Developing Collections to Empower Learners*. Chicago: ALA.

Kowalski, Sue. 2014. "Rethinking the Possibilities @ Your Library: Creating a Library without a Library Space." *Knowledge Quest* 42 (4): E18–E22.

Martin, Ann M. 2015. "Labeling and Rating Systems: Greater Access or Censorship?" *Knowledge Quest* 44 (1): 54–58.

Moreillon, Judi, with Jana Hunt and Colleen Graves. 2013. "One Common Challenge— Two Different Solutions." *Knowledge Quest* 42 (2): 38–43.

Moskalski, Michael D., and Linda L. McBride, introduction by Helen Adams. 2015. "Access to Information: Perspectives of a Superintendent and a School Board Member." *Knowledge Quest* 44 (1): 48–53.

Paganelli, Andrea. 2016. "Storytime in a Digital World: Making a Case for Thinking Outside the Book." *Knowledge Quest* 44 (3): 8–17.

Panzer, Michael. 2013. "Dewey: How to Make It Work for You." *Knowledge Quest* 42 (2): 22–29.

Pendergrass, Devona J. 2013. "Dewey or Don't We?" *Knowledge Quest* 42 (2): 56–59.

Rheingold, Howard. 2012. "Stewards of Digital Literacies." *Knowledge Quest* 41 (1): 52–55.

Rickman, Wendy. 2015. "Collection Development Behaviors in School Librarians: LGBTQ Books and Resources." *Knowledge Quest* 43 (5): 22–27.

Schiano, Deborah. 2013. "Curating the Shelves." *Knowledge Quest* 42 (2): 66–68.

Stripling, Barbara K. 2015. "Creating a Culture of Intellectual Freedom through Leadership and Advocacy." *Knowledge Quest* 44 (1): 14–19.

Additional Sources

Catalano, Amy. 2015. *Collecting for the Curriculum: The Common Core and Beyond*. Santa Barbara, CA: Libraries Unlimited.

Hopwood, Jennifer L. 2015. *Best STEM Resources for NextGen Scientists: The Essential Selection and User's Guide*. Santa Barbara, CA: Libraries Unlimited.

Houston, Cynthia. 2015. *Organizing Information in School Libraries: Basic Principles and New Rules*. Santa Barbara, CA: Libraries Unlimited.

Kaplan, Allison G. 2015. *Catalog It! A Guide to Cataloging School Library Materials*, 3rd ed. Santa Barbara, CA: Libraries Unlimited.

Loertscher, David V., and Carol Koechlin. 2016. "Collection Development and Collaborative Connection Development: or, Curation." *Teacher Librarian* 43 (4): 52–53.

Mardis, Marcia A. 2015. *The Collection's at the Core: Revitalize Your Library with Innovative Resources for the Common Core and STEM.* Santa Barbara, CA: Libraries Unlimited.

———. 2016. *The Collection Program in Schools: Concepts and Practices*, 6th ed. Santa Barbara, CA: Libraries Unlimited.

Valenza, Joyce Kasman. 2012. "Curation." *School Library Monthly* 29 (1): 20–23.

Valenza, Joyce Kasman, Brenda L. Boyer, and Della Curtis. 2014. "Curation in School Libraries." *Library Technology Reports: Social Media Curation* 50 (7): 27–35.

SHARED FOUNDATION: EXPLORE

AASL and ALA Publications

Anderson, Theresa Dirndorfer. 2014. "Making the 4Ps as Important as the 4Rs." *Knowledge Quest* 42 (5): 42–47.

Bowler, Leanne. 2014. "Creativity through 'Maker' Experiences and Design Thinking in the Education of Librarians." *Knowledge Quest* 42 (5): 58–61.

Bush, Gail. 2014. "Fear No Creativity." *Knowledge Quest* 42 (5): 20–23.

Cesari, Lindsay. 2014. "Arranging a Library to Support Adolescent Development." *Knowledge Quest* 42 (4): 44–48.

Cropley, David H. 2014. "From Rhetoric to Reality: Designing Activities to Foster Creativity." *Knowledge Quest* 42 (5): 24–27.

Flint, Lori J. 2014. "How Creativity Came to Reside in the Land of the Gifted (and How to Move It into a New Neighborhood)." *Knowledge Quest* 42 (5): 64–69.

Giffard, Sue. 2016. "Expanding Horizons and Encouraging New Perspectives through Myths: Experiments in Interactive Storytelling in an Elementary School Library." *Knowledge Quest* 44 (3): 18–24, 26–27.

Hanson, Michael Hanchett. 2014. "Converging Paths: Creativity Research and Educational Practice." *Knowledge Quest* 42 (5): 8–13.

McGrath, Kevin G. 2015. "School Libraries & Innovation." *Knowledge Quest* 43 (3): 54–61.

Oremland, Sara. 2013. "Collaboration and Technology for Authentic Research Projects: From Essential Question to Presentation." *Knowledge Quest* 41 (4): 60–68.

Small, Ruth V. 2014. "The Motivational and Information Needs of Young Innovators: Stimulating Student Creativity and Inventive Thinking." *School Library Research* 17. <www.ala.org/aasl/sites/ala.org.aasl/files/content/aaslpubsandjournals/slr/vol17/SLR_MotivationalNeeds_V17.pdf> (accessed October 8, 2016).

Sturm, Brian W. 2013. "Creativity in the Space Between: Exploring the Process of Reading Graphic Novels." *Knowledge Quest* 41 (3): 58–63.

Sullivan, Margaret. 2013. "Build a Successful Library Space with Creative Teamwork." *Knowledge Quest* 41 (4): 52–53.

Techman, Melissa. 2014. "Supporting Creativity in School Libraries: Finding, Sharing, and Connecting." *Knowledge Quest* 42 (5): 28–30.

Wilhelm, Jeffrey D. 2014. "Learning to Love the Questions: How Essential Questions Promote Creativity and Deep Learning." *Knowledge Quest* 42 (5): 36–41.

Willingham, Daniel. 2014. "Making Students More Curious." *Knowledge Quest* 42 (5): 32–35.

Additional Sources

Cox, Marge. 2017. *The Elementary School Library Makerspace: A Start-Up Guide.* Santa Barbara, CA: Libraries Unlimited.

Egbert, Megan. 2016. *Creating Makers: How to Start a Learning Revolution at Your Library*. Santa Barbara, CA: Libraries Unlimited.

Graves, Colleen, Aaron Graves, and Diana Rendina. 2017. *Challenge-Based Learning in the School Library Makerspace*. Santa Barbara, CA: Libraries Unlimited.

Lamb, Annette. 2016. "Makerspaces and the School Library, Part 2: Collaborations and Connections." *Teacher Librarian* 43 (3): 56–58.

Pawloski, Lynn, and Cindy Wall. 2017. *Maker Literacy: A New Approach to Literacy Programming for Libraries*. Santa Barbara, CA: Libraries Unlimited.

SHARED FOUNDATION: ENGAGE

AASL and ALA Publications

Abilock, Rigele, and Debbie Abilock. 2016. "I Agree, But Do I Know? Privacy and Student Data." *Knowledge Quest* 44 (4): 10–21.

Adams, Helen R. 2013. "Passing the Torch: Mentoring to Support Intellectual Freedom in School Libraries." *Knowledge Quest* 41 (4): 28–33.

———. 2016. "Choose Privacy Week: Educate Your Students (and Yourself) about Privacy." *Knowledge Quest* 44 (4): 30–33.

Agosto, Denise E., and June Abbas. 2016. "Simple Tips for Helping Students Become Safer, Smarter Social Media Users." *Knowledge Quest* 44 (4): 42–47.

American Association of School Librarians. 2010. "A Planning Guide for Empowering Learners with School Library Program Assessment Rubric." <www.ala.org/aasl/standards/planning> (accessed October 10, 2016).

American Library Association. 2010. "ALA/AASL Standards for Initial Preparation of School Librarians." <www.ala.org/aasl/sites/ala.org.aasl/files/content/aasl education/schoollibrary/2010_standards_with_rubrics.pdf> (accessed October 10, 2016).

Ballard, Susan. 2015. "Coming This Fall to a School Library near You: The Challenged, the Banned, & the Filtered." *Knowledge Quest* 43 (5): 32–37.

Bray, Marty. 2016. "Going Google: Privacy Considerations in a Connected World." *Knowledge Quest* 44 (4): 36–41.

Bringelson, Carin. 2015. "Essential Intellectual Freedom Resources for School Librarians." *Knowledge Quest* 44 (1): E1-E4.

Cheby, Lisa. 2016. "Search Strategy Instruction: Shifting from Baby Bird Syndrome to Curious Cat Critical Thinking." *Knowledge Quest* 44(4): 48-53.

Chmara, Theresa. 2015. "Do Minors Have First Amendment Rights in Schools?" *Knowledge Quest* 44 (1): 8–13.

Garnar, Martin. 2015. "Ethics Today: Are Our Principles Still Relevant?" *Knowledge Quest* 44 (1): 36–41.

Keeling, Mary. 2013. "Mission Statements: Rhetoric, Reality, or Roadmaps to Success." *Knowledge Quest* 42 (1): 30–36.

Leu, DaNae, and Dee Ann Venuto, introduction by Helen Adams. 2015. "Standing by Their Principles: Two Librarians Who Faced Challenges." *Knowledge Quest* 44 (1): 42–47.

Magi, Trina. 2015. "Newly Revised Intellectual Freedom Manual Makes It Easier to Find the Help You Need." *Knowledge Quest* 44 (1): 32–35.

Miller, Beth. 2016. "Can I Use This App or Website for My Class? What to Know about Instructing Teachers and Students on Digital Citizenship, Digital Footprints, and Cybersafety." *Knowledge Quest* 44 (4): 22–29.

Monteith, Barnas. 2016. "Hacking for Good and Bad, and How to Protect Yourself against Hacks!" *Knowledge Quest* 44 (4): 60–62, 64.

Moskalski, Michael D., and Linda L. McBride, introduction by Helen Adams. 2015. "Access to Information: Perspectives of a Superintendent and a School Board Member." *Knowledge Quest* 44 (1): 48–53.

Pickett, Janie. 2013. "First Steps with a Library Advisory Committee." *Knowledge Quest* 42 (1): 14–17.

Seroff, Jole. 2015. "Developing a Curriculum in Intellectual Freedom: What Our Students Need to Know." *Knowledge Quest* 44 (1): 20–24.

Stripling, Barbara K. 2015. "Creating a Culture of Intellectual Freedom through Leadership and Advocacy." *Knowledge Quest* 44 (1): 14–19.

Additional Sources

Ballard, Susan D., Gail March, and Jean K. Sand. 2009. "Creation of a Research Community in a K–12 School System Using Action Research and Evidence Based Practice." *Evidence Based Library and Information Practice* 4 (2): 8–36.

Center for Teaching Quality, National Board for Professional Teaching Standards, and the National Education Association. 2014. *The Teacher Leadership Competencies.* <www.nbpts.org/sites/default/files/teacher_leadership_competencies_final.pdf> (accessed December 10, 2016).

Hovious, Amanda S. 2015. *Transmedia Storytelling: The Librarian's Guide.* Santa Barbara, CA: Libraries Unlimited.

Part III: Assessment and Evaluation

AASL AND ALA RESOURCES

Bowles-Terry, Melissa, and Cassandra Kvenild. 2015. *Classroom Assessment Techniques for Librarians.* Chicago: ACRL.

Owen, Patricia. 2012. *21st-Century Approach to School Librarian Evaluation.* Chicago: AASL.

ADDITIONAL SOURCES

Harada, Violet H., and Joan M. Yoshina. 2010. *Assessing for Learning: Librarians and Teachers as Partners*, 2nd ed. Santa Barbara, CA: Libraries Unlimited.

Keller, Cynthia. 2016. "Tracking Teacher Librarian Effectiveness Using Digital Portfolios." *Teacher Librarian* 43 (5): 20–23.

Moreillon, Judi. 2013. "Leadership: School Librarian Evaluation." *School Library Monthly* 30 (2): 24–25.

Rajagopal, Kadhir. 2011. *Create Success! Unlocking the Potential of Urban Students.* Alexandria, VA: ASCD.

INDEX

LIST OF ILLUSTRATIONS

FIGURES

TABLES